CROSSCURRENTS *Modern Critiques*

CROSSCURRENTS *Modern Critiques*
Harry T. Moore, *General Editor*

Kingsley Widmer

The Literary Rebel

WITH A PREFACE BY

Harry T. Moore

Carbondale and Edwardsville

SOUTHERN ILLINOIS UNIVERSITY PRESS

For Sons and Rebels
Matthew and Jonah

Copyright © 1965 by Southern Illinois University Press
All rights reserved
Library of Congress Catalog Card Number 65-12389
Printed in the United States of America
Designed by Andor Braun

PREFACE

KINGSLEY WIDMER'S BOOKS on Henry Miller and D. H. Lawrence, as well as his numerous articles whipping up controversy, have pointed toward his study of the literary rebel. This is a volume that performs a significant intellectual service, for it puts together many points never previously assembled, and it does so in a lively and challenging way.

Although himself an academician—he teaches at San Diego State College—Mr. Widmer is far from academic in his approach to the literary rebel, whom he sees as an important and even affirmative figure. "Rebels, indeed, offer something positive and useful: permanent defiance, without which life loses essential freedom and vitality. When the rebel negates the usual negatives, when he denies the stand compulsions and anxieties, he creates positively." Yet Mr. Widmer doesn't blindly idealize the rebel, as his last chapter ("The Limits of the Rebel") shows.

Mr. Widmer ranges across literatures to illuminate a wide variety of literary rebels: The Archpoet of Cologne, Henry David Thoreau, D. H. Lawrence, Diogenes, Feodor Dostoevsky, and others. He shows us that the rebel is no new phenomenon. If we have him with us today, the ancient world also had him, and so did the middle ages.

In one particularly fine section of his book, Mr. Widmer gives a highly valuable re-appraisal of three rebel works of the past: William Blake's The Marriage of Heaven and Hell, Herman Melville's Bartleby, the Scrivener, and Tristan Corbière's Les Amours Jaunes. In other significant chapters, Mr. Widmer takes some more recent rebels, naming names, emphasizing their imperfections. He isn't afraid to tackle the highly regarded Albert Camus, whose essays such as those collected in The Rebel he downgrades (though he likes at least one Camus book—his novel The

Stranger). In a quite different context, Mr. Widmer examines the literature of vagabondage, from Homer's *Odyssey* to Samuel Beckett's *Waiting for Godot*. Mr. Widmer has a wide knowledge of his subject matter—for example, he picks up Jim Tully along the way, and that's really getting into vagabondage.

Mr. Widmer makes many bold assertions, but he usually buttresses his arguments with a full and lively set of notes. Having published work of his before, I knew that he would do this again and attempted to set no limits; he has his own way of working, and should be given a free hand. I think that the readers will find the results highly stimulating.

HARRY T. MOORE

Southern Illinois University
December 21, 1964

ACKNOWLEDGMENTS

SOME EXAMPLES of my indebtedness to other students of the literature and problems considered here—often negative —are given in the notes. Harry T. Moore and the editors at Southern Illinois University Press have shown considerable generosity and tolerance in permitting me some idiosyncrasies of manner and approach. Appropriately, I have no indebtedness to any organization, academic institution, coterie or official for any aid, encouragement or rewards. Thanks are due those periodical editors who published my preliminary studies. One essay, "The Negative Affirmation: Melville's 'Bartleby,'" has been moderately revised from the version in *Modern Fiction Studies* (Autumn, 1962). The other essays have been used only in very brief part or drastically changed: "The Literary Rebel," *Centennial Review* (Spring, 1962); "The American Road," *Univ. of Kansas City Review* (Summer, 1960); "Poetic Naturalism," *Partisan Review* (Summer, 1959); "The Strange Artistic Sophistication of Contemporary America," *Four Quarters* (November, 1961); "Timeless Prose," *Twentieth Century Literature* (Summer, 1958); and "The Existential Darkness," *Wisc. Studies in Contemporary Literature* (Fall, 1960). Essentially part of a continuing argument, I have briefly recapitulated several passages from two earlier books: *The Art of Perversity: D. H. Lawrence's Shorter Fictions* (Seattle, 1962) and *Henry Miller* (New York, 1963). But most of the discussion is new.

I am considerably, and necessarily, indebted to some non-literary sources, found on the rebellious road, etc., and to some sympathetic yet critical anonymous mockers. But my severest loving critic, for this book as for much else, has been Eleanor R. Widmer, who hopes with me for future generations of rebels. To her, to them, and to other authentically rebellious spirits, I apologize for the literary and rebellious limitations of this book.

                                                    KINGSLEY WIDMER

La Jolla, California
July 17, 1964

CONTENTS

PREFACE   v

ACKNOWLEDGMENTS   vii

Some Traditions of the Literary Rebel

1 The Diogenes Style   3
2 Variations of Defiance   17
3 The Marriage of Heaven and Hell   35
4 Bartleby   48
5 Les Amours Jaunes   60

Some Roads of the Literary Rebel

6 The Art of Wandering   77
7 The Hobo Style   91
8 Naturalism and the American Joe   108
9 Contemporary American Outcasts   122

Some Problems of Recent Rebels

10 Rebellion Against Rebellion?   143
11 Ambiguous Rebels on Literature   159

x   CONTENTS

12   Several American Perplexes   175

13   Conclusion: The Limits of the Rebel   199

      NOTES   211

      INDEX   249

SOME TRADITIONS OF THE LITERARY REBEL

1   THE DIOGENES STYLE

LET US START with a literary gesture that marks the perennial attitude of revolt: "I know thy works, that thou are neither cold nor hot; I would thou wert cold or hot. So then because thou are lukewarm, and neither cold nor hot, I will spew thee out of my mouth." [1] This fragment out of Revelation sets the tone of demand and scorn. While much of life and literature necessarily moves in the realms of the tepid, not the rebellious. If one were to do a systematic history of literary rebels, I suppose some time should be spent on pieces from that old anthology, including those of the first identified literary rebels in the Western traditions—Jeremiah and a few of the other prophets. For our purposes, the most modern of the lot, Jonah, might be to the point because he foreshadows the cosmopolitan wanderers in his comic self-consciousness about being a rebel. More generally, it would be hard to over-value for the rebel tradition the significance of the Judaic prophetic mode, including its condemnation of the ways of power, its exaltation of love and compassion as struggle, its expansive metaphoric forms, and its violent manners of lamentation. (Certainly the voices from the wilderness have had their rebellious place in America, not least because the Protestant evangelical movements transmitted rather more of the prophetic fervor than their parochial values could contain.) Modern literary rebels still refract some of the Old Testament rage and repetition—often the first signs of the rebel posture. [2] But much of the Old Testament prophetic mode of revolt does lack modern relevance. Few moderns, rebels included, have the prophets' faith in an ultimately just cosmos, in the sense of personal dialogue with the Divine, or in the engagement to a special historical mission with a peculiar people. There may, of course, come a day when we will find a unique pertinence to the apocalyptic, rather than the moral, passion of the Judeo-Christian prophecies.

The relevance of the Biblical rebel, even in a post-Christian culture, might simply be assumed. Not so, I suspect, with another important and ancient tradition of the rebel voice. The Cynics of the Greco-Roman world, represented by Diogenes of Sinope and his successors, show major parallels with modern literary rebels which may illuminate some of the peculiarities and purposes of even the most recent literature.[3] Though the Cynic does not reveal certain of the self-conscious and syncretistic modern gestures, he does suggest the archetypal pattern of our literary rebels. One obvious reason for his relevance to these times is that, in contrast to many of the Jewish and Christian prophets, the Cynic was the cosmopolitan individualist in a mixed and sophisticated culture and in urbanized and imperial societies. The followers of Diogenes, then and now, may be the sour fruit in an over-ripe time, announcing that rottenness is all. The Cynic program announced most notably a philosophy of failure which also provided a devastating commentary on the fatuous successes of ages of counterfeit. Such rebels are not only disaffiliated from their society and culture but also unaffiliated with any overwhelming religious or revolutionary vision which would create a new society and culture. Thus, the most essential rebel style and attitude, I shall maintain, is just that which reveals rebellion as its central and sustained commitment. Beyond rebellion lies something else, not least the conditions which necessarily produce a new call to rebellion.

While there is considerable variation, historical and individual, in the commitment to rebellion, nonetheless, some generic patterns remain. When, for example, we read the commentaries on Diogenes of Sinope and his followers in Greek and Roman writings, and then read commentaries on contemporary American literary rebels, the arguments seem almost paraphrases of each other.[4] Take the basic image of the literary rebel that was somewhat misleadingly popularized iin the 1950's under the rubrics of an American coterie, the Beat Generation or Beat

Movement—now the almost world-wide figure of the Beatnik. It shows a rather aging youth, usually with long hair and a beard, in the uniform of the disinherited, obviously contemptuous of cleanliness and decorum. While the beggar's cloak and wallet of the Cynic have been replaced, as signs of office, by jeans and paperback book, the rest of the lineaments, and the essential gestures, remain much the same. In prodigal appearance, in casual domesticity, and in outraging taste, both Cynic and Beat seem similar in the ways in which they rebelliously afront the pretensions of the society at large to "gracious living." So, too, with the language of Cynic and Beat which, in and out of literature, fuses the vulgar and the intellectual in a striking mélange of vivid colloquialisms and highbrow abstractions that persistently violates formality and geni- ality. Certainly such speech has intrinsic functions, beyond modishness and group identification. For instance, the yoking of terms of obscenity with those of salvation—a Beat stylization which is also one of the most ancient forms of blasphemy—seems part of a demand that we perceive the incongruities in our ordering of the world. "Forbidden" language, used more or less seriously, serves not only to shock but to re-emphasize natural functions and exalt "common" awareness. Done with skill, curses can provide defiant prayers, obscenity a poetry of outrage. Indeed, a literary rebel whose language does not achieve some such sort of violation in itself is neither very poetic nor very rebellious.

Let us characterize further the archetypal rebel—the shape common to many Cynics, Beats, and others—with particular attention to the Cynics not as an historical phenonmena but as a style of defiance. Many of the Diogenes anecdotes, such as that of his carrying a lamp in the daylight because he was looking for a real or honest man, achieved near universal recognition. In being a tragic comment on mankind, yet given a witty twist and pre- sented with burlesque dramatization, it has the distinctive rebel quality. The same style of didactic verve appeared in Diogenes' dramatic emphasis upon perversely free choice in which he matched his metaphors with direct actions. The reader of "existentialist" literature will be struck by the pertinence of the Cynic's insistence that he was a criminal, a debaser of the official coinage (including the currency of conventional standards), a defender of moral violations such as incest (which were never examined), and an exalter of his role as both actual and internal exile. In his quest for authenticity, Diogenes made what a cultivated society considered both buffoonish and felonious gestures, being intentionally crude and outspoken. The Cynics were noted for their obscenity, in act as well as word, and they reportedly were willing to "be natural" about fornicating and defecating, anywhere. Their notorious "shamelessness" was both part of their lesson and part of a way of life. Many of their self-conscious violations of commercial, bureaucratic and upperclass morals and manners suggest the Cynics as the first to intentionally *épater le bourgeois*. Put in this perspective, we may see such favorite rebel defiance as neither bohemian high-spirits nor part of nineteenth-century class conflict but as a more universal effort to dramatically mock complacent and restricted awareness.

Diogenes had a radical dialectic for every part of his personal life. He went about unkempt, dressed in the uniform of a beggar, slept almost anywhere, scornfully took what food came to hand, refused to work, condemned anxious luxuries but not direct pleasures, and was committed to the simplest sort of life. Even his famed bad manners were as much principle as temperament. "Other dogs bite their enemies, I bite my friends—for their salvation." He was an anarchist when it came to political authorities, a libertarian when it came to social customs, and a cosmopolitan when it came to loyalties ("The only true country is that which is as wide as the universe"). His dog's life, physically mean and rough, intellectually tough and biting, was an outrageous dramatization of radical awareness. Plato reportedly called Diogenes a "Socrates gone mad." But Plato was an authoritarian who refused to recognize tragic absurdity, either by allowing the poets in his republic or in understanding the witty buffoonery of a Diogenes. The Cynic, a better judge than the rational idealist of some parts of human nature, said, "Most men are so nearly mad that a finger's breadth would make the difference."

Diogenes would seem plausibly credited with certain literary traditions—mordant satire of things as they are and a popular dialectic of moral discontent. But the dialectical extremity that he lived may be more important, for he was one of the first to dramatize some rather important values: equality, even with rulers and women; freedom, even from the gods and the economic system; self-sufficiency, even to living a dog's life and masturbating freely; and directness, even in public speech and philosophy. Rather more than Thoreau—one of his descendants—and in the city, he attempted to embody individualistic autarchy and immediacy. His "simplicity" took the form of witty denials of superstitutions, conventions, authorities and ideologies. Naturally, part of Diogenes' significance is confined to the peculiar conditions of his time. As a rebel against Athenian education (a usual dissident focus), he battled over the Greek definitions in the various schools of "virtue," "nature," "reason," and so on.[5] The antiquarian interest in Cynicism's role as "hard primitivism" or as a sort of left-wing Stoicism need not concern us here. The historical Cynics also display a naïveté about "rational" argument and "virtue" which can be related to the Sophists and Socrates but which strikes us as quaint and would certainly be antipathetic to most modern rebels who find their "reasons" in the irrational in an over-rationalized world. Similarly, Diogenes literal insistence on doing all "according to nature" hardly appears so clear anymore since various romanticisms and sciences have inevitably complicated our responses, and faith, in the natural orders.

Of more permanent importance are other curious qualities of the Cynics. For instance, they were harsh realists, yet also some of the earliest "utopians" with an exotic dream vision of a world where simplicity and directness reigned: the Island of Para—perhaps the secularization of sacred myths, later desecularized by less rigorous prophets. Then, too, the Cynics have a special claim on our attention in being one of the few groups of teachers (really *un*teaching in the Socratic manner) not subsidized by state, church, commerce or their own hierarchy, and also one of the few groups of teachers not submissive to those powers.

But more important to the modern view is the clear extremity of the Cynics rebel role. For Diogenes, civilization was to be corrected solely by the individual (that ruled out organizations and politics), in active and iconoclastic confrontation (that ruled out snobs and mystics), in the streets and going institutions (that ruled out esoterics and revolutionaries), and with intense scorn (that ruled out the stupid and bland). We may suppose that the only reason Diogenes was not against bureaucratic authority, mass genteel education-entertainment, the Bomb, etc., was that our technological nihilisms had not yet been invented. Since Diogenes' literary works, apparently outrageous dialogues and burlesque tragedies, have not survived we can see that his greatest creation was a nullifidian style. This philosophical tramp (he usually went south in the winter) and wise buffoon (there must have been some natural appropriateness for all the wise-cracks fathered on him), set standards for the perennial rebel's defiance of how most men believe and live.

The many anecdotes told of Diogenes and Alexander—no doubt apocryphal but quite in accord with the Cynic role—insist on independence and equality. When the King of Kings reputedly stood in front of Diogenes and asked what favor he could grant, and was told to quit blocking the sunlight, or when the ruler of the world flatteringly compared himself to Diogenes, and Diogenes sardonically confirmed the comparison, we see the power of negative thinking. Another series of anecdotes linked to Diogenes provide a mordant last will and testament—a form of tragic wit drawn upon by many later rebels, such as Villon and Corbière, who also used death as the harsh test of conventional values. Diogenes' reputed last wishes have his usual wayward wisdom. One report is that he asked, in a world deeply responsive to Antigone's funereal scrupulousness, to be cast in a ditch and thus do the beasts some good. So much for death, and your pieties, foolish Athenians! Another report has it that he perversely asked to be buried face down. Dialectical to the end, he explained that the world of his time would soon be turned upside-down, putting him the right way up. While few historians will disagree with his prophecy, we should also note a more basic point: the true rebel may be recognized by his commitment to a sardonically apocalyptic vision. The end of a world—and it is always the end of a world for mortal man—justifies the scorn and negation, and the resulting strategies of simplification and intense living.

Most of the direct history of the Cynics, extending from

Diogenes, which appears to continue for at least half a dozen centuries, mocks the conventional successes and anxieties of a period marked by fatuous imperial styles and the pervasive sense of meaninglessness. The Cynics answer was to demonstrate that life could be based on very little, or on a lively nothingness. Thus worldly failure was shown as a choice and a victory—the greatest blasphemy to those in power—and an alternative to the dubious "necessities" and compulsions. But there is more to this style of rebellion. The admirably humane Crates, Diogenes' follower, appears to have been a secular saint—the first of the modern saints without a god that we know of. He gave up his wealth and lived as a simple and compassionate wiseman and teacher. He also mocked the official pedagogy, wrote parodies of accepted morality, and maintained the tradition of contempt for inequality and conventional restrictions. Most delightful of all, Crates made one of the few passionate and equal marriages we hear of in antiquity. Hipparchia, an attractive girl from a "good family," pursued outcast Crates. He honorably tried to dissuade her, finally presenting himself stripped naked in warning that he would provide nothing but a life of honest beggary. Miraculous woman, she accepted, and thus became the first lady philosopher. Their daughter, as a logical result, is one of the first reported sexually emancipated women. Saintly Cynics father pleasure as well as freedom. And much else, for even with the sketchy known history of the Cynics there is a provocative roll-call: Bion, the preaching tramp with a flair for metaphor and arrogance; Menippus, apparently the creator of a major form of satire; Dio Chrysostom, one of the many examples of the wandering Cynic critics of the Roman emperors; Oenomaus, the polemical atheist; and many others.[6] They testify to the greatest creation of Diogenes: the secular prophet. Not Plato in his coterie, not Aristotle in his academy, not the poets at the games and courts, certainly not the priests and magicians, but the Cynic wandering and arguing in the streets is the true forerunner and antitype of the individualistic "outsider" literary intellectual.

In the similar denunciations applied to such rebels in both classical and contemporary writings they are attacked for being outside civilization. Actually, they are right at the heart of it, not only in creating styles of life and intellectual confrontations but literally. Though unpatriotic, except perhaps to the purlieus of the cultural capitals where most often found, they take ideas with both passion and wit. Loafers, culture-bums, hangers-on, parasites, immoralists? Though more or less cultured, rebels do not primarily function as performers or merchants of the arts, institutional intellectuals, or even in most ordinary senses as producers of art and edification. The rebel refuses subordination to social function in assertion of the freely human. He remains "unemployed"—even when working—or as close to it as he can manage for both defiance and self-definition. As a member of the discontented or true leisure class he spends time around about the arts, but many rebels avow that their interest in the arts is secondary to ways of life and states of feeling. That only few rebels are artistic should have nothing of accusation about it, unless one is a pietist to a petty psuedo-religion of art. Why should the rebel produce much art or edification? His vocation is denial and defiance.

The rebel, of course, busies himself with the *mystique* of rebellion, rather more than with the muses. Outside organizational conventions and the usual rationalized self-interests, he justifies himself with his nagging and arrogant "why not?" Main principles, from Cynics to Beats, seem to be claims for individuality, voluntary poverty, simplicity, spontaneous feeling, ingenuous communication, intense sense experience, and a general heightening of immediate life. These qualities the rebel supports with considerable invective against official society. The mark-of-the-kind may be that when asked for his identity, the rebel most often defines himself by attacking the nonidentity of the prevailing others.

The official society, in turn, often displays an irritated fascination with the rebel, taking much righteous delight in what it calls his barbarism, crudity, immaturity, sickness, immorality and perversity. Most of our knowledge of the Cynics (as with Christian heretics and later rebels, through the Beats) comes from the perplexed or denouncing reports by the unrebellious. These public apologists insistently attack—perhaps with the morality of envy—the rebel's economic and sexual libertarianism. It is curious also that while official teachers scorn the rebels for their lack of significant productivity and for their corrupting effects, the accusers as a group are most open to those very charges. If there were no rebels, public apologists would have to invent them.

At a common-sense level, the attacks on rebels for economic parasitism and lack of social productivity seem the most irrelevant. Even a meager economy could tolerate the simple needs of a rather considerable number of bearded malcontents. Our ornate modern Western societies could, and do, comfortably support vast numbers of people who fit no simple rational needs for goods and services. The hostility of official rhetoricians (and police, employers, welfare services, etc.) to rebels, of course, has little to do with economics or social utility. Similarly, in societies with varied or changing erotic ways, the rebel's views—usually uncoercive demands for sexual directness —do not require more than a modest tolerance. Since rebels, in obvious fact as well as almost by definition, are small in number, why the insistent fuss about their ways in such things as work and sex? Could it be that which hardly any of the contemners of rebels grant: much of the society despises its meaningless labors and burns against its arbitrary restrictions?

Many of the other charges against rebels, from Cynics to Beats, seem equally curious. For example, the recurrent disgust with the rebel making an exhibition of his failure and maladjustment must be based on the requirement that one be miserable only in standard ways. The argument that the rebel denies "civilized life" often rests on some weird definitions of "civilized" which give primacy to impersonal powers, social anxiety, individual repression, warfare, and similar sorts of "progress." The awesome fear that rebels, unless put down, will encourage vast numbers to throw off work and orderly life is more a condemnation of the society than of the rebels. For real defiance of conventions and their conveniences is usually too arduous for all but a few strong souls, and if vast numbers really seem ready to imitate the rebel mode the social order is about to flip-flop anyway. Surely a surplus of bearded bad poets is more desirable than a surplus of clean-shaven bad policemen, even to pietists of the conventional authorities. The "universalist fallacy"—the argument that goes by way of "What if everyone were a rebel?"—is usually sheer anxiety or fraud.

Some anti-rebel arguments have considerable merit.

When rhetoricians of things-as-they-are, for example, attack rebels for being tediously noisy little failures who are not really very rebellious, the contemners are using, and thus justifying, real standards of rebelliousness—and the more candid will learn from them. And the quite true charge that the rebel style attracts a number of the pathetic, the incompetent, the pathological and the fraudulent, provides an admirable discriminatory emphasis even more applicable to the commercial and political and academic styles of life. Equally useful is the persistent anti-rebel contention that the latest manifestation of defiance repeats the same old stuff, not really new or original. Perhaps so, for the first modern literary rebels, the Cynics, may have been an essential part of the first full civilization in our Western traditions, and such rebellion thus remains a positive continuity of civilized tradition. Literary wildmen and arch-bohemians hold as permanent a part in our heritage of response and understanding as the supposedly more honorific roles of humanistic and scientific and political hero types. Though often discussed as mere bellwethers of artistic faddishness, the gropings of the young, and moral and political discontent, the significance of the rebels seems rather greater than the topical issues they raise in the public minded. The rebel's style and distinctive identity remains, and becomes its own justification, an existential choice for meeting the comic incongruities and tragic absurdities.

But confronting what is said against literary rebels could be endless; there might be more pertinence in emphasizing what is said by the rebels themselves. The difficulty here may be found in the somewhat perplexed relation of the rebel to literature. The Cynics were called "philosophers," and their simple vagrant life, polemics against convention, dialectical buffoonery, long hair, and careless dress provided a dominant image of the philosopher for some centuries. That such rebels would not be called philosophers today might be taken as a damning comment on the Cynics' antagonism towards science, epistemology, metaphysics and grammar. Put with other emphasis, it might also be a damning comment on the genteel technologism of much contemporary philosophy. Almost certainly anyone fitting the Cynic image would now be popularly identified as a stock "artistic" or "literary" figure.

Men of letters the Cynics certainly were, though not in the
debased polite sense which the phrase acquired in the
eighteenth century. Diogenes and Crates were known for
paradoxical dialogues and perverse tragedies. Other Cynics
may have created, and certainly practiced at length, the
diatribe, the satiric sketch, the anti-conventional fantasy
(often a descent into Hades), the idiosyncratic potpourri
(the sort of satiric scrapbook later called Varronian), and,
of course, all sorts of parody and outrageous anecdote. The
so-called "great" or "major" literary forms—epic, tragedy,
formal lyric, history and complex tale—were obviously not
for them. Since epic is based on a warrior aristocracy,
tragedy on a perplexed religious questioning of the universe, formal lyric on a refined class society, history on faith
in an unfolding order, etc., the forms themselves are in
good part antithetical to the spirit of radical revolt.
Aesthetes still charge rebels with failing in the literary
forms of established society, of shockingly violating the
great artistic canons, quite missing the point that the rebel
view must (even if unconsciously sometimes) invert and
twist most of the accepted literary forms. A true rebel
could hardly do a "straight" job on a tragedy, an elegy, a
social novel or a hymn, even if he were so inconsistent as to
want to. Granted that rebels, confused by accepted
literature, the critics and the powers that disseminate
literary materials, sometimes attempt the unrebellious
forms; however, the results generally turn out to be
inversions or burlesques of the accepted and official modes.
For rebellion, like any other fundamental commitment, is
not just an argument or taste but a whole way of engaging
reality, including the literary organization of it.

Though we have very little of the Cynics' literature—
history usually being no more kind to them than they were
to history—the evidence seems clear that many of them
wrote much. Yet they were not literary as dedicated artists
but rather as dedicated rebels. They lacked aesthetic
emphasis, if that means a form of contemplation of form,
since they contemplated immediate life and denied most
of the forms. And they were also not literary in directly
making money, fame or identity from the profession of
writing as such. Apparently for the Cynics, literature was
largely a homiletic and iconoclastic supplement to rebel
teaching and living. With certain important qualifications

(which we will come to) that would still seem to be largely true of rebel literature. Like other teachers, rebels often fall into repetition, over-insistence, lesson mongering, insular monologues and professional self-pity. And as with all forms of intellectual assault, iconoclastic force often over rides finesse. These characteristics point to the inevitable weaknesses their role put upon their literary efforts. For literature was part of the expression of their function, though perhaps less "self-expression" in the modern sense than counter-expression. Critical and aesthetic theories rarely give sufficient place to the impetus to mock, confute, overturn, outrage and defy as actual and important artistic principles. But theories of literature, rather more than the practice of literature, tend to be justifications of conventional responses and authorities, even at their best making moral and moderate the more extreme ways of thought and feeling. While there are many positive artistic virtues—as well as fundamental truths—to rebel literature, what needs first emphasis is the quite special and peculiar expectations appropriate to the literary rebel as rebel. Both the merits and limitations of rebel literature will be, and often have been, confused, covered up or explained away by the simple application of unrebellious literary standards.

Nor is the distortion of the literary rebel merely the work of modern institutional intellectuals. For example, in his orations on Cynicism—"To the Uneducated Cynics" and "To the Cynic Heracleios"—the Emperor Julian (called the Apostate by Christians) pretty clearly "purifies" the Cynic heritage, as one would expect from a sympathizer in power. So, it would seem, does that polite philosopher Epictetus in the moral pedagogy of "On the Calling of a Cynic." More recent discussions, I suspect, also give the Greek austerity in which Diogenes propounded his anticonventional and libertarian defiance an undue puritanic emphasis, which does not really fit the tone of the literary fragments we have.[7] Though there are naturally some corruptions appropriate to Cynicism, such as notoriety-seeking, the renunciation of direct individual gratification should not be primary. Or put it this way: keeping the rebel emphasis in mind, the modern terms for what is usually translated as the "pleasure," "luxury" and "honor" which Diogenes attacked could be "blandness," "security," and "ambition." The rebel has always been opposed to the stolid world, above all.

Certainly many of the Cynics were notoriety seekers, showmen of the absurd, with the vices appropriate to their emphasis on the immediacy of life. Diogenes and his tub achieved a fame about equal to his contemporary Alexander and his empire. There is a literal example of the sameness of the way up and the way down! Four centuries later we have the intriguing case of the Cynic Peregrinos, satirized by the cynical Roman Lucian in the second century and unsatirized by the cynical French novelist Henri de Montherlant in the twentieth century.[8] Peregrinos appears to have been a strikingly modern neurotic ideologist, a Greek philosopher of questionable character who turned to Christianity and became an admired and noted leader in Palestine, then turned again, along the way becoming the polemical critic of a rather decent Emperor that the nice intelligent people weren't critizing (there are some obvious modern political parallels here, too). Peregrinos was thrown out of Rome, apparently got in several other imbroglios via his teaching and writing in Greece, and finally committed a fancy suicide. After four years of public preparation and a good many literary farewells, which kept the rebel passions going in his old age, he immolated himself at the Olympic games in A.D. 167. Lucian nastily delineates Peregrinos as a notoriety-hunting scoundrel and confidence man. Montherlant draws Peregrinos as an aristocrat of the spirit, a master gamesman-mocker in converting and deconverting, and a wise fool in adopting in Rome "the principle that no truth should be left unsaid, which is the greatest crime against society." Montherlant grants that Peregrinos sought fame, but argues that he was a true poet about it. Not only did he announce that he was going to turn himself into a Phoenix in the suicidal flames, but he made the supremely cynical gesture of sacrificing his life without any other purpose than the defiant desire of dying his own way. In Montherlant's autobiographical treatment of the Cynic, it is a case of romantic will hopelessly defying the contemptible crowd of clever Lucians. Peregrinos was a "genuine fraud," argues Montherlant, for "true greatness is greatness that has no point." Here is a strikingly desperate, and contemporary, last twist given to our view of cynic defiance.

The other side, and even more desperate and twisted cynical modern view of the Cynic rebel, may be found in Franz Kafka's parable about Diogenes.[9] In explaining to his self-divided self "why this man [Diogenes] must torment and distrust himself, why he must renounce, why he must not live," the sickest of all interpreters judges that Diogenes must have been "gravely ill." In Kafka's horrified reversal, Diogenes did not scornfully ask Alexander to quit blocking the sunlight but "frantically begged" him to. After all, "Which of us would not have been happy under Alexander's radiant gaze?"—preferring the light of the psychopathic conqueror to the light of the natural sun. In the labyrinthine justification of such abasement to authority, only the Grand Inquisitor of inner fear can be trusted. In the rest of the parable Kafka insists that both the active and conscionable parts of himself must submit —"under the most severe pressure" and a faith which is more "fear" than "understanding"—to the beatification of unlimited power. How dare one do otherwise? For the possibility of, and desire for, revolt are total and absolute, and can only be put down by an equally capricious and extreme longing for authority. So Kafka lucidly exalts the true antagonist of every rebel and the one real justification of all power, the god Anxiety.

The contrasting poetic views of archetypal Cynic rebel by Kafka and Montherlant seem disinctively modern because neither rebel nor anti-rebel can believe in values independent of his consciousness. Rebellion thus becomes capricious negation, finally flamboyant and suicidal. Authority becomes endless power, totally anxious and abasing. The ultimate paradigm represented by these typically self-conscious and exacerbated twentieth-century literary nihilists of rebellion and faith may well be true. Even so, I think we might see, and choose, the rebel case as promising a certain heroism and affirmation of life in its perverse individuality. More moderate men will justly shudder, and finally have to deny that they can see any Cynic and Emperor, allow any rebel and god, understand any deep commitment to rebellion or to power. Such moderate men may often be right, but they, too, are nihilists in denying the tangible extremes. However pleasant to have around, such bland ameliorative souls lack relevance to important parts of our literature and to the rather more drastic events and meanings of our lives.

BEFORE SCANNING some analogous gestures of literary rebels, we might note a more direct extension of the archetypal rebel style of Diogenes. Significant parts of Cynicism, or a closely related way, were taken over by Christianity; its mendicants took up the voluntary poverty, simple life, wandering beggar vocation, bizarre didactic anecdotes and impassioned homilies against conventional life which had been presented with such radical verve by the Greco-Roman rebels. The lively side of Christianity was not only the work of Middle Eastern vagrants, though the image of one dark Galilean, as we have it through a collection of outrageous anecdotes, powerfully maintained rebellious traditions. The Christian version of the Cynic, of course, acquired unrebellious otherworldliness and oriental ritual, an ornate guilt psychology and Roman bureaucratization—among other power devices—which were hardly compatible with defiant spirits. Thus rebellion as such was probably not maintained by monks and saints (though such as the friars certainly furthered it in their best period) but by heretics. The recurrent fusion of wild words and revolt may be found in the radical interpretations of scriptural writings and the imitations of Christ by many of the schizmatics, in the recurrence of passionately eccentric doctrines like the sexual pansacramentalism of the Brethren of the Free Spirit, and in the special ecstasies of such as the troubadors. In later centuries, especially since the works of more rebels have survived, we can find a great number of profoundly protesting heretics, from Sebastian Frank—"Stand against and you stand with God."—to the later Leo Tolstoy—devastatingly aware that most men's lives were "most ordinary and therefore most terrible." [1] We may recognize a fairly continuous heritage of revolt in Western religion, in spite of the attempts to institutionalize rebels, from Jesus to the present. The heretical modes are still with us, though—for reasons to be discussed later—their contemporary forms tend to be more fragmented, obscure, syncretisic and uncertain than in many times past. Norman Mailer, in commenting on one of the tales of the Hassidim, puts the point with traditional succinctness: "To learn from an inner voice the first time it speaks to us is a small bold existential act, for it depends on following one's instinct which must derive, in no matter how distorted a fashion, from God, whereas institutional knowledge is appropriated by the Devil." [2]

Antinomianism is usually the religious direction of the literary rebel. Those who deny institutionalized meanings in terms of immediate and individual intensified awareness follow the ancient wisdom of superseding morality with grace. Heart and conscience are not only more radical than authorities and conventions but less destructive. Subjectivity rebels against whatever objectification has achieved, the spirit against its own categories once they have become impersonal and self-generating forms. [3] Despite the differences in antinomian illuminations (variously attributed to God, conscience, sexual orgasm, compassion, etc.) the result usually seems to be vitalistic, egalitarian, libertarian and intransigent. Even when communal in its emphasis, antinomianism becomes necessarily individualistic and, as one of its more prudent historical commentators noted with understatement, "formed sensitive and determined personalities." [4] That is no mean justification. This, and the insistence on rebellious truth-as-action, may strike us as more important about the antinomians than their idiosyncratic theologies or the times they played revolutionary roles in history (those Medieval groups attempting to create a heavenly communion in this world; Münster and the Anabaptists violently resisting the embourgeoisement of the Reformation by Luther and others; the sectaries of the seventeenth-century civil wars deciding to forcefully build Jerusalem in England's green and unjust land). The divinization of human life and the denial of convention take intriguing form in a Joachim of Flora, a Jacob Böhme or a William Blake. In their writings we see antinomianism not as a temporary product of especially chaotic historical circumstances, or as an almost inevitably inadequate political movement, but as a perennial and absolute prophetic defiance of the false fixities of life.

Rebels not only tend to supra-political libertarianism and the religious anarchy of inner illumination but, as we uncomfortably discover in getting close to them or deeply involved in their writings, to all sorts of eccentric tastes. Diogenes, it is reported, ate raw octupus, apparently arriving at that affinity by his sarcastic hyperlogic in which he would attempt anything that might be appropriate to the natural order and inappropriate to conventional standards. Other rebels that we have mentioned in passing went in for vegetarianism, nudism, group concubinage and nihilistic gnosticism—whether in the upward or downward way to wisdom is not always clear.

A similar impetus seems to be at work in the esotericism often found in literary rebels, which may also be part of a Western avidity for wandering into someone else's school. Thus it was reported that one of Diogenes' followers reached India and was convinced that he found a people (Yogi?) who were leading a true Cynic life of directness and simplicity. Thus, too, the American Beats made much of the individualistic and unpuritanic immediacy of the monks of Zen Buddhism—the wine drinking dharma bums. The contemporary voraciousness for Zen, and other exotic ways of thought and feeling, has often been misinterpreted. Very few Beat writers, for example, take over Zen's extreme social quietism, involuted technical disciplines, esthetic of ellipsis and understatement, or ritualistic and authoritarian context. The Western rebel's interest in the East is less ponderous fusion of East and West than of rebel seeking other rebel.[5] The drive to search out "alien" and unusual modes is rarely done in terms of logic, but rather in terms of literature. Literature often suggests ways of rebellion against orthodox and accepted modes of response, including the writings of those earlier rebels who have ostensibly been accepted in one's own traditions. Thus some modern rebels read oriental "cynics" as their dramatic types for the style of defiance and the insistence on direct experience. The *Tao Te Ching*, says one scholar, might for Americans be called a "nonconformist ballad." [6] A witty and sardonic Taoist

like Chuang-Tzě, who denied authoritarian powers, rituals, manners and morals, was a master of paradoxical
parody, dialectical anecdote and a vivaciously independent life style—an oriental Cynic. The moral may be presented in the words of a couple of Taoist "True Sages"
who loved wine and women to one who urged rational
prudence and moral restraint upon them.

> It is strange to suppose that we were waiting for you to en-
> lighten us. Life is of all things the hardest to meet with,
> and death the easiest to encounter. [You recommend that
> one] degrade life, so hard to come by, to a level below
> death. . . . You recommend that by deference to morals
> and manners we should pander to the world, by doing
> violence to our natural desires should court reputation. But
> in our view death itself would be far preferable to such a
> life as you propose.[7]

The problem, then, is to find what one truly desires, to
make that the pursuit of life, and to deny the compulsions
and anxieties which conventions and authorities would
seek to impose on one. This has always been good rebel
doctrine.

Even given only a slight acquaintance with oriental
literary rebels, we must also note a fundamental difference
from occidental rebels. For the Westren traditions, in
contexts which have encouraged intellectual dynamism
and psychological aggressiveness, for better and for worse,
often show an assertiveness, an exacerbation of sensibility
and an angry nihilism which may be distinctive. The
sarcastic Cynics and the outraged Christian heretics—
unlike the usually quiet dharma bums and the dry
Taoists—were frequently harsh, wild and overwhelming.
Partly for this reason, I believe, the Western rebels have
often been misunderstood as revolutionaries. Cynics and
antinomian heretics manifested a drastic discontent, an-
tagonized political and social authorities, scorned public
rituals and pieties, and on occassion incited crowds of the
disinherited to revolutionary actions. But most of the historical examples seem to show that individualistic rebels
engaged as revolutionaries ended not only in contradictory and futile mass violence but helped to create new
rigid orthodoxies which destroyed rebels and demanded
new rebellions. This does not deny that rebels, especially
the Western ones who have been less quietistic about

social evils than oriental rebels, help create crucial social changes. But most essentially, rebels modify society by providing styles of discontent and disaffiliation, not by revolutions.

The more or less Socratic intellectuals who followed the Diogenes way found a wandering and peripheral but also stimulating and educating role. That in Roman times many of the more intelligent slaves slipped their bondage and took up the egalitarian scorn and exilic liberty and license of the Cynics shows a major practical utility to the doctrines. Furthermore, Cynicism, much more than most of the classical philosophies and religions, provided a mode of rebellion against slavery. The monastic and mendicant styles of Christian life functioned to provide ways partly out of enslaving social hierarchies. Later literary rebels, in creating bohemianisms, provided cynosures to give a way of life for refugees from commerical-utilitarian enslavement and displaced persons from middle-class morality. A distinctive style of nonconformist living—even if it becomes a minority conformism (but remains open to new recruits)—provides both the wisdom of a voluntary choice of life and a lively social dialectic, as we in an increasingly homogenized world become all too boringly aware.

The marginal mode of the rebel serves as the antithesis of the uniform society, whether conservative or revolutionary, oligarchic or democratic. The accusation that the rebel wishes to overthrow the social-political order may be righteous fear or a trick of those in power. For the rebel wishes to escape from the pattern of the dominant society, to bottom out, where the revolutionary wishes to take over society, to get on top. Where revolutionaries tend to be moral puritans seeking all power, rebels tend to be amoral libertarians mocking all power. Rebels, unless corrupted into something else, can hardly be revolutionaries since they make absolute criticisms of authority and power and emphasize kinds of individual autarchy which can never be the aim of major social and political organizations. The "politics of the unpolitical," [8] in Herbert Read's phrase, provides values by going against all politics. Generally libertarian and egalitarian, pacifistic and antibureaucratic, insisting on direct freedom of expression and on personal autonomy, the rebels provide a varied and protesting cluster of anti-political alternatives. Total politicalization, of whatever ostensible coloration, naturally must deny the rebel. Moderate and rational politics, whether "conservative" or "liberal," recognize their own limits and thus allow (and perhaps even draw upon) the unpolitical and anti-political values. However, a liberal or a conservative who denounces rebel separateness and varied protest and individual defiance thus reveals his doctrine as totalitarian and his temper as authoritarian, regardless of his "traditional" or "progressive" camouflage.

By the persistence and ultimacy of his rebelliousness, the rebel provides acute tests of power. The perpetual radicalism of mocking and denying any existing authority and ethos dramatizes the permanent revolution in all of us—the fundamental and inherent dissatisfaction with most collective purposes—which can never be fully embodied in any actual social-political ordering or reordering.

The fascination of some rebels with revolution, however inconsistent and short-lived, expresses temperament rather more than ideological politics, as we can see in some of the heretics with the Reformation wars, some of the Romantics with the French Revolution, some later rebels with liberal-nationalist conspiracies, and a number of rebels in the past century with "Marxist" revolutionary movements. The charge that most of the literary rebels were not really revolutionary ("terrorists of the library," "parlor pinks," "bourgeois deviationists," etc.) seems true enough—they were concerned with the expression of discontent, not with its corruption into ideological power. A revolutionary who glitters somewhat like a rebel may appeal to some rebels until the police state politico tarnishes through. But the differences between rebels and revolutionaries are not really very subtle; revolutionaries are those who, in contrast to the more plodding ways of long established authorities, *quickly* deny, condemn and destroy rebels.

While rebels may sometimes confuse their counter-dialectics with a counter-politics, rebel demands usually show too much directness and too much absoluteness to be acceptable to mere revolutionaries. Rebels mock even the best forms and aspirations of civilization. To the rebel's candid eyes, history is more disgrace than promise. Though he may be aware that the securities and luxuries of a fully elaborated culture can be intriguing, he insists that the price is too high for these pretentious goods. Manners may make complex discriminations possible but they even more efficiently produce hypocrisy and meanness. Morals may provide a semblance of justice and order but they also provide more than a semblance of distortion and repression. Ideals of a "high culture" create principles and hopes but they just as clearly rationalize the authorities and disguise the realities. Like an unabashed child, the rebel will go to almost any length to expose the common frauds and display his disenchantment and disaffiliation. The rebel, then, gives theatrical shape to the truth that even the best society and highest civilization will be enemies of individual directness and aliveness. Therefore, rebellion is a permanent need and response, not to be reduced to revolution nor shuffled under particular histories and the partly varying habitations and costumes in which it can be found.

But rather than continue to pursue a general discussion of the religion and the politics of the rebel (both of which we will return to in specific cases), we might in an introductory sense briefly suggest a series of rebel motifs and representative rebels. An obvious instance of the rebel who belongs with the Diogenes tradition is Henry David Thoreau. Note Thoreau's rebel extremity of religion and politics, he who speaks for "absolute freedom and wildness, as contrasted with a freedom and culture merely civil." [9] Thoreau is the angry antinomian in the modern sense: "where there is a lull of truth, an institution springs up." [10] His contempt for politics and government, in "Civil Disobedience," combined with radical but unrevolutionary ways of protest, illustrate several of the points made earlier about rebel politics. Thoreau's scorn for business, official culture and work, and his sardonic dismissals of moral justifications of these, put him quite in line with the Cynics—as did his often wry ways of dramatizing his rebellion. Thoreau's mystique of simplicity in good part serves as a defiance of conventional living and anxieties. His use of nature often provides a nihilistic heightening of sense experience, the exaltation of "the gospel according to this moment." Such points, I suppose, are generally recognized about Thoreau. Yet a natural corollary, Thoreau's rebel aesthetic, often gets obscured by discussions of Nature, Emerson, New Eng-

land and Transcendentalism. Thoreau's works take the
same defiantly idiosyncratic directions we find in most
literary rebels—individual, iconoclastic, eccentric, hyperbolic. *Walden,* and the major essays, consist of
anecdotes and homilies, mocking aphroisms and parodies
of accepted rhetoric, burlesques of his neighbors and
outrageous denials of ordinary sentiments—all with the
pervasive tones and gestures of individual defiance. This is
not to deny Thoreau's local coloration—his Puritan fear of
the flesh and the domesticated romanticism of his botaniz-
ing—which weirdly allow him to be taken as a genteel
garden saint. How odd that so many discussions of
Thoreau make him out as the pietist of an innocuous
worship! Henry Thoreau, much more likely, would have
agreed with Henry Miller that "the rebel . . . is closer
to God than the saint." [11]

For a twentieth-century rebel-buffoon like Henry Miller
belongs to the same tradition as Thoreau, even though his
solitary walks and ruminations lead through the flora and
fauna of the Parisian streets. Miller's hyperbolic journal of
a year's ecstatic self-discovery, *Tropic of Cancer,* is, also
like *Walden,* an egotistical collection of anecdotes and
diatribes about seeing and being off the conventional path.
At his best, Miller's outrageousness has the Diogenes
verve; his iconoclasms are also much the same as those of
Thoreau. The essential gestures of *Tropic of Cancer* could
provide justifications for living in the Athenian streets or
in the Walden woods as well as in bohemian Paris. Miller's
shouts, like Thoreau's eloquence, relate the joy of directly
engaging life, of rebellious reversal of conventional justifications. This is not to deny Miller's local coloration—his
fractured sensibility and Brooklyn boy pretenses—which
weirdly allow him to be taken as a profound literary artist.
How sly that so many discussions make him out to be a
great writer instead of a comic rebel! The early Miller
would undoubtedly agree with Thoreau (in *Walden*) that
"I did not wish to live what was not life, living is so dear";
I wished instead "to drive life into a corner, and reduce it
to its lowest terms, and, if it proved to be mean, why then
to get the whole and genuine meanness out of it and
publish its meanness to the world." Thus one defiantly
comes "to front only the essential facts of life."

Rebels like Thoreau and Miller cannot be held up as

adequate artists in the usual senses since they were often uneven, tedious, peculiar, and not the practitioners of "great" literary forms. Their value comes from the whole rebel stance, of which the artistic nature of the work was but a small part. The imitation of Thoreau in American nature, or of Miller in the bohemian purlieus, provides appropriate accolade. Pedants will be left confused by this since they can only, somewhat uncomfortably, accept a past defiance if it produced a lot of autonomously fine artifacts. The true rebel illustrates a more sophisticated naivete in which an intense style of living serves as its own justification.

This might also be the appropriate place to raise briefly, and reverse, four other charges often made against rebel literature—the nastiness, the lack of humor, the lack of positiveness, the weird philosophizing—since these come up with almost every rebel discussed. At the only serious level worth considering, the charge that rebels, from Diogenes to Henry Miller, are nasty, is true, if it be recognized that it serves as a demonic strategy. Many rebels certainly seek out the dark powers of forbidden desires which provide much of the iconography of the demonic in Western traditions. Obviously a technique for questioning, inverting and shocking, the demonic also does something else. "Evil be thou my good" serves as more than just a twisted response when official morality and religosized authority succeed in making devils the repositories of fully human qualities and freedoms that have been denied. Ancient cults of repressed worship, romantic Satanism, the diabolism of the Symbolists, the rebellions by way of violation, crime and madness in European Surrealism and American Hipsterism, and such contemporary styles of sacramental wickedness as that of Jean Genet, attempt to break restrictions in the enlargement of experience and the heightening of response.[12] Certainly rebellions by ways of evil can turn into destruction for its own sake, yet that would seem to be rare and limited. Almost all the great historical crimes—the Slaughter of the Innocents, the achievements of empires, the "great" religious wars, the inquisitions, the revolutionary Terror, the campaigns of fratricide and revenge, the Stalinist purges, the Nazi genocides, etc.—claimed social, moral, historical and divine ideals. When men consciously pursue evil to its violent extreme, the results would seem to be mostly individual and temporary, and probably the most likely end is some form of self-destruction. No historian seems to report a time when rebellious demonics have been a major social problem; the rankest violences and horrors have always been pre-empted by those with the most exalted claims to the public good. Since the demonic searches for new areas of knowledge and intensities of experience, even his most outrageous taboo violations will more likely lead to incest than to rape, to drug-taking than to torture, to suicide than to murder. (Rape, torture and murder—pain generally—as De Sade suggests, are attributes of power.) While the possibilities for acquiring purposive power to carry out some ideal program, as with dictators, are endless, the possibilities for acquiring unusual experience and knowledge, as with demonics, are drastically self-limited. So, indeed, are the very number of demonics since they are only definable as perverse rebels against the generally acknowledged good.

It is not my purpose to justify rape, torture or murder (a worthy case can sometimes be made for incest, drugs and suicide); but, on the literary evidence, neither do most demonics. A De Sade or Genet wants, almost in spite of his fantasies, reciprocal relations which markedly limit the destructive possibilities; even more evident, the most thorough reversers of values want to create new realms of fantasy, beauty and sincerity as well as states of extreme feeling and awareness.[13] A thoroughgoing pursuit of the demonic is as creative as it is difficult. Those who see only the "nastiness" may be blinded by their own needs. But no simple affirmation of the demonic comes to issue here, for discrimination must also be applied when it comes to devils. The shabbiness of much of the romantic and symbolist Satanism comes from reversing a rather shoddy religion as well as from incapacities for full rebellion and adequate metamorphoses of Satan. A demonic like D. H. Lawrence certainly shows a good bit of nastiness but, with the palpable religious feeling that obviously informs any authentic demonic, positive intensities supersede the nastiness, even in his obsessional Black Mass of a Christ and a priestess of Isis copulating on an altar in *The Man Who Died*. For the positive affirmation against restrictive and distored values dominates, no matter how negative or perverse the way of rebellion. As the Russian novelist Zamiatin insists in *We*, even a vision of future resistance to a totalitarian anti-utopia requires that rebellion in the name of individual sexual and religious values take the shape of the revolt of the "Mephis" (the new followers of the ancient Mephistopheles). Rebellious "energy," says Zamiatin, provides the only antithesis to the social law of "entropy," and finds its natural style in demonic and perversely individual traditions.[14]

A Mephisto as a spirit of denial in the literary intellectual's study may strike the contemporary reader as quaint to the point of comedy. The devil might make a more suitable wager in a laboratory or an administrative office since most of our soul-selling takes bland and banal institutional forms. Granted, too, that there is often sad farce in the post-Rimbaud artist making himself into his own pathetic demon or, as Ibsen shows it, using a demonic pretense as a bathetic "life-lie." Contemporary rebels also suffer from modern dehumanization and trivialization in the attempt to create demons who are not quaintly anachronistic fools. Bedeviling our indifferent and manipulated cosmos becomes absurd humor. But there is a tradition of such laughter for the rebel. For while our public comedy, such as the castrato styles of mass entertainment, comes out merely genial at best, buffoons, jesters and fools play an important role in the iconography of rebellion.[15] Diogenes not only played the wit but magnified his denials of convention into crowd-stopping burlesque. The "holy fool" provides the mold for the heretic. Rebellion, even in its demonic excesses, often takes on additional poignancy by its defensive slap-stick. The "stupid" buffoon, from his "simple-minded" misunderstanding of primitive ritual into his contemporary "confusion" about regulations, plays a rebel role. As with Jaroslav Hasek's *The Good Soldier: Schweik*, every act of obedience can be foolishly carried out as a wise mockery of false order. If men will not perceive the tragic incongruities, they can at least laugh at one who pretends to follow the farcical logic of authority. Fools, it is generally agreed, raise difficulties about morals and manners, employ techniques for the break-through of the repressed, and cast laughter on things as they supposedly are. Falstaff, the most common focus of debate on humor, can reasonably be viewed not just as the wise-buffoon educator of a mythical hero but as a satirized Diogenes gone to pot, with his grossities only partly masking his astute "counterfeit" of conventional morals and his penetrating mockeries of the fatuous code of honor. (Shakespeare, of course, is no rebel, though often a disinterested nihilist.) [16] Grotesqueness provides not only a devastating comment on the rebel but on all pretensions to order and meaning.

The too familiar arguments that comedy is corrective, commonsensical and essentially conservative often come out of special pleading based on a narrow selection of material. For example, arguments for the social reasonableness of neoclassical satire rarely probe the extremities of an Earl of Rochester, who turns creation into an absurd void ("Upon Nothing"), so savagely slashes his own desires as well as his contemporaries that no saving joke remains, wittily undercuts not only the unreasonableness of his society but any claim to good sense ("A Satire Upon Mankind"), and literally played the noble-buffoon in and out of rhyme and reason. To think of Rochester as merely a "court wit" of the charming Restoration is to mistake the ill-fitting costume of his radical discontent for the reality.[17] Rebels as aristocrats, whether in the historical dress of the devastating Earl, or in the dream fineries of Nietzsche's Zarathustra, practice a defiant, if feverish, humor which roughens their poetry and rejects far more than it affirms. The "superior laugh" provides the most bitter and disruptive confession of all.

The Golden Mean, so often identified as the moderating and solacing spirit of comedy,[18] may most likely and properly be found only in the fabled Golden Age. Decorous and restrained comedy surely exists, such as those pleasant forms sweetly ending in the marriage festival—a polite version of the Saturnalia and orgy. By the "logic of comic form," the "gang shag" is as appropriate, if a bit more savage and honest, ending than official nuptials. Partly disguised mockeries, like contemptuous submission, reinforce rebellion. Fools and comedies and laughter, including the cosmic jokes of human creation, rarely have decorous morals. Thus the truisms that comedy affirms and "rebels lack a sense of humor" (or saints or dictators, for that matter) comes out of sheer bigotry of *le homme sensual moyen* who smugly concludes that humor, too, is his special prerogative. Specifically rebellious humor, of course, may often take a quite peculiar cast: mordant, "irresponsible" in its lack of sentiment and decorum, bitter, outrageous, nihilistic (epitomized, perhaps, in the savage incongruous shots of the cinema of Luis Buñuel). In contemporary literature, it has been pointed out, the "dissociation of sensibility," the disparities of our civilized mixtures of blandness and horror, and "absurdist" philosophies produce a humor of fragmented incongruities [19] —really the art of schizophrenic laughter.

Current literary rebels sometimes carry this to hysterical extremity in which all the oldest beliefs are the newest farce. Whether, as in the harsh comedy of an Ionesco or a Beckett, we take this as a distinctive tragic-burlesque vision, or follow the dadaists in seeing nonsensical chaos as the untoppable joke, or surrealistically see *"humour noir"* rising out of the freed derangement of the post-Renaissance psyche, or more generally suspect that the Pelican laugh was first given at the gates of Paradise and that cosmic mockery and jaundiced amusement were simultaneous with the moment of creation, there is no end of rebellious comedy.[20]

Thus any discussion of the literary rebel must allow the varied shapes of the demonic and dark humor, involuted irony as well as simple naturalism, and similar complications of motive and motif. This also rules out certain common and too easy objections to the rebel. The standard plaint that rebels and their works—especially recent ones—are too negative, destructive, and lacking any positive value, may strike us as especially American, though it would seem to be common in any literal-minded and bumptious place as well as to authorities everywhere. At some levels this longing for the positive cannot be answered because it simply misses the whole mode of the rebel; those who do not see fundamental falsities, injustices, absurdities and mortalities cannot even imagine what the rebel is about. No better are those well-intentioned ameliorists who view rebellion as symptom of some current social malaise, correctable by well-administered dosages of money or education or psychiatry or reorganization. Perhaps most obtuse of all are those middle-brow moralists who see rebels as slightly ill-tempered liberal reformers. If rebellion is not recognized as an ultimate response to the very conditions of existence, it seems to be mere bad manners.

Rebels, indeed, offer something positive and useful: permanent defiance, without which life loses essential freedom and vitality. When the rebel negates the usual negatives, when he denies the standard compulsions and anxieties, he creates positively. Since the rebel tends to treat all forms of power as anxiety compulsions—not just authority and ideology but luxury, security, fame, talent, art, faith, honor and even virtue—rebellion becomes the living individual dialectic against all impersonalized claims. The rebel may often be counter-accused of having the power of righteousness, if not of rightness. Circumstances also sometimes appear to turn deviant ways of living and expression into more direct powers. Occasional rebels obtain what the unrebellious consider success. Once, it is said, a saint became a pope, but sanctity did not reign; there are a few claims for philosophers having become kings, but not that politics became wisdom; similarly, rebels with ordinary power have no claim on rebelliousness. For if the rebel achieves ordinary power, it must be negative so to maintain his positive vocation. The issue gets confused because those in power think mostly in power terms, and thus miscomprehend rebellion as directly competing power—and treat rebels accordingly. So we see a rebel tendency to exaggerate his defiant peculiarities in the effort to reinforce his own terms, his defiant rather than competing self-definition.

Rebels must also reply to those in power that they "refuse history," that their choices of moral libertarianism and idiosyncratic art and social directness and intellectual iconoclasm were not aimed at practical power, whatever the circumstances. The point seems incomprehensible to many of those, whether presidents or clerks, who feel themselves wired up to the manifest forces of their times. On the one hand, those rebels who turn to power and success and conformity with overt history do so only by negating their rebellion. On the other, the consistent rebel must even mock rebellion and truth—his appropriate claims to esoteric power; many do, with an ultimate (though hardly maintainable) nihilism which provides the rebels' unique terror, and strength. Paradoxically, the rebel cannot have direct power, or he ceases to be a rebel; yet he must have some significant relation to, or effect on, power, not only to avoid futility and capriciousness but to define himself against.

Many rebels, such as those we have been discussing, actually rest their case on their positiveness, on their direct intensity of experience and feeling and action, on their responsiveness to the immediate universe of nature, God, sex, despair, anger, sympathy and desire. The rebel demands to be present with the thing-itself. Diogenes, we learn from some of the favorite anecdotes, was given to rather wry illuminations—a burst of joy as to how simple and direct life could be and thus how false were the pleasures and fears of most men. Once thirsty but without a cup, Diogenes realized that a child was showing him the way by drinking out of his hands. Just as Diogenes exalted in the pleasure to be found in that simple drink of water, so a William Blake exalts in the imaginative world seen in a grain of sand, Thoreau in the wealth of a walk in the woods, Lawrence in the reverberations of a sexual touch, Jack Kerouac in the luxury of a can of hot beans. Admittedly, part of the point is again negative: Diogenes was mocking the crippling by civilized manners, Blake unimaginative scientific vision, Thoreau the Puritanic-competitive work ethos, Lawrence dead responsiveness, Kerouac dully affluent suburan living. The rebel attempts to answer, with a usual mocking twist, the query about what life means by an angry finger directing one to fully taste, see, hear, feel, think this, *this* right in front of one.

Such a fusion of intensified desire and insouciance to the usual concerns, however, seems to require occasional supports. Here is where the literary rebel becomes peculiar —"cranky, lunatic fringe." Historically, the supports for intensified immediacy include various exceptional and even recondite disciplines: nature worship, visionary initiation, orgiastic music (such as jazz), romantic love, demonic practices, derangements of the senses, drugs and metaphysical visions, among others. Such, even with rebels, appears the disproportion between simple human ends and the ornate means used to reach them. The very outcastness of the rebel increases the temptations to build labyrinthine places to house his lonely defiance. Heretics, as we see in the reformation antinomians, indulge in home-brewed mythologies. The later Blake said, "I must

create my own system or be enslaved by another man's."
Rimbaud, and many of the later Symbolists, ransacked
occult lore to furnish, and over-furnish, exasperated images.[21] D. H. Lawrence wrote almost as much strident
"pollyanalytics" as fiction to justify his insights. Henry
Miller does obeisance to almost every form of murky magic
he encounters. Many contemporary literary rebels take on
Zen, Vedanta, theosopy, Reichianism, alchemy, fantastic
science, Jungianism, the less popular forms of Christianity,
various types of jazz, Tibetan ritual, poeticized drug-
taking, and dozens of theologized literary works. So many
and such indiscriminate supporting systems make some
contemporary American writers seem the victims of, rather
than rebels against, a confusedly acquisitive culture. But
even so, rebel nostrums often display a more amusing
fancifulness and less viciousness than the popular forms of
piety, technology and entertainment.

The "philosophers" utilized by literary rebels frequently
turn out to be literary rebels themselves, and perhaps
deserve attention as just such a continuing tradition. Read
together the sixteenth-century Paracelsus and the
twentieth-century Wilhelm Reich and one finds that both
of these rebel doctors and explorers of the physiological-
psychological fringes show touching similarities.[22] The
medicine of Paracelsus turns Medieval astrology and
emblematic lore into insights in homeopathic therapy and
psychosomatic diagnosis; the medicine of Reich turns
physiological Freudianism and Marxian revolution into
therapy for orgiastic impotence and diagnosis of rigid
social character. The dross—Paracelsus' absurd medica-
tions and demonology and Reich's "orgone accumulators"
(undersized telephone booths for increasing orgiastic
potency) and cosmic sexual mysticism—appear equally
fanciful. In further parallelism, both Paracelsus and Reich
wisely made much of marginal experiences, both were
megalomaniacs who took their metaphors with fantastic
literalness, and both ended in a partly justified paranoia.
The learned and troublesome rebel doctors violently
parodied the sciences of their times, authored voluminous
obscure messianic pronouncements and notably influenced
a number of literary rebels.

Strange rebellious minds like Paracelsus and Reich
deserve to be taken seriously but not literally. But that

applies to most rebels. Rebel philosophies might be seen as serving styles of defiance, in living as well as in ideas, rather than as atomistically verifiable truths or as part of any ultimate universal harmony. No rebel truth is a science or a metaphysic; it may often be something much better—the experience of, and the way to, revolt against the false ordering of life. The mythopoetics of past literary rebels, which have been of considerable interest to recent unrebellious literary scholars (under headings of occultism, symbolism, orientalism, monomyths, vision, etc.) take drastic forcing to come out as a body of thought, feeling or history separate from the denials and defiances which engendered it. If the literary rebel is, as I have been arguing, a rebel first and foremost—and rebellion is its own justification—then we exalt rather than reduce him by demythologizing any unrebellious claims made by him or for him. Some are due. The antinomian religion, the anti-politics, the sardonic humor, the demonic explorations, and the positive negations insist that no metaphysics, no power, no art constitute the rebel's primary purposes and products. Granted that there are ex-rebels who take up all sorts of trades and vices, and that no man plays a pure role. But rebellious wisdom, starting at least with the violent lucidity of Diogenes, shows an awareness comparable to that of tragedy: life is limited, choices are decisive, the world and awareness deserve a defiant passion.[23]

BUT RATHER THAN continue this here-and-there commentary on the rich traditions of the literary rebel, we might focus in some analytic detail on three examples. They come from one of the great and pertinent ages of rebellion, running from the last part of the eighteenth century to the last part of the nineteenth. I suggest William Blake's *The Marriage of Heaven and Hell*, Herman Melville's *Bartleby, the Scrivener* and Tristan Corbière's *Les Amours Jaunes*. Besides matters of taste, these seem appropriate because of their diverse national, personal and literary origins, because of their diverse ways of rebelling, and also because of their similar intriguing merits. To my suspicious eye, these works of Blake, Melville and Corbière have also suffered considerable misemphasis by unrebellious readings (which my commentaries seek to reverse). Our subject, then, is no local or parochial tradition. These three, out of many possible choices, especially highlight rebellion against the very nature and limits of literature. And all three have had—though Corbière is not always given his due—a powerful influence on rebellious twentieth-century literature, some of which will be our later concern. Our heroes are always what we make of them, but these should make appropriately contumacious masters for any rebellious education.

3 THE MARRIAGE OF HEAVEN AND HELL

WILLIAM BLAKE's *The Marriage of Heaven and Hell* [1] should be seen as an idiosyncratic, nearly unique, work, defying both usual literature and ordinary responses. Some of the ostensible admirers of Blake dislike it; [2] other unrebellious students of Blake blandly dissolve parts of the *Marriage* to wed themselves to one or another version of Blakean metapoetics (thus at least testifying to its importance); [3] and yet other critics falsely ameliorate Blake's most extreme gestures into reasonable art. [4] *The Marriage of Heaven and Hell*, the most quoted and quotable of Blake's works, shows his most distinctive qualities. This grotesque, satiric, didactic, and fervent pot-pourri survives as both one of a kind and yet as an excellent example of just what we might expect from a literary rebel. Its mixture of argument and anecdote and fancy belongs with the Cynic-heretic-*épater* tradition; indignation and perversity provide its tone and method. Drawing on major gestures and figures of rebellion, and angrily assaulting pseudo-rebels and authorities, Blake endlessly opposes the things that supposedly are. Only his extremity of opposition, and his justification of it, provide the coherence of *The Marriage of Heaven and Hell*.

Among the toppled turtles are conventional reason. Here Blake calls upon traditional literary rebels, including the Old Testament prophets and Diogenes. In the second of the anecdotal prose-poems called "Memorable Fancies," Blake wryly describes himself dining with Isaiah and Ezekial, and he inquires about their hardly believable speaking with God (Blake, at this level, shows post-Enlightenment scepticism). Isaiah replies that he didn't see or hear any literal God but "discovered the infinite in everything" (the largest meanings) and that "the voice of honest indignation is the voice of God." If one wants to discuss Blakean metaphysics, here lies the rebellious crux. The fanciful anecdote continues with an emphasis upon "firm perswasion." But since many appear not to be capable of a rebellious firmness about anything, the argument leads into the question of its authenticity. Blake, antagonist of institutional religion and authoritarian transcendence, and heir of radical antinomians and poetic subjectivists, here raises the difficulty of the atheistic religion he poses throughout the work: how be sure that the prophetic urge, lacking external revelation and institutional discipline, gives the truth? The two prophets answer by explaining that they lived arduously, naked and directly and intensely, like the American Indian shaman and "our friend Diogenes, the Grecian," in "the desire of raising other men into a perception of the infinite." Blake thus insists that the rebel's ground for his truth comes from his rebellious commitment and his extreme way of life. Such extremity produces a passionate indignation which violates ease and ordinariness so that the heightened response of individual conscience is "the voice of God," the truth.

This point, I believe, becomes crucial in understanding Blake's drastic antinomianism. The rebel's truth of "honest indignation" stands antithetical to most ways of truth. Its insistence on passionate conviction and desire opposes what is usually meant by mysticism, as well as the rationalist's analysis and contemplation. The disinterestedness, objectivity and common verifiability of scientific methods get fully excluded in the impassioned, personal and exceptional means of prophetic discovery. Is this "firm perswasion," then, mere arbitrary subjectivity? Hardly, since it required arduous preparation in terms of a whole rebellious way of living, demanded unusual persons, and rejected the errors of prudence and self-interest ("I cared not for consequences, but wrote," says Blake's Isaiah; and, asks Blake's Ezekial, "is he honest who resists his genius of conscience only for the sake of present ease or gratification?"). The rebel's truth, then, does not fit the usual standards of knowledge, but is also no easy whim, selfish fantasy or capricious deduction. There is, we might say, arbitrary subjectivism and profound subjectivity, and

Blake here sketches the latter which provides human truths quite distinct from the conventional ways of knowledge. Those who disagree, Blake seems to suggest, better avoid the biographies of all great prophets, and better hold to moral and prudential order as more important than truth. Put another way, Blake believes that prophetic wrath provides exalted awareness, and that is why the rebel demands a different way of living and responding. Thus intense defiance leads to wisdom.

Currently, it is an anti-romantic commonplace to deny that the artist needs any special way of life and feeling, and in so far as he be artist that may well be correct. But Blake, even when he speaks of "Poetic Genius," means rebel rather more than artist; the rebel—here rightly represented by Diogenes and the Indian shaman as well as the Judeo-Christian prophets—must live and react differently. It is also a scholarly commonplace that Blake, struggling against materialist and empiricist philosophies, re-creates an aesthetic idealism (variously restated in Platonic, Neoplatonic, occultist, humanist-Christian or "visionary" terminologies).[5] Confining the argument to the *Marriage*, that also leads to misinterpretation. (Even in Blake's mostly awkward, ornate and confused long metapoetic works, the ideal myth is not always the crucial thing for one sometimes rebelliously "striving with Systems to deliver Individuals from those Systems."[6]) Blake's insistence that "honest indignation is the voice of God" cogently tells us what a good many rebels are about, including Blake.

The Marriage of Heaven and Hell is an anthology of eighteen parts: an opening and a closing rhetorical poem, five prose-poem fables ("Memorable Fancy"), seventy aphorisms called "Proverbs of Hell," half a dozen very brief catechisms or essayistic declarations, three separated aphorisms, and a brief statement of principles called "The Voice of the Devil." By its very rebellious nature, it does not, and probably could not, take an over-all formal shape. Call it a scrapbook on some related themes, or a polished notebook, or a poetic anti-poem. One can, of course, attribute a shape to the work, but the shape will either be vague abstraction—such as formal musical analogies for a work in which musical analogies are not in any other way appropriate—or otherwise fail to take into account the specific gestures and tones of the work. The *Marriage* often gets labeled "satire"—an easy category in which to shove many angry rebel writings—but the mockery of Swedenborg, or that of other figures such as Paracelsus and Böhme whom Blake also draws upon, does not control the work as Blake sketches various caricatures and expounds his wrath. Of course almost everything in the *Marriage* aims against something, but that defines rebel rather than satire. Literary rebels rebel against as well as in literature.

The opening and closing poems do not determine the work's shape since their style appears markedly different than those of the pieces between them, and those pieces could easily be rearranged in various possible sequences. The opening poem, entitled "The Argument," announces, I take it, the need for prophetic wrath because the just man has been driven into the wilds by the hypocrite. But it is not a very good piece in its own terms or in comparison with the rest of the anthology. The imagery is weak and stock (serpents are sneaking, paths are perilous, humility is mild, death is a vale). Weak, too, is the uncertain mixture of Biblical and homemade machinery which suggests a cycle of creativity and barrenness—a "myth" made much of in Blake's shifting later poems but mostly irrelevant (and ignored) in the *Marriage*. The weak final piece of the *Marriage* is also a poem (the rest are heightened prose), "A Song of Liberty." This may well not belong with the *Marriage* since it uses the different style, and attitude, of Blake's cosmic rhetoric. "A Song of Liberty" does carry the opening poem's individual rage into a universal apocalyptic process, but to find much further linkage would be just ingenious. Some declarations, also used elsewhere, suggest the power of Blakean rhetoric— "Nor pale religious letchery call that virginity that wishes but acts not!" But most of this "Song" rants against authority with too much godly roar and fire and thunder in the images. There are obscure political elements here, though Blake essentially lacks politics.[7] When he says, "EMPIRE IS NO MORE! AND NOW THE LION AND WOLF SHALL CEASE" he refers not to the British empire of his time, nor even generally to imperialism as such but, as the imagery tells us, to the whole ravening quality of power itself. But Blake sometimes thought he dealt with tangible politics and fell into its rather hysterical bombast on the revolutionary side. Such enlargement of defiance, a frequent temptation to the rebel, Blake elsewhere aptly set aside with individual rage: "General good is the plea of the scoundrel, hypocrite & flatterer." [8]

The rest of the *Marriage* takes a sharper style, especially if we do not twist this rebel into quite unrebellious political, aesthetic and methaphysical patterns. Let us comment, for examples, on the three fine aphorisms that Blake significantly sets out in isolation: "For everything that lives is Holy." "One Law for the Lion & Ox is Oppression." "Opposition is true Friendship." Their partly paradoxical and enigmatic suggestiveness cannot lie in their truistic interpretation. "For everything that lives is Holy" certainly should not be taken as the unrebellious spiritism or pietism which Blake attacks. Given the *Marriage's* extreme religious humanization ("All deities reside in the human breast") and Blake's angry atheism, the proverb insists that life itself—energy, anger, sex— remains ultimate and sacred. Contrary to such an adage's use in an unrebellious mouth, the holiness of tangible existence remains a passionately anti-moral assertion.[9] The most exalted quality belongs to all aspects of immediate responsiveness.

"One Law for the Lion & Ox is Oppression" states a double ethic, itself also an attack on moral universals, which we find again and again in rebels.[10] Blake's lions and tigers belong, in both imagery and attitude, with Nietz- sche's *"übermensch"* and his animal friends (the moun- tain scene in *Thus Spoke Zarathustra*) and with D. H. Lawrence's "dark heroes" and their animal states. This aphorism may also be partly explained by the preceding Memorable Fancy which argues that we should love "the greatest men best . . . for there is no other God." The usual connotations of "great men," of course, do not apply; Blake shows no partiality for historical greatness in the realms of power (rulers, military heroes, revolutionists, social leaders). Prophets of indignation (those figures most abhorrent to middle-class culture) represent what Blake means by greatness in all the examples he uses. The one in this Memorable Fancy is exactly to rebel order for it is Jesus Christ—made demonic (unlike the more evan- gelical Christ of Blake's later works) since He broke all the

Ten Commandments and "acted from impulse, not from rules." The law for the lion is passionate, angry and demonic experience; rules fit only the plodding parts of life.

"Opposition is true Friendship" may have been erased by Blake from some copies of the *Marriage* because he later did not want the friendship of opposition with Aristotle, Swedenborg and the other angels of moral convention he mocks throughout the work. Anyway, the truth of opposition is the major theme of the entire collection. Blake's more abstract statements, such as "Without Contraries is no progression," are simple variations on the positive assertion of contumaciousness and opposition. To reduce pedantically the quality of exalted opposition and make the contrariness into some balanced, reasonable dialectical system violates the tone and meaning of most of the work.[11] Blake's gestures, and most acute and emphasized statements, throughout the *Marriage* come out less corrective than corrosive, less dialectical than damning. Only to oppose is to find and be the truth for this rebel.

That Blake means much more nay than yea—or means his yea to be a nay—appears quite emphatic in the third brief section of the work entitled "The Voice of the Devil." Using the usual demonic technique of reversing accepted doctrine, he contrasts orthodox Christian moral principles of dualism (body *vs.* soul, energy *vs.* reason, good *vs.* evil) with his contraries of monism, vitalism and amoralism, which patently hold true for him. The emphasis here should be on Blake's insistently demonic oppositions and not on any equilibrium between orthodoxy and heterodoxy. Blake does not juggle or moderate between reason and energy but creates a new angry reason, called energy, of which the old reason is a small, restricting and conforming part. The contrariness of the contraries provides, for Blake, the real "Eternal Delight." Delight—pleasure, desire, free play—brings the ultimate. Thus, in the final Memorable Fancy, he turns Christ into all energy and burns up the orthodox angel who disagrees with the poet. The angel then becomes a prophet and finally a devil who is Blake's demonic muse and "particular friend." *That* is how opposition becomes true friendship.

In the first brief Memorable Fancy Blake seems to wryly

and delightedly identify his own mirror image as that of the "mighty Devil" producing this very book. His affirmation of "Infernal Wisdom" provides the most consistent point of view in the *Marriage*. Of course this is not *mere* Satanism since Blake's Devil, also, belongs to no orthodoxy but came from being a "burned-up" angel. But to over-qualify this demonic insistence by plumping heavily on it as an ironic literary device or as a dialectical part of Blake's earnest moralism belongs with "the cunning of weak and tame minds which have the power to resist energy." Such "Devourers," as Blake calls them in one of the catechism sections, belong with the oxen in a deathly fixity against the energetic "Giants" and rebels ("now in chains"). "Religion," he scornfully comments on the ameliorism of his day, "is an endeavour to reconcile" the giants and the devourers, the lions and the oxen. But "whoever tries to reconcile them seeks to destroy existence." This, contrary to many learnedly devouring and amelioristic commentators on Blake, makes rebellion an absolute.

Blake's demonic Christ ("Messiah or Satan or Tempter") does not reconcile the ox and the lion, the rebel and the complacent. Granted, the later Blake partly abandoned rebellion and fell into various snares of religious reconciliation—perhaps because of his own Protestant-guilt heritage, his sexual difficulties with his wife, or his paranoid sense of defeat in an uncongenial time. But the rebellious Blake belongs with the "father-killers," that major psychological drive of the Western rebel, and the figure he sometimes calls Nobodaddy or Urizen (God, Reason, Virtue, Empire, Order, or whatever other names fit paternal authority), must down. Probably some of the hostility to Swedenborg and his engineer's Protestant super-rationalism, which provides part of the focus of the mockery of the *Marriage*, may be explained by Swedenborgianism's earlier role of intellectual fathering to Blake. He now condemns Swedenborg for his anti-rebellion, his justifying "Providence" as against the "Active Life." [12] Similarly with the image of Milton, that literary father, whom Blake condemns for casting out "Desire" and, in the famous passage, puts as a true poet of "the Devil's party without knowing it." (Understandably, Blake was not prepared to accept Milton's rebellion against civility and individuality in the form of creating a horrendous and

static authoritarian deity.[13]) In this section, too, Blake
does not balance Reason against Desire but exalts desire as
the source and quality of right reason.

Blake's views on restraint and repression must lead to
assault on all systems of power authority. Any institutionalized idea—church, monarchy, sect, official style—becomes a priestly system (as he points out in the seventh
piece) and then grows autonomous from, and antagonistic
to, individual human truth and desire. Following this
emphasis, we might see Blake's doctrine of expanded sense
perception as less idealist metaphysics (though it may have
led to that) than something more literal.[14] The main point
in the pair of verses closing the first Memorable Fancy—
"How do you know but ev'ry Bird that cuts the airy
way,/ Is an immense world of delight, clos'd by your senses
five?"—is in the "Infernal wisdom" of heightened sense
awareness. For when, in a later section, Blake also states
the demonic-rebel point that the apocalypse "will come to
pass by an improvement of sensual enjoyment," this points
less to aesthetic idealism than to tangible human desire
and delight. As with the Blake who wrote, "Embraces are
Comminglings from the Head even to the Feet,/And not a
pompous High Priest entering by a Secret Place," [15]
heightened imagination takes consequent place to heightened and enlarged sexual orgasm.

Blake, I am arguing, really is a rebel, and rebels should
not be reduced to distant metaphysical blandness or
ameliorative liberal humanism. Wrath, denial, intensified
sexuality, institutional and religious anarchism, absolute
opposition—these provide the appropriate direction. In
"The Proverbs of Hell"—yet another demonic section—all
golden means seem to be Blake's antagonists, and it is
hard to subvert such exultant adages as "The road of excess
leads to the palace of wisdom" (No. 3). Why not mocking
"shack" instead of hopeful "palace"? Because Blake really
believes in the royalty of extremity. When we turn to the
final proverb of the collection we may see the issue of
interpreting Blake in a simple crux. It reads: "Enough! or
Too Much" (No. 70). Some polite citizen-readers inter-
pret this as saying , in effect: I've gone far enough, or even
too far. More clever literary gentlemen take the adage as
ironic, with Blake saying, in effect: I've gone far enough
with my mocking proverbs, and so most will feel that I've

been excessive. But, the major form of Blake's proverbs is paradoxical parallelism (opposition *is* friendship) in which the two sides of the aphorism tend to equal each other. Given this, and Blake's insistent emphasis on extremity, "Enough! or Too Much" should be paraphrased thus: excess (too much) is precisely the right amount (just enough). Nothing less than excess provides the "norm" for the true rebel, like the Blake of the *Marriage*, because anything else would be an acceptance of the basic logic of things as they are.

While we need not discuss all the demonic-reverse strategies of Blake's proverbial extremity, at least a little excess in commentary might be appropriate. It is sometimes said that gnomic wisdom, as in folk sayings, lacks meaning because the statements cancel each other. But this misses the multiple focus of such wisdom. The point applies to Blake's proverbs. For example, he uses "pride" in contrasting ways: "Shame is Pride's cloke" (No. 20) might be a shrewd comment on neurotic guilt. "The pride of the peacock is the Glory of God" (No. 22) might be an affirmation of human sexual attraction. Both the negative and the positive uses of "pride" here do not cancel each other because they take different aspects. We must also ask what the rebel opposes to get the full force of his gestures; in both cases here Blake seems to be inverting Puritanical morality. Many of the other proverbs similarly attack the various facets of the repression of human desire and energy, as in those which praise lust, wrath and nakedness (Nos. 23, 24, 25). Even the apparently prudent aphorisms —really parodies of Biblical and other cautious advice— should be viewed in the appropriate perspectives. Thus "In seed time learn, in harvest teach, in winter enjoy" (No. 1) praises a "natural" sequence of responsiveness and twists prudence so that it culminates in joy. Some go ironically against prudence, as "Bring out number, weight & measure in a year of dearth" (No. 14). Here the only justification for a measured and rationalized set of responses is an emotional drought. Otherwise put, in a hardworked pun, "Damn braces. Bless relaxes" (No. 57).

Blake's anti-proverbial proverbs directed at social forms take the libertarian perspective which aims not at reform but at the radical rejection of the very basis of institutions:

"Prisons are built with stones of Law, Brothels with bricks of religion" (No. 21). "As the caterpiller chooses the fairest leaves to lay her eggs on, so the priest lays his curse on the fairest joys" (No. 55). An angry insistence on the psychic price to be paid for codes and institutions of repression comes out in many, including several of those famous ones which have been called "Freudian": "He who desires but acts not, breeds pestilence" (No. 5) and "Sooner murder an infant in its cradle than nurse unacted desires" (No. 67). All through the *Marriage* "act" becomes the very identity of man, in contrast to "essence" idealism. And action must flow clearly, unimpeded, from response and desire and energy in Blake's denial of the entire guilt culture: "The soul of sweet delight can never be defil'd" (No. 53). Blake's affirmation of freedom, as so many of the images insist, depends above all on sexual rebellion.[16] Traditional idealists and moralists should be outraged, for Blake supports active "sin," so long as it is individual and authentic.

Even the negative attacks on the prudential in the honor of excess draw a sexual focus: "Prudence is a rich, ugly old maid courted by Incapacity" (No. 4). The range of assaulted restraints is not only institutional, moral and religious; the conservatism which appeals to the past gets turned over: "Drive your cart and your plow over the bones of the dead" (No. 2, etc.). And, of course, Blake repeatedly comes back to that central emphasis on rebel anger as wisdom, which we have discussed: "The wrath of the lion is the wisdom of God" (No. 24) and "The tygers of wrath are wiser than the horses of instruction" (No. 44). We also repeatedly come back to the double order of existence, deriving from the special role of the rebel in his anger, sex and joy: "The cistern contains; the fountain overflows" (No. 35). We not only get contrasting existences but contrasting knowledge: "The rat, the mouse, the fox, the rabbit watch the roots; the lion, the tyger, the horse, the elephant watch the fruits" (No. 34) and "The eagle never lost so much time as when he submitted to learn of the crow" (Nos. 39; & 9, 12, 27, 41, 44, 50, 54, 65). Blake's insistence here, I believe, reflects a basic difficulty of the rebellious: once you knock down the usual repressive social, moral and metaphysical distinctions, what "standards" or discriminations remain valid? The rebel an-

swers with images drawn on the qualities of rebellion itself
—anger, isolation, stubbornness, sexuality, defiance, etc.
—and uses them as the categories of discriminating
awareness. The rebel principles are, by usual standards,
*a*principled; even "bad" energy (the lion or tyger) is
"good." "Exuberance is Beauty" (Nos. 64, etc.), writes
Blake in affirming a refusal of form which could be the
justification for this very work. Waywardness also becomes
the highest form of awareness; "Improvement makes
straight roads; but the crooked roads without Improvement are roads of Genius" (No. 66). Or even more
emphatically, "If the fool would persist in his folly he
would become wise" (No. 18).

Several of Blake's own follies come out in the occultist-
alchemical images of man, such as "The eyes of fire, the
nostrils of air, the mouth of water, the beard of earth"
(Nos. 48, etc.). Combine this with evangelical feelings
about the powers of imaginative faith—"Everything possible to be believ'd is an image of truth" (Nos. 38, 33, 36,
69)—and the result may well be the often tiresome
phantasmagoria of cosmic mythology which so obsessed
Blake.[17] Such peculiarity may be one of the prices to be
paid for rebellion. For I suspect the word "know" in the
following "Proverb of Hell" to mean, for Blake, knowledge
in the Biblical sense of "to be": "You never know what is
enough unless you know what is more than enough" (No.
46). The rebel can easily fall into one of his incomplete
excesses such as revolution or religion. Rebellion is precarious.

Blake, it intermittently becomes clear, was reaching for
"far out" experiences, sexual and cosmic ecstasies, in which
things are no longer ordinary restrictive reality. "Excess of
sorrow laughs. Excess of joy weeps" (Nos. 26, 60).
Extremity, then, defies the world's order so to create new
experiences. For full rebellion must reach the nerves, be a
condition of body as well as of mind, perversely heighten
desires and sensations as well as heighten the truths of
opposition. To reduce this process to the bland categories
of mysticism, or the euphemisms of "vision," or the
de-energizing structures of idealism would be to obscure
the rebel emphasis. As the very form of so many of the
"Proverbs of Hell" show, opposition and excess themselves
become the intensifying experience we can only properly

call rebellion. In savaging traditional "wisdom" (including the Old Testament proverbs created by the prudently fearful scribes of an authoritarian bureaucracy), Blake denied any gnostic order, any encompassing myth.

Even in the two most elaborate Memorable Fancies (to conclude our commentary on *The Marriage of Heaven and Hell*) where Blake becomes involved in his epistemological allegories, the rebellious side of the cosmic mythology remains crucial. In the "Printing House in Hell" fancy Blake has six chambers for his parable of the cave—an infernal reversal of idealist theory of knowledge?—with emblematic figures (perhaps Dragonmen of sensual passion, Vipers of reason, Eagles of aspiration, Lions of wrath, and Unam'd Forms of genius). This parody of the six days of creation—and perhaps of some of his esoteric sources [18]—may be partly serious to Blake but also results in comic anticlimax. For this elaborate cycle of the creation of knowledge is how books are made and "arranged in libraries." Since all the other Memorable Fancies and, indeed, most of the *Marriage*, mock and satirize, Blake must be taken as partly sardonic here in his images of how "knowledge is transmitted from generation to generation" in entombed sensibility.

Rebel opposition more clearly over-rides metapoetics in the longest Memorable Fancy, a satiric cosmic journey with a nastily orthodox angel. This not only parodies the order and restraint of the philosophers (Swedenborg and Aristotle, and perhaps others) but stands forth as metaphysical "phantasy" in a Swiftian savage indignation. Here the cave of knowledge is clearly negative, as are the stable of social common sense, the church void, the mill of reason, etc. Blake displays passive self-consciousness as a place full of spiders (so, later, did Dostoevsky), and a pious angel brought him there. But a vaster creature with "all the fury of a spiritual existence" (thus a positive image for Blake) disrupts the self-contemplating nihilism. Blake, unlike Job, dare understand this exuberantly colored Leviathan. The angel flees the demonic cosmos of Blake's imaginative fury, and the scene of horror transforms itself into a pastoral idyl. Here a rebel harper sings against the intellectual status quo that creates nastiness, and also justifies Blake's rejection of his former intellectual fathers: "The man who never alters his opinion is like standing water, and breeds reptiles of the mind." So Blake ignores the consistent serpents, journeys back to reason, catches the orthodox angel and drags him into the pit of the Bible and an apocalypse where stinking monkeys copulate and cannibalize in the chained torturings of conventional self-consciousness. Blake has amusingly mocked the dubious heavens and hells of moral and metaphysical impositions, and demanded the excess that transcends—or better, trans-descends—such limits and order. He has, of course, implicitly provided a major justification for prudential repression and the thought which makes heavens-and-hells—and one which he dabbled in himself in other works—for the rebel desperately needs a lucid and dramatic order to rebel against. Thus the far-flung knowledge, the theological cosmos, the almost esoteric parodies, and the demonic strategies. Thus, too, opposition affirms the fullest sense of the past and the most richly active response to the present.

The title, *The Marriage of Heaven and Hell*, we should realize here, also mocks those psychic states produced by the impotent angels of convention and the nuptials of metaphysical monkeys. Blake's own hell, which is paradisical for rebels, defies all other heavens and hells.[19] By reading the Bible and other literature in its "infernal or diabolical sense," by burning angels into devils, by twisting prudence to glorify energy, by honoring repressed and demonic awareness, Blake illustrates the positiveness of denial. Wrath, Desire, Excess—and the rest of the rebellious cluster in Blake's metaphysics of defiance—provide the values of Blake's philosophical *The Marriage of Heaven and Hell*, and lead to the quite literal actions of more refusal, more anger, more sex, etc. The very parodistic, grotesque, outrageous shape of the work attest to them. More tangible realms remain to be explored, but in the glow of energy as "Eternal Delight" the opposition unto defiance becomes a positive faith in the truths and experiences of rebellion as against all other truths and experiences.

"ALWAYS BE READY to speak your mind and a base man will avoid you," goes one of the optimistically rebellious "Proverbs of Hell." Blake's own limitations and abstractions made him not always capable of the indignant directness he recommends. But who is? If one could and did fully speak out, would there be any need for literary writing? For art, too, provides a cultivation of inadequacy and a restriction of truth. (And if one could fully act, commune with one's body, why even speak?) The sense of restriction of the literary act would seem to be part of what impels the rebel, such as Blake in *The Marriage of Heaven and Hell*, to refuse literary "form" in an effort to avoid base men and their subterfuges by insisting that a rebellious man in all his individuality of mind is speaking. But both literature and rebellion can take more devious ways, not excluding that ultimate rebellion against the word which some ancient saints and modern nihilists approach: utter silence. Between the act of indignation and the silence of total accusation falls most of literature, though in the word-frenzied contemporary world the revolt into some literary equivalences of silence—Dadaist noise, the efforts of Surrealism to break through consciousness into primordial images, expressionist gesturing, and the mimicry and dumb show of "theatre of the absurd"—seem especially relevant. The failure of other modes of relatedness, and the falsifications of rhetoric, have put an intolerable burden on the word.

Herman Melville's *Bartleby, the Scrivener* turns about a rebellion into silence in Melville's own, post-heroic, gestures of quiet defiance.[1] The novella could well be described, in twentieth-century terms, as comedy-of-the-absurd or Kafkaesque metaphysical expressionism. With its touches of Dickens and garrulous detailing, it is a parody of pathetic realism. For despite some caricatural mannering, it has nothing to do with the tangible world. Its scenery, for example, consists almost entirely of an abstract "Wall Street" in which Melville plays upon the pun rather than upon the economics. Somewhat portentously, windows look out upon dead walls. Barriers of incomprehension rise up everywhere. And the final scene caps the metaphors of silent confinement by Bartleby's perversely willful death within the heavy and silent masonry of the Tombs prison—the final extension of his mostly silent refusal to accommodate himself to the conventional walls and identity.

The main characters in Melville's odd-angle fable of desperately quiet rebellion consist of a decent and reflective attorney and a weird copyist briefly employed by him. More accurately, we should note that there is only one character, the narrating attorney, whose first person account provides and tones the wryly philosophical monologue. His enigmatic copyist, Bartleby, does little more than to appear mutely forlorn and perplexingly repeat, "I prefer not to." Melville's narrator warns us in the opening paragraph of retrospective narration not to view Bartleby as a person or character in the usual senses since he is "one of those beings of whom nothing is ascertainable." Bartleby simply stares at walls and perversely prefers not to do what common sense and custom, selfishness and morality, rationality and hope, dictate—or what the attorney, as conventional benevolent rationalist, thinks they dictate. Bartleby does all the refusing; the narrator does all the reasoning for both; and the peculiarities of his self-arguments, against Bartleby's rebellious silence, provide the meaning of the grotesque comedy.

At risk of belaboring what should be obvious, but is not in many studies of the novella, we must insist on the given order of Melville's art: the metaphoric abstract scene, the first person self-argument, the avoidance of biographical and social dimensions for Bartleby, and the revealing progression of the narrator's account from jocular rumination to agonized grandiloquence. These means emphatically direct the focus upon the narrator's consciousness and his representative limitations. Bartleby is neither more nor less than the bland attorney's specter of rebellious and irrational will, whose authenticity he denies, and who therefore haunts and defies him. A major point of the novella would seem to be the primacy of that perverse will. Or, to further generalize its significance, what Melville revolts against, I shall argue, is the metaphysical and human inadequacy of the liberal rationalist. All the civilized decency of the narrator fails to adequately confront Bartleby, and this indicts the best traditions of moral reasonableness, in Melville's time and in ours.

Some of the studies of the novella, and what seems to be the prevailing critical emphasis, provide cases in point. To circumvent the moral unreasonableness raised by Bartleby's nihilistic rebellion and the narrator's inadequacy, social and biographical "explanations" have repeatedly been proposed. They make the story a document of mere pathos. Those, however, who view *Bartleby* as dramatizing the irrational center of human existence tend to see the piece as having the rebellious brilliance a good many apt readers have found in their responses to it.[2] Those who find metaphysical revolt distasteful find the novella wearisomely ambiguous.

The external evidence for biographical interpretations is well known. *Bartleby* immediately followed the public failure of *Pierre*, which followed the public failure of Melville's heroic gestures of metaphysical revolt in *Moby Dick*, which confirmed Melville's sense of his own plight as the alienated artist in complacent mid-nineteenth-century America. Clearly, too, the story says it is about "Wall Street" and Melville had a distaste for the commercial world (and perhaps for an uncle-attorney in Wall Street) and so must be writing social criticism. The further, and less factual, logic of the biographical allegorizing critics seems to go as follows: Melville was a forlorn writer; the forlorn Bartleby is a scrivener; scriveners write (actually, this one, like other law scriveners, only copies); in short, Bartleby is Melville as American artist.[3] If one adds quasi-Marxist mythology, the narrating attorney is the "boss" in the headquarters of American capitalism where most writers (the two minor comic scriveners in the office) are submissive "wage earners." Melville's theme, then, satirically goes beyond "the sacred right of private prop-

erty" to an "unequivocal case against Wall Street society
for its treatment of the writer." Somehow, too, Bartleby's
perverse nihilism is taken by such critics as expressing
"hope" for the "average man" because of Melville's
self-directed "rebuke to the self-absorption of the artist,"
who apparently should have been delving into the class
struggle instead of metaphysical rebellion.[4] This opportunistic moralism would turn a subtle rebel into a sick
revolutionary.

Such dogmatic interpretation deserves attention only
because it represents a gross example of a widespread
fashion in undercutting literary rebels. The irrelevance of
"boss," "wage earners," "private property," "case against
Wall Street," and similar Marxist mythology to the
language and tone of the novella, as well as to Melville, the
rebellious metaphysical poet, seems obvious. Surely a
"case" against Wall Street can be made much more adequately than it is in *Bartleby*; if the novel is such obtuse,
and largely irrelevant, allegory, it raises more weird ques-
tions about Melville, as both person and writer, than it answers. Other critics note that equating Bartleby with Melville reduces the novella to a trivial and elaborately obscure
personal document.[5] Since the roles of writers were rather
various, especially in the nineteenth century, socio-
economic alienation at such a crude level provides the least
adequate biographical perspective. Biographical allegorizing, within a reductive social morality, makes embarrassing
assumptions about art as conspiratorial camouflage for
self-pity and usually best fits bad literature by the most
conventional of writers.

But, of course, there are no end to those who anxiously
wish to negate negations. Perhaps the best counter-
emphasis would be to accept Melville's directions of form
and take the narrating attorney's perplexities as substantial. In analyzing this evocative and wry story, let us
focus on the conflicts of the figure who characterized
himself at the start as "an eminently *safe* man" whose two
"grand" qualities were "prudence" and "method." When
his reflections, following Bartleby's denials, lead him to a
sense of his albatross-clerk's horrible "solitude" amidst
"dead wall reveries," his response violates all method and
prudence: for "the first time in my life . . . overpower-
ing . . . melancholy seized upon me. The bond of a

common humanity now drew me irresistibly to gloom."
Bartleby's perversity has forced the narrator to recognize
the nihilism of life which he has systematically denied.

In the ruminations that follow, the narrator becomes
aware of what the reader has already perceived in his
actions; the labyrinthine responses of even the decent and
prudently rational man "whose pure melancholy and
sincerest pity . . . merge into fear [and] . . . repulsion."
Though the narrator soon falls back into usual "prudential
feeling," and applies to Bartleby his conventional utilitarian reasoning, he has for a moment reached towards a
harsher wisdom. Like Benito Cereno, Captain Vere, and
other Melville characters, he found the pessimistic insight
that man's repulsion-suffering does not flow from the
moralist's "inherent selfishness" but "rather proceeds from
a certain hopelessness of remedying excessive and organic
ill"—the malaise awaiting the radical rebel. Such pessimism also "disqualified" the narrator, for that day at least,
"from churchgoing."

In the next major episode the narrator persuasively tells
his copyist to leave, and generously offers him a present
(later he admits to himself that it was a "bribe"). Then he
congratulates himself on his "masterly management" in
getting rid of the "incubus" that defied his decency and
reasons. "I *assumed* the ground that depart he must; and
upon that assumption built all I had to say." But Bartleby
prefers not to leave. Desperate, the rationalist then carries
his calculated decency contrary to fact; he would force
Bartleby to leave by assuming, in front of Bartleby, that he
has left. To the unintentionally humorous narrator, "It
was hardly possible that Bartleby could withstand such an
application of the doctrine of assumptions." But the
incubus, for the seventeenth time, replies, "I would prefer
not to." Or, as he earlier put his defiance of reason by will:
"I would prefer not to be a little reasonable."

Why doesn't the narrator use force to remove this
passive resistor of a copyist who refuses to copy but insists
on standing in his office? One of the other scriveners
suggests it, and the narrator—no Southern gentleman—
acknowledges but rejects the alternative of calling the
police. The story operates only within the assumptions of
the decent and rational mind. When those assumptions do
not work, the narrator, too, falls into despair, as he does
here. Soon after, he looks into "Edwards on the Will" and

"Priestly on Necessity." Bartleby, we see, is *the* intellectual dilemma for the narrator who, nicely civilized, wishes not to confront rebellious irrationality by personal decision but by bookish moral logic.

One of the careful students of Melville has suggested that these learned citations provide the main "hint for the hunter" of the meaning of the novella.[6] A recent syncretistic study implicitly follows out the "hint," concluding that Bartleby is a story "in which predestination undoubtedly predominates."[7] But the critics, like Melville's narrator, seem to suffer from an excess of the "doctrine of assumptions." The contrasting but related necessitarianisms of Edwards and Priestly are soon set aside by Melville. The narrator, because of the disapproval that Bartleby raises in his associates, simply moves to another office, leaving Bartleby and metaphysical necessity behind. Predestinarianism is but one of the narrator's, and the critic's, expedient and decent rationalizations of metaphysical negation. Need we add that Melville's bookish clue was ironic? It merely points up—and shows up— reason's irrelevance to the will.

The attorney's obsessive preoccupation with his forlornly defiant scrivener has led more than one critic to speak of the tale as a study in "schizophrenia."[8] Perhaps more appropriate than the clinical category would be the related motif of the "double," as we find it in other tales of Melville's (Delano-Cereno, Claggart-Budd, Ahab-Ishmael, etc.).[9] The fusion of the pragmatically moral attorney and the mutedly demonic scrivener would appear, then, as a grotesque parody of the Faustian duality of consciousness. In this comedy of incomprehension, Bartleby's perverse will is put in the modest and even decorous terms appropriate to the rationalized decency of the attorney. Without his demon, the narrator would be incomplete and meaningless. Thus, though on the surface horrified by the scrivener's defiance, the attorney suddenly acknowledges: "I burned to be rebelled against again." And he pursues Bartleby so that he may be defied again and again. This provides the completing rage to his prudence, the covert rebellion to his "profound conviction that the easiest way of life is the best." The image of the ever-resistant clerk completes the human totality of the ever-adapting attorney, for metaphysical rebellion is at the heart of every man's existence.

Early in the story, the attorney becomes the victim of his scrivener, reversing roles to read his own copy, slinking away from his own door, ultimately "to stagger in his own plainest faith." Yet he cannot stop, as an act of faith, from trying to fit Bartleby into his calculated conventional decency. At one point the attorney convinces himself that Bartleby must be "demented"; as if to confirm his judgment, Bartleby altogether gives up the copying which has provided, until then, the rationale for keeping the otherwise insubordinate clerk. Of Bartleby's new refusal, the attorney righteously demands: "And what is the reason?" Bartleby coolly replies, "Do you not see the reason for yourself?" None is self-evident, but, with comic alacrity, the narrator "instantly" comes up with a reason to justify the even more fantastic behavior of the figure he just previously denounced as demented. He assumes that Bartleby must have "temporarily impaired his vision" by his copy work. It is a kindly, practical and logical explanation; it is also totally unsupported by any fact or even any assertion of Bartleby's, and appears particularly gratuitous at that moment. The decent rationalist will have an assumption that properly explains otherwise rebellious behavior, no matter what.[10]

However, shortly later the attorney asks Bartleby to do something not at all dependant on his eyes. The scrivener still refuses. Then the narrator poses to Bartleby, hopefully, the possibility of his doing copying sometime in the indefinite future when his eyes are perfectly normal. Bartleby, totally ignoring the narrator's proferred rationalization for his defiance, simply refuses for all time to copy. Another reason up, another reason down; the perverse negation remains, and so does the gulf between the narrator's practical reasoning and Bartleby's defiant choosing.

Let us turn from the narrator's rationalism to his closely linked benevolence. *Bartleby*, like another mid-nineteenth-century grotesque monologue obsessed with irrational rebellion in terms of a perverse clerk, Dostoevsky's *Notes from Underground*, is a sustained mockery of the great Enlightenment heritage of benevolence by way of rational self-interest. Where Dostoevsky's exacerbated melodrama against Euclidean moral reasoning goes on to affirm the desire for suffering, Melville's absurd comedy against benign moral practicality goes on to affirm the inevitableness of perversity.

Absolutist Bartleby, who asserts the freedom of the will but denies it any specific reason or moral value, lacks all self-interest. Repeatedly through the story the attorney triumphantly resorts to offers of money, better employment, letters of recommendation, travel, a home, friendship—any selfish desire with which the enlightened human being might be manipulated—but Bartleby remains unamenable to all the appeals of calculated selfishness. Early in the tale, as an almost comic decoy of what is to come at a more profound level, we are briefly presented with the more laughable irrationalities of the other two scriveners. These Dickensian humor-caricatures provide a comic perspective on utilizing individual selfishness for the rationalized common good. Turkey, a confirmed drunkard, works as a good copyist in the mornings, but is of no use at all after his liquid lunch. Nippers, bilious and ambitiously irritable in the mornings, resigns himself to productive tedium in the afternoons. Since the scriveners thus alternate in their selfish weakness, the narrator manages to construe it as "a good natural arrangement," and so obtains a usable day's work in which conflicting individual motives produce a parody of Adam Smith's general harmony and welfare.

With Bartleby, however, the narrator cannot discover any usable selfishness. He prudently tries to incorporate the perverse negations within his utilitarian economy by raising the issue to a moral level. So long as Bartleby, however insubordinate, will copy, the attorney can bear with him, demonstrate his liberal tolerance of the unfortunate, and thus "cheaply produce a delicious self-approval" of "conscience." When Bartleby refuses even to copy, and the attorney's rational efforts to explain and expel the scrivener have failed, he attempts the balm of a higher morality. He stays his rage against Bartleby by recalling a parabolic situation.

> I remembered the tragedy of the unfortunate Adams and the still more unfortunate Colt in the solitary office . . . and how poor Colt, being dreadfully incensed by Adams, and imprudently permitting himself to get wildly excited, was at unawares hurried into his fatal act.

In this Cain-and-Abel motif we amusedly note the decent rationalist's reduction of murderous rage to imprudence. The narrator adds a theological moral to his fable by remembering, as a result of the ancient story, "the divine injunction: 'A new commandment give I unto you, that ye love one another.'" It is, of course, mockingly too neat: the Adamic curse of solitary man ("this old Adam of resentment," says the attorney) is redeemed by Christian *caritas*, reduced to a Wall Street prudential goodness.

> Yes, this it was that saved me. Aside from higher considerations, charity often operates as a vastly wise and prudent principle—a great safeguard to its possessor . . . no man, that ever I heard of, ever committed a diabolical murder for sweet charity's sake. Mere self-interest, then, if no better motive can be enlisted, should, especially with high-tempered men, prompt all beings to charity and philanthropy. At any rate, upon the occasion in question, I strove to drown my exasperated feelings towards the scrivener by benevolently construing his conduct. Poor fellow, poor fellow! thought I, he don't mean anything; and besides, he has seen hard times, and ought to be indulged.

This passage seems fairly representative of the tale's craft, and crafty parody: the revealing "prudent" once more; the moralistic self-congratulation; the professional rationalist's pompousness in "benevolently construing"; the too easy pity for the perplexing and defying; the purely gratuitous assumption of environmental causes ("hard times"); the reiterated and reductive generosity which reveals both incomprehension and contempt. *Caritas* as the product of "mere self-interest" shows the obtuseness of such rationality and the brutality of such decency. Yet something else has happened to the benevolent rationalist, to the unacknowledged side of his mind and feelings represented by Bartleby. As he leaves his old chamber to get away from the specter haunting him, he notes to himself: "strange to say—I tore myself away from him whom I had so longed to be rid of." We need not rehearse his remaining strategems, when he sees Bartleby again, of bribes, appeals to self-interest and prudential charity, for they follow with comic excess the forms already indicated. The silently accusing denial remains. Bartleby, hauled off to prison by others when the narrator has fled, remains self-aware, adamant, refusing to eat, to change, to ameliorate his forlornness—refusing not to prefer not to.

The attorney, upon his return, visits Bartleby in prison, with kindly and guilty concern. On his final visit he meets the final denial, and pronounces the epitaph over the figure who preferred not even to live anymore. Melville has, throughout, established a secondary tone in the narrator's ruminations, ranging from early comments about Bartleby as the most "forlorn of humanity" through recognitions of his monumental "common humanity" to several quietly magnificent comparisons. When, for example, the attorney finds Bartleby in prison, once again silently facing the usual dead wall, he is deeply moved by such solitary resistance in a hostile world, and comments, "I thought I saw peering out upon him the eyes of murderers and thieves." The sacrificial rebel, who knows what he is and where he is, and yet has no message and forgiveness, takes on the largest connotations in the narrator's consciousness. When the attorney finds Bartleby, for the last time, lying solitary amidst the "Egyptian" masonry—the largest and most futile walls of all—he concludes that Bartleby sleeps "With kings and counsellors." The phrase probably comes from Job's rebellious curses (3:14) of an unjust and inexplicable cosmos. The majesty of negation and quietly defiant defeat becomes unmistakable to the narrator, and the reader.

Then follows the perplexing concluding paragraph of the novella, suprisingly fervent in tone and apparently providing an environmental explanation for the whole story. The ending is badly anticlimactic, says one shrewd critic, saving the tale from its moral. The conclusion, he notes, provides the single significant violation of tone in the entire novella.[11] Certainly the final eulogistic line, universalizing the moral of forlornness, suggest high Victorian sentiment: "Ah, Bartleby! Ah, Humanity!" The conclusion, however, need not be reduced to a single resonance. Surely it is, as several have noted, prepared for by the narrator's increasingly impassioned view of his scrivener, and the secular beatification of Bartleby, forlorn saint of defiance, does not violate the cumulative sense of his universal significance. *Humanity*, here, must have somewhat the same significance as when Melville writes in another of his stories: "Humanity, thou strong thing, I worship thee, not in the laureled victor, but in this vanquished one." [12]

But Bartleby is humanity in just two fantastic ways: as

forlorn defiance and as the obsession of the benevolent rationalist's consciousness. Perhaps here we may, for a modest moment, let the biographical and social critics back in; Melville's preoccupation with and glorification of heroic failure, the necessary obverse to the perception of the morally rationalized American aggrandizement, certainly is a force behind the fable. And that final pean is not spoken by a heroic failure but by a legal, rational and moral defender of the dominant American faith. The "ah, humanity" may, then, also function as a final tactic of dubious understanding, the last moralizing and rationalizing gesture of a representative American confronted with the perverse negation which is contrary to benevolent manipulation.

A similar explication might be made of the narrator's posthumous explanation of Bartleby. He has acquired, the attorney says, a "vague report," never verified, that Bartleby once worked in the "Dead Letter Office."

> Conceive a man by nature and misfortune prone to a palled hopelessness, can any business seem more fitted to heighten it than that of continually handling these dead letters, and assorting them for the flames? . . . from out the folded paper the pale clerk takes a ring—the finger it was meant for, perhaps, moulders in the grave; a bank-note sent in swiftest charity—he whom it would relieve, nor eats nor hungers any more.

Are we to take this passage literally? [13] Or has the narrator, yet again, fallen into a moralistic excess of the "doctrine of assumptions"? In tone and maudlin incident, this section is fully consistent with the narrator's character, whose kindly incomprehension has been so fully dramatized. Either we have another mocking twist, or we have, if the passage be identified with Melville rather than his narrator, a mawkishly sentimental ending. In short, defiant or bad. And that causal (environmental) method of explaining that hypothetical ex-postal clerk Bartleby? It is woefully inadequate, if taken literally. True, Melville has a characteristic weakness in most of his fictions, an alternately facetious and portentous historical documentation: in most of the early novels, in *Moby Dick*; in *Benito Cereno* and *Billy Budd* (with their involuted meditations on sea-law obscuring the affirmation of innocence). Part of this seems a wry but often too heavy labyrinthine puzzle-

ment about actuality and its uncertain relation to multi-
tudinous analogues—the nihilism of the overwhelming
American reality that runs through so much of our
literature.

If we take the arbitrary and limiting conjecture that
Melville equated the Dead Letters with his own writings
(confusing source of an image with its meaning) and
himself with Bartleby (or Bartleby with the American
writer, and thereby himself), then the ending is a personal
and anti-climactic intrusion on a strong and self-sufficient
metaphysical fable. We may, however, read the ending
in terms of its speaker, of Melville's dominant themes
in the novella proper, of his ironic craft and style, and his
pervasive affirmation of defiant *isolatoes*; and save the tale,
if not from Melville's intriguing biography, at least from
unrebellious rationalizing biographers.

Melville may falter into final ambiguities, in ways
altogether characteristic of a self-made and self-doubting
American writer, but the mythographer who demonically
created a whale as large as God did not make the absurdly
sainted Bartleby as primarily an image of self-pity in a
social tract. The wryly sad "Story of Wall Street" is an
endlessly suggestive defiant comedy, perhaps even a father-
son story done by an aging father killer. But most
importantly it is the confession of a decent, prudent,
liberal representative man who finds in his inner chambers
the incomprehensible, perverse, negative, irrational demon
of his denied humanity. The narrator attempts to exorcise
that rebellious image with common sense, authority,
rationality, theology, prudence, pity, charity, resignation,
causality, flight, morality, and even, at the end, reverence.
But the melancholy enigma, and the walls of incomprehension, remain. And it is that modest demon of irrational
and defiant will, Bartleby, approaching the silence of the
ultimate passive resistor, who "prefers not to" give in to
civilized pretenses and forms, and thus forces benevolent
rationalism up against its limits of common humanity.
The perversely human is exalted in Melville's amusingly
sad demand for a heroic humanity in a grotesque universe.
In this sardonic existential comedy it is the rebellious
negation which provides Melville's real affirmation.

5   LES AMOURS JAUNES

THE DISTINCTIVELY modern forms of literary rebellion often take exacerbated directions, perhaps partly out of desperation in Western societies which developed a remarkable ability to assimilate and attenuate rebelliousness. Particularly emphatic are the styles of the "young rebels" which mix "bad taste," anguished buffoonery and shrewd mockeries in odd combinations of defiance and pathos. Brilliant adolescents create an anti-literature to force awareness of savage discontent and annihilation. Of the poets of nihilism, I prefer discussing Tristan Corbière, most virile, amusing and least pretentious of the young rebels in post-Baudelairian despair. For he never lost the self, as did his contemporaries—Rimbaud in mystical self-violence, Lautrémont in pathological disorder. Though surely the sick poet, and one turned in upon himself, he retains the defiant exuberance and outrageous humor which, I have been arguing, mark our main rebellious traditions. Even more isolated than Blake and Melville—and without the abstraction of the one and the ambiguity of the other—and less able than they to settle into quiet corners in the ordinary world, his rebellious perversities become more frenzied and poignant. Some motifs from his one volume of poetry, Les Amours Jaunes (1873),[1] may suggest how mordant individualism and the radical criticism of life are devastatingly directed at one's self, and the gratuitous existence of all selves.

Such rebellious involutions provide the distinguishing twisted qualities which pervade Corbière's images, syntax, ironies—as they did his body and character. Sensitive and crippled only son of a strong and successful but aged

literary-adventurer father turned solid bourgeoise—an image of authority both imperturbable and indulgent—
Corbière never quite grew up, and died before he was
thirty. He seems simultaneously the spoiled brat, posing
and playing, and the oldest beast in the jungle, disillusioned and destructive. Self-conscious rebelliousness
drives the verse of this energetically dying eccentric as he
devilishly burlesques and parodies all. He especially delighted in railing antitheses and is a master of the bitterly
clever paradoxes of one who has sympathy without hope
and perception without purpose. In a recent stock phrase,
Corbière was an authentic case of the rebel-without-
a-cause.

Self-defined "poète contumace," he twists even the
Diogenes role. Identification with a mendicant-dog,
whether in strength or pathos, was a favorite gesture. In an
elegy for one of his hounds, he calls the animal "Maître-
philosopher cynique," and with misanthropic wit praises
him above men for his sincerity and freedom.[2] But in "Paris
Nocturne" his outrageousness takes a more bizarre turn.
There the degraded Diogenes, lantern necessarily in hand
for the dark purlieus of bohemia, scavengers the streets of
death where "perverse poets" fish up images of horror.[3]
Corbière, at the time playing mock-bohemian in Paris, is
one of his own perverse poets, piling up in this poem
shocking tropes (perhaps partly in parody of Baudelaire).
This goes beyond a Breton sailor's attack on the vicious
megalopolis, full of *poète maudit* hysteria and images of
satiated sadistic love, harpies of poverty and dead gods.[4]
For as the epigraph (and the other Parisian poems) bitterly points up, Paris is the world. Even in the sun, in the
parallel "Paris Diurne," the great capital gets presented,
with melancholy violence, as a skid-row hell; in a world of
scorching injustice, the poet prefers the shadows of alienation and the cold pot of failure.[5] While the Parisian poems
quick-step between hysterical pathos and bitter bemusement, their attitude centers on rebellion against a capricious world.

A deep compassion directs a large part of Corbière's
subject matter and concern. With a cauterized self-pity
and a sympathetic honesty, given form in the wryly
colloquial monologues of outcasts, he presents those
defeated by the brutal indifference of man and the

universe. In the section on the sea, "Gens de Mer," it is a more obviously pervasive fate than the cruel city which victimizes the apprentice sailor, the shipboard hunchback, the aging coast guard, the outlaw shipwreckers and the other dying or cast-up men identified with the sea. His maritime proletarians gain much of their verve not from Corbière's social indignation but from his anti-romantic bravado. In many of the pieces praising seamen, such as "Matelots" and "La Fin," the harsh awareness of reality which separates Corbière from the romantics (and here takes the forms of a brutal awareness of death) achieves a twisted affirmation of the actual by the parodistic humor of reversing operatic and sentimental images. In Corbière's bravura definitions of what it means to be a man, the grandiloquent views of love, adventure and longing are played off against the reality which justifies itself by its nihilistic truth and propounds the vigor on the other side of despair.

Naturally, much inverted sentiment crops up in Corbière's poems. "Le Douanier" is not merely an ignored and cast-up isolato hero but, with comic pathos, an artist of life—"Poète trop senti pour être poètique." [6] In their very roughness—rather than in spite of it—the men of "Matelots" are a "poème vivant." Thus Corbière makes the rebel's demand for a poetry of life over the Parnassian's and symbolist's poetry of poetry. Also, the repeated growls of misogyny (in "Bambine" and "A Mon Côtre 'Le Négrier,'" as well as in many of the Paris poems) show twisted sentiment: adolescent erotic uncertainty heightened to a perverse cry for love in a world in which love is itself perversely rare. While a better case can be made for sentimentality inverted than straight—the upside down requires effort, sometimes of heroic proportions, which can rarely be found with stock sentiment—it must be granted that the side-of-the-mouth plaints for love sometimes achieve only pathos (as in the message to the mother on the death of a young sailor, "Lettre du Mexique" [7]). But his perverse imagination elsewhere raises the love cry to a powerful bitter compassion, as in "Le Bossu Bitor." [8] This grotesque narrative of a mistreated hunchback in a whorehouse, followed by his apparent suicide out of shame, ends with images of the swollen, cannibalized and mocked cadaver—and the savage comment: "Le pauvre corps avait connu l'amour."

In his sea poems, Corbière equally insists on the man-making and man-breaking forces of the impersonal universe. With the lemonish wit of one who sees himself as ugly and unlovable, crippled and dying, he undercuts his own sentiments to insist on the gratuities of outcast state and death. Corbière follows the romantics in making the sea the locus of heroism and grandness, but makes them synonymous with alienation and annihilation. Joy comes from the harsh reality rather than the sentiment. So, too, with the Breton world of the section entitled "armor." The bleak landscapes, the folklore of death and the lives of simple misery become the poet's positives. The humor and harshness hold inseparable in the lament of the mistreated conscripts ("Le Pastoral de Conlie" [9]), the horrible ironic hymn ("Cris d'Aveugle" [10]) and the masterful ballad-painting of the pilgrimage of pious cripples—at once grotesquely sympathetic and a wryly savage indictment of God—"La Rapsode Foraine et le Pardon de Sainte-Anne." [11] One of the lesser pieces from "Armor," "Un Riche en Bretagne," [12] illustrates in a simple way Corbière's fusion of compassion and mockery. The title is a joke, for a *bon riche* in Brittany is a *vieux pauvre*. This professional tramp may be one of the happily simple-minded, though shrewd enough to get a bit of food in the villages by saying a Latin prayer, in Hebrew. Corbière sees him as a mock-Diogenes, the *philosophe errant* of the Breton countryside, or, in a typically reversed comparison, a leisurely *rentier moins l'ennui de la rent*. By also using some disproportionately witty and learned religious comparisons, Corbière heightens the nobility of this self-appeasing outcast and lordly bum who leads a life of simple misery. No doubt he has tongue in cheek, when he isn't sticking it out at Christian piety, Breton prudence and literary bucolicism, but his richly poor wandering fool also stands as a wise outcast hero.

Corbière's sensibility, profoundly wedded to outcasts, beyond tramps and seamen and deeper than crippling and cynicism, reaches the very perversity of selfhood. In "Gens de Mer" it is "Le Renégat" [13] who illustrates the *contumace partout*. The hard paradoxes and burlesqued melodrama with which he portrays the outcast of outcasts achieves a curious gusto in which the renegade among men does all and is all. For Corbière's renegade is not the victim of love or hate or vice—he is not stupid, comments his similar author—but of an even greater passion: his fated genius for alienation. To be a renegade "est un-tempérament . . . un artiste de proie." And with yet another sardonic leap, the poem concludes that to be a renegade is a victory, an achievement of reverse virtue: "Pur, à force d'avoir purgé tous les dégoûts."

That the stranger to the community of men desperately achieves this purity of selfhood by rebelling against all limits also appears in the poem "Paria." This provides the penultimate piece in the central, and crucial, group of poems entitled "Raccrocs" (flukes, chance shots). Corbière's autobiographical pariah was born "par haz-ard" [14] in a world of godless accidents. In his monologue he mocks what passes for liberty—the supposed freedom of public yokes and domestic nests; the pariah, that oddly different bird, sings of a more desperate freedom, "toujours seul. Toujours libre." His country is the world which, being round, is also endless; consequently, his land lies wherever he plants his feet, when he can stand. When he lies down, his country is his lonely bed, and a woman—whom he does not have. His horizon is the beyond; he's homesick for a home never seen. Some follow their road, but his road follows him, indifferently. His past is what he forgets, his present that which becomes his past, his future that which follows. True existential voyager, he is what he does, which is unknown. What he says echos emptily, saying nothing—that is his point. The only thing he holds tight is one hand in the other. The homeland of this ultimate cosmopolitan is simply the dirt that will hold his unshrouded bones. Thus, beyond love, hatred, even ego-tism, the pariah provides the nakedly human. While the above incomplete paraphrase loses some of the lively nihilism, it may be clear that such absolute estrangement by this master of negative freedom strips liberty of any claims to ideology and order and comfort. Freedom becomes the defiant despair of pure individual being.

In "Liberta," another of his sardonic "Raccrocs," he establishes his typical burlesque tone by a footnote saying that the word appears on the gate of a prison.[15] He plays with liberty as being a voluptuous creature found only in a prisoner's yearnings, an ideality and eternity of longing locked in with the condemned and quite beyond those bent-backed ones supposedly at liberty outside prisons.

The authenticity of freedom must be discovered most fully in the extremity of its denial. As with some of the brilliant young rebels in the fictions of Stendhal and Dostoevsky, Corbière finds freedom in confinement, individuality in its negation, and therefore discovers the most intense responses. So with other values: God, in a slashing little prayer to that "vieux monsieur sourd," exists only in his indifference and absence.[16] Love, in the series of "amour jaunes," turns out to be jaundiced duels in which man struggles with the enchanting beast so he can recognize his separateness. Reality, reached by antithesis with any ideal hope, reveals itself as incommensurable with life.

Nor is this just an exotic awareness to be found in ships and prisons, by renegades and pariahs. For Corbière, the gratuitous and perverse are the very stuff of daily life— discovered in his simple folk (even though they don't recognize it) and in himself (even in his most impassioned and earnest longings). When birth and death are only odd flukes, and living and loving weird tricks (though for Corbière desire and anguish are immediate and substantial), incongruity becomes tangible and pervasive. So he takes the insomnia that racks him and, sardonically aware of literary conventions of the erotic muse, turns his sleeplessness into a tantalizing black goddess of the "damnés-de-lettre," the poets-for-themselves. With his usual cathartic twist of pathos-to-mockery in "Insomnie," [17] the apostrophe to that bizarre female of sleeplessness concludes with a plaintive mock-plea to her: "Nous dormirons ensemble un peu." In this characteristic turn of hysteria to humor, he has wryly twisted the poetic convention and knowingly exploited the sexual yearning which tortures his bedding, and his verse.

With his natural tendency to doubling, Corbière frequently wrote two versions of the same theme (renegade-pariah, Paris by night and by day, two epitaphs, etc.). The other insomnia piece, "Litanie du Sommeil," [18] is a prayer to protean nothingness, a hypnotic verbal eruption: 147 lines of conceits and reversals on the fecund and contumacious nature of the deity of sleep, by one who longs for her. Insomniac outrage comes forth as imagistic outrageousness, and sleep, the great escape from reality, becomes the super-reality scorning the fervent poetic worshipper. In rebelliously naming the capriciousness of

the universe, Corbière makes it hilariously and horrendously rich in his affirmative despair. "Litanie du Sommeil" has been viewed by the surrealists, those programmatic revolutionaries against the refinements and rigidities
of continental artistic traditions, as a surrealist poem with
an outpouring of unconscious frenzy and imagistic au-
tomatism.[19]

The case can easily be over-stated since Corbière is
often a hard-nosed and nose-thumbing rebel whose rage, as
we can see in so many of the sly images, ends not in
fragment and association but in striking paradox. Certainly
the poem is "un-French" and "anti-poetic" in drawing out
an incantatory sweep of comparisons. But the images may
be less the mechanism of the unconscious than the
mordant recognition of the world of consciousness itself.
Wit and rigor, however turned by defiant violation, keep
the poem on the lucid side of surrealist self-hallucination
and ornate depersonalization. With Corbière, verbal
intoxication submits, as it often does not in those who
pursue the wild word, to a tough delight in appraised
incongruities. For unlike much of surrealism and other
revolts into the disintegration of the self, the Corbièrian
gestures of revolt affirm the distinctive self as the center of
mockery of the past and convention (much of which are
always invertedly present). His extreme idiosyncrasy of
image and tone and style thus heighten and affirm, against
all impersonal forms and fates, his individuality.

Corbière's weakness goes quite another way—into mannered self-pity. "Un Mort Trop Travaillé," [20] for example,
is a poem over-worked for effects within its adolescent
fantasy of shooting himself (for the unadolescent reason
that he is soon going to die). Its self-lacerating elaboration
ends in the farce of a misfire and self-conscious triviality.
Apparently, as title and exclusion from his book indicate,
Corbière knew it was an over-strained piece of would-
be anti-pathos. In the more or less parallel poem about the
young poet who is going to die, "Un Jeune Oui S'En
Va," [21] the lament of one who hears "Le vide chante dans
ma tête" is partly saved from fingered self-pity by some
shrewdly objective mockery of poets who indulged in the
metier de mourir. By thus refusing the solace of literary
mannerisms,[22] and by again sarcastically setting himself
out as the stranger to accepted responses, he defies the

reduction of his life and death. But when not rebelliously detaching himself from himself in this poem, or in his charming but sometimes sentimental romantic lament, "Le Poète Contumace," Corbière does slide into arch self-pity.

What most commentators object to in Corbière are the harsh "Raccrocs," the burlesque "Sèrènade des Sèrèndades," and the nastiness of some of the love poems—for bad taste, diabolism, course jokes, slaps in the face. Readers who wish to find literary charms rather than rebellious gestures are naturally outraged. But these very negative qualities give Corbière his remarkable ability to project himself into "unpoetic" materials and awareness: the blind and deaf on the streets, love as a self-lacerating contempt, the hunchback in the whorehouse. In thus purging self-pity in a disinterested compassion and bitterness, he expands, as only a rebel against accepted subjects and styles can, the range of sensibility. Granted that many of the minor pieces are sarcasms and jokes and insults— offensive to those who demanded seriousness and an artiste rather than rebelliousness and a man: the double-entendre sexual pieces ("Venerie" and "À Ma Jument Souris" [23]), the two contemptuously perverse monologues about himself by the woman he supposedly loves ("Femme" and "Pauvre Garçon"), the burlesqued troubadour "pop-tune" which ends with the crudely candid request that the woman open her legs ("Chanson en Si") and the swaggering song that insists on his ugliness ("Guitare"). As in "Le Crapaud," a poem for Corbière is not a moment to reveal beauty but himself as a toad. Classical responses, such as those over the Italian Pilgrimage—Corbière made and caricatured the journey—lead him to treat Naples, Vesuvius and Mount Etna with images of familiar pettiness and disgust, which also have their truth and appropriateness.[24] His good taste, as he several times notes, is in his distastes. And his defiant gestures break out of any possible moralism and aestheticism to demand that the self confront grotesque reality.

Disgust, sex, rage, suffering break the conventions, and prettiness, in the attempt to supersede mere art. Corbière is in consequent danger of being caught in conventional reversals and gestures for their own sake. When his singular vitality of language and feeling falter he ends as the strident *enfant terrible*. Conventional anti-conformity and petty perversity are, if you wish, aesthetic and moral sins, though more promising ones than conformity and pettiness. And if we grant the literary rebel his rebellious place, rather than confining him to moral and aesthetic decorums, we may see—as with many of Corbière's intentionally minor gestures—that the precarious verve of one "en dehors l'humaine pistc" has carried him to new reaches of truth and awareness.

Some of the devices, for example, of "Rapsodie du Sourd" [25] are obviously hard-pushed inversions, such as the title since the newly deaf man, in his anguished fear that he will sound like a screeching clarinet, a duck, a scraped bone, offers anything but a rhapsody. The contradictoriness carries through the epigraph—put at the end of the poem!—the saint's horrendous irrelevancy, "Silence is golden." But the poem is something more than this, more, too, than the comically grotesque dramatic monologue of an "acoustical Tantalus." Once the certainty of communication is lost, all speech and even gesture become threatening. And each fear of mishearing and ridicule puts one in a dark cell in which the metamorphosed self becomes obscure. Fearful of responding, "Je suis là, mais absent." The one communion left is with the idol of the imprisoned self, "oubliant la parole," in a terrifying awareness of the lost relation with men which is also the loss of the self.

Thus the straining for effect and reversal in Corbière comes from a poetics of radical separation, a fearful attempt to make words go beyond words, to use an exuberance of rebelliousness and pity in a fantastic pulling at language to get through the human deafness. (Corbière was right in a literal sense; his book was completely ignored; his flukish re-discovery a decade later, and exploitation by Verlaine, then Laforgue, then Eliot and Pound, who viewed him in terms of their own dubiously rebellious purposes, substantiates Corbière's kind of irony.) Rather than pursue the high muse (whom he turns into a naive streetwalker), the rebel poet wants to violate the mute desperation of the world and break out of the dark self. The finale is sad—as sad as Bartleby. In the last poems, the "Sonnet Posthume" and the five "Rondels pour Apres," his desperate lyric flights from nothing lead into a child-land of poetic magic.[26] In the pathetically defiant rondels he can only yearn for a way out of the dark cell by such vague roles as "snatcher of sparks" (voleur d'etincelles") and "trimmer of comets" ("peigneur de comètes"). Rebellion becomes a lingering curse ("Pour les pieds-plats, ton sol est maudit"). No one really hears or sees for long as the darkness closes in. Desire and death are a desperately incommunicable poetry, and the words really fail in the attempt to catch the sparks and shape the burning moments.

In his more usual burlesque treatment of his literary role, as in the prefatory "Ca?" [27] in which he poses and wise-crackingly answers a series of mock-questions about the book, his defensive sarcasm is used to deny any relation to conventional literature. His work, he says, fits in none of the usual categories, genres or motives; his drolleries are of the street, neither classical nor French, stray shots of one who is neither known by nor knows Art. Corbière's staccato and broken rhythms of exasperation, his joking eccentricities of punctuation and idiom, his parodistic use of verbal association and disparate vocabularies, follow from this anti-artistic stance. His rhetoric of defiance exists right in his outrageous oxymorons and reversing puns. He utilizes incongruities as a means of denying the adequacy of both literary and commonplace norms of response. There is a rebellious awareness here which goes beyond personal anguish and sardonic taste if we recognize the pathos of most art—historically and aesthetically fortuitous, physically and socially a vitalistic excrescence, ultimately contumacious gestures which are equally "rien or quelque chose."

Corbière follows the Blakean wisdom of persisting in his folly, exploiting his uncertainty, defiance and self-contempt in a series of wry and poignant gestures. Perhaps the best known, but certainly not the best accepted, poems are the musing self-mockeries, paradoxical attempts at self-definition, which provide a series of epitaphs.[28] ("Paria" and "Renégat" are oblique epitaphs; the dramatic monologues of the deaf, blind and crippled are symbolic epitaphs; it takes no critical forcing to read all of *Les Amours Jaunes* as the mortuary graffitti of one insistently aware of fecund death.) The long poem entitled "Epitaphe" [29] which, with usual inversion, he uses as a preface, is a series of contraries, via puns, sudden shifts of levels of meaning, reversed contrasts, burlesque antitheses and outrageous declarations, such as that "his only regret was not to have been his own mistress." Others: nervous, without nerve; lively, for a cripple; soulful, but no violin; lover, and a bad stud; an idealist, without an idea. This philosopher of the perverse is a poet, in spite of his verse—his false lines were his only truths; crying, he was a singer in genuine falsetto. An unfunny clown, an actor who didn't know his role, a drifter against a headwind. Dryly drunk, he was always natural—as a poseur; without posing, he posed as unique. Thus by posing all the way yet mocking each of his poses, this precisely unkempt dandy *in extremis* passionately makes and comically undercuts his gestures to point beyond any limiting pose and gesture to the authentic remainder—the direct self. To catch the gratuitous qualities of existence we get passion when we expect pose and grimacing gestures when passion is in place. For the rebel, the shortest distance between himself and the truth is a series of cater-cornered turns.

There is a fine innocence here, elsewhere frequently caught in Corbière's equal acceptance of savagery and yearning. It is an innocence which knows better, and is therefore all the more pure because caught by no standards, delusions or hopes. "Trop naïf, étant trop cynique;/ Ne croyant a rien, croyant tout.—Son goût etat dans le dégout." The method, of course, is very simple: the truth is always in back or underneath—but always! Despite those who see in this merely the mechanics of paradox, the antitheses and reversals build up a distinctive awareness, which insists not only on the merging of opposites but on the reality of the incongruous. The *is not* remains the most important part of every *is* in this mock-logical way of getting at the irreducible illogic of selfhood.

In turning himself over and over, Corbière finds underneath devastating insights, such as that he suffers most in being too much himself. Oh heartless heart of one with too much heart! To find the delight in this suffering, the success in this defeat, the self in this denial—just as he finds the community of outcasts in his estrangement and the art of poetry in confounding all art—provides the unmistakable vigor of his work and himself. Painfully amused by the fact that he is "dying to live, and living just to die," he insists on the intense awareness, without solace, of the universal precariousness of individual existence. While he longs for a fuller existence and completion, which he is too knowledgeable to believe in (being his own mistress), he undercuts all attempts to get outside the self. Therefore Corbière chooses the permanent personal rebellion of failure, including mocking his role as a failure, which he rarely faults: "Trop réussi—comme raté."

Or as he coolly remarks in another of his self-epitomizations, "Décourageux," [30] "voir est un veuglement." He knows what he does, in the modern rebel's self-conscious and pathetic concentration on himself—in contrast to the simpler Cynic who focussed on the outer world. In "Décourageux," a burlesque of himself for his artistic awkwardness and pathos, he sarcastically starts with a slash at all poets, including himself: "Ce fut un vrai poète: il n'avait pas de chant." And he sadly ends with oxymorons about the "Sublime Bête." The beastly sublime of the modern song of nothingness creates an art of desperation in which the rebel revolts against himself. He insists, with the precocious disenchantment which suddenly includes us all, that his art, his passion, exist in his not truly being a poet, a lover, and a man. Here, I think, is how the modern nihilist carries out both the exaltation and purging of the person which, we are told, has been the profound central individualism of the Western religious heritage. Saint Tristan? Corbière, no doubt, would have appreciated the deeply contumacious joke.

For a final example of Corbière's amusing and crushing strategy, we might conclude with his witty *ci-gît* parody, "Laisser-Courre," [31] another of his untranslatable "Raccrocs." It is a testament catalogue of what he has left, playing upon the puns of left in the senses of legacy, left-behind, left-over, etc. In his running dog defiance he leaves his mistress to the cuckolds, credence to his creditors, liberty to the cops, hope to the old (grown childish), his truisms to the stupid, and so on. What is left? "Puis me suis laissé moi." In getting to that savage legacy of the naked self, he mockingly uses and leaves behind various styles of response (Villon's gallows, Baudelaire's devil, troubadour love, chivalric bravery, authority, faith) leaving the self without role, aid, or saving style. As if to say: "Life is Beautiful and Meaningful? Stand up Beautiful and Meaningful! Ah, Nothing!" So one finds himself: "Laissé, blasé, passé,/ Rien ne m'a rien laissé. . . ." "Rein," as well as "laissé," I believe, must be understood, in Corbière's repreated and insistent use, as almost a pun. *Nothing* is the *something* that the rebel finds, simultaneously a bitter loss and a wry victory—an emptiness and a desperation which are yet a style and a meaning.

Corbière brilliantly perceives that the rebel's truth cannot be an unresponsive "no!" but must be an endless, and even comically contradictory, process of passionate refusal. The pathos, of course, lies in refusing that life which is refusing you. Lucid, analytic, scornful, Corbière wishes to be more impassioned, mad, even beastly, to break through his self-consciousness, though knowing that it is the only self he has. Too responsive and intelligent to romanticize, except by inversion, the heroic sea and the bohemian city, Corbière cannot use nature or art to escape from the directly human. But because of his crippling, brilliance and outsideness, that human could never resign himself to accepting a place in the fortuitous world. Tristan brimmed with the sexual yearning, sympathetic revolt and involuted self-awareness of the young man—the young man about to die. He wants all, and yet perceives that all is but a parody of what he wants. Disgusted with himself, his jaundiced love poems full of need, hostility, shrewd physical awareness and harsh mockery, he also knows that the contemptible woman and degraded muse is life itself. Artifice he is on to, he who twists his ennui into his amusement, his insomnia into a game, his outcastness into his communal bond, his hysteria into humor, and his nothingness into his meaning. And the artifice of literary art? That provides one of the most elaborate jokes. If he must play it—and what else?—he will double-play it, just as a sailor he preferred to take his cutter to the rocks in stormy weather, as a painter he did caricatures marked to appear damaged, as a dandy he dressed like a slovenly corpse, as a lover he pursued the hardly admirable mistress of a friend in a weird *menage á trois*, and as a sensitive soul he played the gross *blagueur*.[32]

Truly sceptical and religious, intimately knowing *nothing*, Corbière knew how unseriously serious the outrageous joke of life and death is. Or, if you wish, a sad case with an exasperating lack of moral ideas and illusions;

a young man too self-conscious and intense, obsessed with
sex, incongruity and death, joking and pitying in bad taste,
a bitterly clowning anti-litterateur, quite incapable of
perceiving the ordinary order and sense of the world. In
short, a fine example of the still contemporary literary
rebel, and the poet as stranger who knows that the true self
is that which accepts by refusing.

The LITERARY REBEL? Certainly my few examples so
far—Diogenes, Blake, Melville, Corbière, and some others along the way—do not cover all the possibilities of
literary rebellion. Many another case can, and perhaps
should, be made for some of the varied forms of revolt,
literary and other. After all, the conditions of life almost
always deserve much refusal and anger and opposition. (In
the following chapters, I partly switch focus to a broad
rebel subject and group of experiences—"the road.") But
central to my concern are some of the themes, the
perplexities and the qualities of those absolutely rebels—
the rebel not adequately comprehendible without a sense
of commitment to defiance, involvement in ancient ways
of denial and an identity most essentially seen as contumacious. As some believe in God, these believe in rebellion.

To consider how far the nihilistic awareness and disorderly wisdom of the past are traditional (just as well as
piety and orderly wisdom) might be salutary since most
arguments for "traditionalism" have been pre-empted to
other ends. How far, too, can parody of others, mockery of
the accepted, and art as extra-artistic revolt succeed as
literature? The literary role of the rebel, I have argued in
some detail, is inherently precarious, and therefore may
require some awareness and discriminations not common
to the usual biased assurance of literary discussion. The
same emphasis applies to the moral anti-morality of the
rebel, to an extremity so alien to most moral conventions
that we may do better to think of it in other than moral
terms—as the special style of the rebel which is his
ultimate social and metaphysical sanction. Is it really so
strange that the mode of response of the rebel should be
distinguishable as its own purpose and meaning? High
moralists praise the fusion of means and ends; individualistic rebels are among the few to engage that order of
merit, however desperately. Many more points might well

be made on the ultimate nature of the rebel and rebellion as its own end, past as well as present. The emphasis on the past traditions of the rebel serves not only to help define the present rebel, by breaking through the current and parochial into the recurrent and fundamental, but, also, the past has its main value in providing a place to stand when confronting the present. (It is all too common in the literature on the rebel to mistake contemporaneousness for rebelliousness; thus rebelliousness can also be explained away in terms of limited and temporary circumstances.) Such is my argument. But arguments can overwhelm perceptions, and so perhaps we should affirm again the humane positiveness of the rebel tradition: *the* true rebel, as my examples should also illustrate, not only has a hard rage but an essential tenderness for what it means to be human. Extremity of defiance is a way of compassion for an inherently inadequate world, society and self—which are made even more inadequate by the refusal to rebel against them. The tradition of refusing much of life-as-it-is affirms and achieves life.

SOME ROADS OF THE LITERARY REBEL

A CONSIDERABLE PART of the subject matter of literary rebels, past and present, is linked with the road. This does not just derive from the aesthetic aptness of the outsider to mirror life on the highways and in the low-ways of society, but comes also from the glorification of the outcast as hero, the kaleidescopic picaresque modes, the rich amorality of pariahdom, the radical perspective on the established order, the almost mystic negative freedom and terror of the wanderer—indeed, a whole complex of related ways of showing man not at home in the universe. Of course most tramps have not been poets. Vagabondage has usually been a sufficiently miserable existence, exacerbated by punishment, destitution and despair, that we should be quite reluctant to sentimentally aestheticize it.[1] Yet, with wandering blind Homers, peripatetic Cynics, homeless rhapsodists, drifting jongleurs, mendicant goliards, rhyming beggars, fluent picaros, itinerant preachers imitating Christ, literary students on a *wanderjahr*, restless romantic poets, footloose folk singers, exiled revolutionary memorialists, artistic mariners, professional literary hobos and aspiring hitchhiker novelists—among others!—large parts of our significant literature have found the muse on the road, if not down-and-out in the streets. Unquestionably, experiences and perspectives connected with the road take on a crucial literary and intellectual importance. Some of the greatest types in literature, such as Odysseus and Don Quixote, largely define themselves by their wanderings. Many of our most profound probings in art appear through the eys of restless Ishmaels. Much of "travel writing," from the Biblical accounts through those of

D. H. Lawrence, was not so much about traveling or places as part of a flight to a deeper awareness. And at least from Whitman's exaltation of the "Open Road," through Jack London's hobo adventures, then down Hart Crane's "Macadam" that reaches "towards a shore beyond desire," then into the saintly delinquency of the highway by Jack Kerouac, we have a century in which the road appears in American literature as a rebelliously identifying image of our yearnings.

Surely not all who made much of the road can be considered rebels, literary or otherwise. But wandering itself seems to provide a degree of exile from, and violation of, established society, and therefore an implicit defiance. The perennial hostility of established authorities to free individual wandering confirms the point: the punishment of "exile" and the usual lack of recourse of the "fugitive" in classical societies, the repeated official "degradation" and "repudiation" of the *ordo vagorum* by the Medieval Roman Church, the truly vicious vagrancy laws of the Renaissance and after (including present day America), and the quite paranoid insistence of modern national bureaucracies on residence and passport and permit and job justifications.[2] Yet wanderers receive magical sanctions in primitive and heroic societies—recall the obligations toward the stranger and "sojourner" in most epic literature—and the major religious writings claim an exalted place for holy vagabonds. The repression of wanderers runs deeper even than bourgeois societies' puritanical and commercial righteousness against those with disorderly and improvident ways. The restriction of identity to technical functions and institutional loyalties is not the innovation of our mass-bureaucratic-technological societies, though we have given them peculiarly impersonal and pervasive forms.

Once again, most of the official justifications for restraining and punishing outsiders reveal disguised nastiness. Vagrants are unproductive and parasitic? At their worst they never come near equaling the aggrandizement of military and priestly and other bureaucratic castes. Drifters are thieves and robbers? Big crime has usually been organized, rooted and closely linked to the authorities. The rootless are violent? Really significant violence has always been the prerogative of those controlling the technology;

executioners kill more than assassins, churches more than sects, governments more than gangs, and only the "greatest" powers can practice death camps, saturation bombings and nuclear warfare. But are not alien drifters often dirty, sick, disrespectful, unpatriotic, anarchic, disgruntled, antisocial and even blasphemous? True, and for these crimes they get thoroughly punished. Those on the road are clearly immoral, if morality be confined to the categories of the settled and powerful. When wandering within organized society reaches large scale—as with the mendicant friars, the beggar brotherhoods and the American hobos—remarkably decent (and relatively unpoliced) codes of conduct have often been evident, however inadequate they may be from more genteel perspectives. Order and morals do not provide the genuine issue between those inside and outside. Part of the antagonism against those without the settled pattern of the society must be a hostility, sometimes of pathological proportions, against the very state of being outside.

Many of those who have bought into authoritarian institutions somehow paid such an intellectual and emotional price that they feel compelled to present righteous damage claims to those who will not or cannot make similar investments. We need hardly rehearse the tiresomely irrelevant charges against the vagrant based on "general economic welfare" since vagrants take very little and, in their intermittent labors and servitudes, get much cheated. The arguments against the unsettled in the holy names of "civilization" or "culture" also belong to ancient bigotries. The cultural values of restless bohemianism, whatever they might be, are probably greater than respectable salesmanship; more art seems to be created by marginal than by solid citizens. Awareness of the basic nature of the society—its miseries and generosities, its crucial boundaries of freedom—seem far more incisive among bums than among bureaucrats (a major reason why modern novelists dwell far more on the down-trodden than on the up-riding). New ecstatic modes, from which the major historical styles of thought and feeling develop, probably arise on the restless peripheries rather than in the settled suburbs. Thus the opposition of power groups and their moralists to wandering is less economic and cultural than a matter of ideological defense and psychic fears.

That few societies grant more than a minimal toleration to those without the "fixed abode" of land, employment, money or authority reveals a fundamental antipathy to a large area of freedom. Perhaps the social powers have a prudent wisdom in so doing; they recognize that those on the road implicitly deny the claims to freedom and worth made by the ostensibly civilized. In brief, those on the margins are so often treated as rebels against "civilized forms" that inevitably some of them become self-conscious rebels. If the very structure of civility bars the vagrant—or the artist or the religious—and insists on his peculiarity and outrageousness, then his self-definition will demand that he expoit some of the peculiarities and outrageousness. The heroism of outlaws, when they have it, is partly forced upon them by the dubious nature of the laws, and those within the law.

Some obvious distinctions must be made between the passive and active negators of the civilized order.[3] Most of the literature of the road separates the merely defeated from the defiant wanderers. Professional beggars, most criminal groups, Bowery bums, and so on, do not naturally rebel; most of them also travel little, unless forced to, since their denials have taken narrowly self-protective and self-destructive forms (the end of the road: perhaps a state most permanent wanderers must reach). The closer a man feels to pure victim, whether from destitution, addiction, psychosis or belief, the less of a rebel he is. To be in revolt seems to require some sort of self-consciousness (though not mere intellectuality) at least partly free from inner and outer compulsions. The literature of the road almost invariably emphasizes not just the forces which compel the writer to wander, from unemployment to wanderlust, but the sense of radical liberty from being driven and obliged, an almost ecstatic freedom (however grim in details) which becomes one of the nuclear experiences of the road.

A recent report by Philip O'Connor on vagrants (including himself) denies that men wander from free will, then rather thoroughly undercuts the denial by emphasizing the sense of freedom. Other major and crucial responses to the road that he discusses also insist on radical senses of freedom, such as the wanderer's loss of competitive and egotistical identity, his hostility to "the top heavy wedding-cake" of our civilization, the cosmic but also diffuse affect of being without parochial loyalties, the terror and heightening that go with total separation and the awareness of universal human precariousness, and a religious intensification—both frightening and blissful— that follows from the very role of being "outside." [4]

The more vigorous outcasts of the literature also sometimes insist on roles which further justify, even exalt, their vagabondage: preacher, poet, student, philosopher, revolutionist, or moral and artistic tourist. That many wanderers must claim an honorific role rather than wandering for its own sake—for why shouldn't wandering in itself be a good?—seems also to reflect the antagonism of the settled. Congenital tramps pretend, often for decades, to be temporarily unemployed, though more basically they live as mobile hermits. Quite a mixed lot of Medieval wanderers justified themselves as pilgrims, as Chaucer slyly tells us. Most American hobos were never more than part-time laborers at best, yet often claimed otherwise and, under the impact of ideologies, even pretended to be the Working Class of modern political mythology. Odysseus, ostensibly eager to get back to Ithaca, had a whole warring cosmogony to justify his wanderings; Don Quixote even persuaded Sancho that ideal journeyings would show a certain hard profit. Many of our restless contemporaries pass as perpetual students, reverse vacationers (working for short periods), or neo-innocent American explorers after "something better" in the spiritual geography of opportunity. Such justifications of vagabondage naturally tend to become rationales for a way of life, obscuring the purer impulses to restlessness and rebellion, since a disguise will eventually deceive its wearer. If the footloose justify themselves as political moralists or literary artists, a political movement or literary cult may follow. But we may still suspect that the implicit ideology of individual rebellion remains most essential to the wanderer. The Christianity of many pilgrims, the socialist doctrines of many hobos, and the poetics of many Beats often turn out to be nothing more than fancy dress, somewhat musty from self-sanctification, for the more basic impetus to rebellion. Taking to the road has for long been the *Ding-an-sich* of the discontented.

Whatever their stated reasons and roles, the ways of

those on the road can be seen as objections to the prevailing conditions of life. The arduous wanderer's "laziness" is crucial: "The tramp or hobo, the Bohemian and many nomadic or sporadic workers [in contemporary society] may be held to be protesting not only against the lack of free time but against other things too, like the regularity of the work world." [5] Probably the wanderer in all periods protests by his flight the vitiating or vicious falsifications of a genuine relation to work, whether found in Classical slavery, Medieval serfdom, modern mechanization or contemporary bureaucratization. In present day America, most of significant leisure—the pursuit of ecstasy or truth or style in their own right—is inevitably marginal. To subvert an institution, by cultivating independent thought and feeling and life-style within its interstices, comes hard. Not only do modern bureaucracies—universities provide good examples—specialize in subtle tests of allegiance in which they above all "know their own" and eliminate the intransigent and peculiar, but the rebel within also gets trapped in inner compulsions. The restrictions such institutions manage by a mixture of ornate pressures and calls upon the culture's standards of puritan moralism, efficient benevolence, anxious geniality and rationalized power-ambitions become enslaving.[6] The inherent tolerance of formal institutions for rebels of intelligence and passion is quite limited, and a good many will inevitably be forced into either more fully counterfeiting the settled style—often to their own defeat—or into more bitterly nomadic and sporadic ways of life. The fascination with the literature of the road also testifies to the incipient drama, the yearnings, for such a crux. America is a free and open society, as they say, which means that temptations and distractions are greater, compulsions more confusingly ambiguous, and the spirit of rebellion more uncertain as well as subvertible. But American freedom also means that traditional sense of being able to refuse, throw it up, let them have it, and take off down the road.

In the commentaries on hobos, peripatetic bohemians, wandering students and other forms of self-conscious vagabondage, there often appears the odd assumption that these are very few in numbers, which is dubious, and are, like more necessitous men on the move, the products of compulsion—instead of rebels against it! The vagrant, intellectual as well as physical, gets dismissed as the victim of social malaise. Certainly there exists a correspondence between mass wandering and social conditions: in Classical times, slavery, political punishment and war; in Medieval times, heresy, serfdom and war; in modern times, unemployment, inadequate social welfare and war.[7] In times of peace and prosperity in welfare states the problems raised by migrants and vagabonds appear markedly lessened, though this may mean in part that the problems take less calamitous and more disguised forms. But such discussions rather too exclusively define wandering in socio-economic terms, which miss the point as much as earlier definitions that moralized with the jargon of "sin" or "insanity." The reductive morality common to social scientists that wanderers must be understood as social victims or sick deviants lacks logic as well as sensitivity. While most contemporaries no longer seem to believe, with a few generations back, that vagabondage comes from bad genes or special forms of madness, they now blame alcoholism and similar addictions, Oedipal and other sexual difficulties, or simply syndromes of failure. That lack of "vice," *a*sexuality and syndromes of success are not more suspect indicates a denatured, and dull, view of human possibility. Whether drinking, homosexuality and character neuroses really dominate wanderers more than comparable settled folk, or just appear more direct and evident, remains uncertain. Clearly, the more elaborate "addictions" are unsuitable to outcasts; and some of the nastiest sexual "deviations," such as identification with superiors, must be less common among vagabonds than people in corporate structures. Adaptability, responsiveness, intelligence, education and character have not been in short supply among the nomadic and marginal. In much of history, and not least in the present, the argument can well be made that the blandly accepting and conventionally ambitious are the sickest deviants of all from a significant image of the human.

Wanderers, then, should not be reduced to socio-economic malaise (though they significantly express it) or the psychologisms of deviant behavior (though they dramatically show them). Vagabondage draws on very basic values. That current social ethics allow little place for those who, by temperment and/or belief, want to be outside the official productive order is a disguised authoritarianism. Considering the meaninglessness of the majority of modern jobs in factory and office and school, and the anxious dullness of the dominant patterns of living, the assumption of the automatic elimination of the marginal and outcast—by improving psychic health, social welfare and education—mocks all sense of human liberty. Gratuitous choice, the bedrock of freedom, gets thickly silted over with benign functionalism. Current ideologies of endless consumption, deranged productivity for its own sake, and status and acceptance anxieties do everything possible to confuse and confute the longings for irregularity, the love of individual liberty, and the defiance of the social-moral order which have long been represented by the freedom of the road.[8]

But to thus push against the arguments which attempt to negate the rebel on the road, and deny any inherent validity to a whole type of subject matter, would be endless. My basic point is simple: wandering may be many things, but most certainly includes fundamental expressions of human awareness and aspiration. Of those filling the role of literary wanderers—quite literally the spokesmen for millions of other wanderers, as well as for many who long to wander—the Cynics, we have already noted, used their errant way of life as part of a radical individualist attack on the first principles of conventional morals and manners. A good many wandering literary intellectuals have been less programmatic. The goliard poets of the high Middle Ages, for example, were only mockingly didactic in their burlesque recommendations to follow the fraternal ways of begging, gambling and drinking. They were not, however, merely the whining and lyrical victims of an educational surplus in one of the great periods of the universities. Granted, they practiced a literature of complaints and flatteries to possible patrons, but they often did so with a mockery quite foreign to any practical conformity. When Primas (Hugo of Orleans) plays the repentant beggar ("Dives Eram Et Dilectus") his tone is far more wry than penitent. When the Archpoet of Cologne denounces the pleasures of the flesh as sins ("Estuans Intrinsecus") he has a gambit for praising their delights. Such poets, and the authors of the *Carmina Burana*, carry the usual rebel satire, burlesque and parody to its natural blasphemy in which drunken gaiety becomes the *summum bonum*. That strange but recurrent rebel mysticism of the bottle, combined with the exaltation of carnal delights and the love of irregularity, made wayward-ness their discipline and devotion. It has rightly been noted that the *clerci vagi* "were rebels against authority and sometimes against decency." [9] Reform, personal or public, was not their primary meaning (though they may have contributed significantly to doubts about the reli-giousness and authority of the church); and their wander-ing mockeries, ecstasies and miseries defied any order except that of their own disorder.

Naturally, the wandering scholars of the Middle Ages illuminate for us their times, providing some apt awareness of the corruption inherent in a religious bureaucracy, the persistence of Christly vagrancy, the repression of direct life inhering in much of official Christian ethics, and the odd mixture of exacerbated physicality and delicate senti-ment of high Medieval sensibility. But what history we learn from them should not be the only measure of what they were. Another quality they teach is what I take to be one of the essential marks-of-the-kind, the notable tone of rebellion in which pity and anger merge into the perfected sardonic gesture. We may see it also in Villon's famous "Quatrain" preparatory to his hanging in which he mocks both authority and his miserable fate, and concludes that his neck will soon find out the weight of his ass.[10]

The same defiance of all less candidly human standards might be emphasized about some of the Renaissance literature of the picaresque, which does something more than present crime and the seams of social reality.[11] From *Lazarillo de Tormes* on, those wandering rogues incisively show the underside of life with an energy that is in itself rebellion against the usual sense of restriction on life. The picaresque writers, of course, especially mock the social hypocrisies in ways which demand that one have no lesser allegiance than that to the road which runs all the way out of conventional acceptance. And there again appears that crucial tone: "At long last I was prosperous, and at the zenith of all good fortune," [12] concludes the account of Lazarillo, after describing how he had to play the stupid and cunning cuckold to a rich archpriest. The attitude here cannot be encompassed by terms of "social realism" or criminal roguishness. Even a commentator not much given to admiration for literary vagabonds has properly noted: "Le picaro détest l'ordre social et met sa gloire dans sa friponneries." [13]

The authors of the picaresque, from the beginnings through such rambling twentieth-century versions as those of Pio Baroja,[14] insist not only on the special authenticity of the down-and-out and drifting but also on that stance and style which curiously combines sympathy and cynicism. The rogue achieves this tonality by a sort of mock-innocence which contains both affirmations of energy and of social outrage. As with Grimmelshausen's Simplicissimus, he is a fool "because he telleth everyman the truth so shamelessly; yet are his speeches so ordered that they belongeth to no fool." [15] Simplicissimus was fortunate, he sardonically notes, in suffering the horrors of the Thirty Years War because that gave him a chance to learn so many fine things, such as irrelevant Christian piety. The wise-fool discovers pervasive falsity, as in those "mighty deeds" which are "accomplished with the destruction and damage of other men"—civilization being mostly based on such "mighty deeds." [16] Characteristically, too, the rebel plays the bard of protean form; Simplicissimus was a peasant boy turned hermit, then a roguish variety which included jester, page, brigand, soldier, hunter, enchanter, seducer, scholar, merchant, quack doctor, diplomat, etc., ending as a hermit among peasants. What means this usual form of the picaresque? No social roles and positions ever are, or ever can be, adequate.

The point still appears strongly in the somewhat portentously overdone modern rogue of Günter Grass's *The Tin Drum*. The drumming dwarf, Oskar, telling his story from his insane asylum bed, is a demonic Jesus of the "Barbaric, Mystical, Bored" Teutonic side of the twentieth century. He takes many of the equivocal forms of the perpetual delinquent, represented by his dwarf state in this archly symbolic *mea culpa*. Most essentially he mocks, as one of his verse refrains puts it, "the bourgeois-smug"—both parent and child of the Nazi horror.[17] This symboliste-picaresque author puts his version of the principle of rebellious plenitude in the analogy of the artist being like the "partisan" fighter, incorrigibly revolting against what his revolt has just created.[18]

That no moral program can be extracted from a Goliard or a Villon, or be given to a Lazarillor or a Simplicissimus, or be focused on the wandering literary forms of a Baroja or a Grass, comes not from a defect in their art but from their very rebelliousness. Thus many of the contemporary attempts to find a poetics of the road or to redo picaresque modes may attest to the fundamental defiance found in these literary traditions. The monotonies and splendors of the road intensely set off the inadequacies of ordinary order. The commitment to non-commitment, represented by the hero on the highway, includes the joy as well as the terror of alienation, the wisdom as well as the waywardness of being outside.[19]

The types embodying such miseries and ecstacies are far broader than the explicitly picaresque. For example: that ancient sufferer, the Wandering Jew, who in Christian folk legend searches the world for repentance because of his denial of saving grace (sometimes he was identified with the disciple Thomas), becomes a hero to those of rebel temper.[20] The Jew as the suffering yet comic, sensuous yet self-conscious, prophetic yet ironic, alien believing in communion becomes a positive exile.[21] Quite rightly, the heroic Jew in acute modern literature is not an Israeli but a wanderer who has found that the whole world is a ghetto. As Jeremiah insisted, exile sharpens true faith more than the Chosen Land. The contemporary British anarchist Alex Comfort thus develops in his novel On This Side Nothing a dialectic of refusal in which he contrasts the "Man-Jew" with the "Law-and-Order-Jew." [22] The Diaspora ironist versus the smug Zionist turns out to be a somewhat flatted allegory of the permanent rebellion of the self-conscious man. To be a Wandering Jew in the fullest sense less reflects the history of a dogged and persecuted minority than the imaginative state of refusal of parochial solace. Or as Leslie Fiedler dramatizes it in one of his rather hysterical paradoxes in The Second Stone: "I'm the real Jew," victoriously says the Anglo-Saxon-Protestant-American and bohemian failure abroad to the Jewish spokesman, "the real Jew, Rabbi, if to be a Jew means to live on the margins of the world in failure and terror, to be an exile." [23]

Why this ennobling of failure and exile and wandering? Because the rebel has a religious sense of man's precarious existence. At a simpler level, patterns of power and authority dedicate everyone to success and homogeneity and fixity. The contraries require antithetical experiences as well as forms. The criticisms from outside—quite different from those of a competing power group or a "loyal opposition" or reformers—tend to be total and absolute. The wanderer forever denies the idolatry of things-as-they-are. The outsider's heroism shows the usual heroic excess in making demands that can never fully be met and in transmitting intensities of life which can never fully be contained.

Another Wandering Jew, Jesus Christ, similarly appeals to modern rebels. Several Beat poets aptly take Christ as a comic scapegoat, an image of heroic and outcast absurdity.[24] In Nikos Kazantzakis' rather over-fervent Last Temptation of Christ, the Christ's commitment to failure is his major virtue and power. At somewhat prolix length, Kazantzakis dramatizes the ultimate temptation as the success of ordinary and conventional good life. To create God is to resist, to be the complete alien, defeated, outcast, crucified. So, too, with the Christ of D. H. Lawrence's The Man Who Died, a seasonal wanderer who renounces his ministry of love, even his regenerative demonic passion, and all settled order to perpetually follow the sun into exilic freedom. Or as Kazantzakis puts it in his meditations: God is "the Great Vagabond" who best loves those brooding "on rebellion, on the endless road." [25]

But aren't some conventional lives good, some settled morals and manners better than others? Surely, within the relativity of conventions there may be meaningful shadings. But the rebel, as rebel, demands something else, some tone to existence only perceivable in motion. Thus he must break beyond conventions into the disfamiliar world of bloody and dark and icy and golden shades; and thus, like the hero of Kazantzakis' ornately painted metaphysical rebellion in The Odyssey: A Modern Sequel, he becomes the total voyager. This requires a search beyond muted tones to the violent colors of the despised and outlawed. And any more than momentary success would be real failure for the rebel since any truth which is not exiled would be a lie against human mortality.

The men identified by the road, then, are not just deviants fleeing into the mindless flux, or searchers after romantic paradises around the given corners, or the discontented riffraff who unmake civilized sensibility. The rebel on the road chooses his ambiance with its sense of extremity—though it often looks as if the road chooses him—to achieve a certain awareness which does not readily come in other ways. This grounding (and limiting) of knowledge by special experiences is, after all, fairly accepted in common sense. We also know that the responsive man who has been an infantry private in a modern army despairs of ever quite adequately explaining his cynicism about authority to officers or civilians, though his outrage against arbitrary power has been an almost obsessive subject of a vast array of American novels about two world wars.[26] From this perspective, the military (or similar) organization is, no matter how relatively good, bad. Thus, too, the aware individual who has undergone time in a prison or concentration camp struggles to communicate the utter despair of confinement and the absolute beauty of freedom. What is mere freedom, that negative thing? say pedantic Pilates. But they have never "done time" (apt mortal phrase) for their felonies, or they dare not remember. Almost any responsive piece of the literature of confinement seems a rebellious work, regardless of the avowed (and sometimes irrelevant) morals of the author.[27] Certain subjects lead to qualities of awareness, of art (despite the aestheticians), in and of themselves. It may also be true that only those authentically know the reverberations of "liberty" and "freedom" who are, in fact or in intense analogous experience, exprisoners.

So, too, with benign moralists' logic that we "all belong to minorities," and thus should assert common humanity with the persecuted.[28] It is not the same humanity, unless we can existentially realize—as the accounts from the road so often insist—some of the uprooting, contempt, outrage and even paranoia and self-hatred which provide a distinguishable wisdom of those really separated out from the larger communities and engaged in the particularistic consciousness which gives a fundamentally different (instinctual? perplexed? anguished?) cast to awareness. Apparently, some experiences, such as full sexual orgasm, or pregnancy and childbirth, or mystical illumination, or—I am arguing—the outcast state, tend to the ineffable and surely are incommensurable with all other states. That almost all rebellious literature draws heavily, nay, obsessively, upon experiences of confinement and escape, failure and wandering, exile and persecution, must not be accidental—nor a technique of art. Therefore there exists a deep imperative to present those extremes for the creation of the self, as well as for others. While it might be desirable that everyone should be for a time a rogue, a Wandering Jew, a convict, an indentured servant, an infantry private, a Negro (black or white) and a tramp— motherhood and sainthood may be a bit more specialized—our more limited concern here is their literary significance. The most simple point might be that we should not defensively or fancifully translate the vagrant and outcast, in or out of literature, into something else. The rebellious wanderer's journey, for example, usually forms no "quest" with a grail-purpose and a salvational ending (his journey is "open" rather than "closed"). Being outside provides truths of its own, often just obtusely falsified by social moralities and religious allegories.[29] Liberty and authority, for example, can probably be uniquely apprehended from the road where the gratuitousness of both show more fully. The arbitrariness of our social arrangements—not least in America—seems primarily a perception of those traveling the edge. The anxiety and narcissism of power seem clearest to those on the margins. The pettiness of most of what calls itself "culture," and the exorbitant prices demanded in heuristic terms of civilization, stand out when one wanders beyond them. Such self-defining states as freedom and solitude and sufficiency demand equivalent experiences. Ancient wisdoms advised that love or virtue or faith provide a unique sense of life. To be a rebel on the road, however foolish or degraded, may also provide such a distinctive perspective. Currently, the traditional wanders—whether in theologized vagrancy or socio-economic trampdom— seem in marked decline; but their significance remains, not only in the evident diffusion of their attitudes to many others sceptically discontented with our civilization but also in providing archetypal ways of awareness and defiance for those who feel the desire to opt out. The true voyager, says Baudelaire, goes for the going.[30] What he finds are the intensifications of appearances and dreams, some nihilistic truths underneath, and the road right out of any easy acceptance.

LET US FOCUS on the modern American tramp as an image of rebellion. The "hobo" is a common figure in our twentieth-century literature. We may ignore here most of the origins before the late nineteenth century, though obviously there were tramps from the colonial period on, not only as a continuation of European styles but also as indigenous responses to the open frontier, to a partly declassed society, and to such notorious American characteristics as rootlessness, guiltiness, and the naive aggrandizement called "opportunity." Many of these wanderers go by the euphemistic names of explorers, scouts, frontiersmen, forty-niners, hunters and cowboys; they were frequently puritanical and violent versions of what Europeans call vagabonds and rogues. Even now, the mythologies developed about them too much turn waywardness into bland opportunism—"creating new frontiers," "winning the West" and similar gaudy imperilisms—and into the nasty-innocence of American Manicheanism: "good guys" and "bad guys." Our patterns of vagabondage for both the primary and secondary frontiers take a generally paltry cast. Part of this may inhere in the actuality, as well as in the counterfeit "mass culture" which corruptingly controls and manipulates our legendary images. The fantastic expansiveness and technological change of all the American frontiers created the rebellious types only to quickly and grimly displace them, leaving us with fragmentary images of already anachronistic styles of individuality and heroism. "Western" literature, from Twain's anecdotes to Clark's *Ox-Bow Incident*, shows little adequacy in its art and perception, though the best of the cinematic Westerns, with their lonely and laconic figures caught between ruthless economic societies and a vast alienating natural world, do visually suggest some of the significance.[1] But these essentially atheistic American frontier heroes, with their rigid codes of work-and-battle in place of any larger way of responsiveness (and a pistol in place of a penis) mostly adumbrate a desperately uncertain and violent wandering without very enriching possibilities.[2]

What, then, might be the other sources of our contemporary image of the rebellious wanderer? Thoreau, in part of "Walking" and "Life Without Principle," aphoristically creates a role of philosophical tramp and rebel (he also disparages less highfalutin tramps) but seems not to lead to the primary American type. Nor are Melville's wanderers quite in the dominant form, though his sailors were maritime tramps (like Melville himself, and many others until economic developments in recent decades drastically restricted shipping out).[3] Whitman's "Song of the Open Road" is often made much of by tramping litterateurs. It does point to some of the essential qualities with its exalted "Allons!" for taking to the endless and enlarging road in negative freedom: "From this hour I ordain myself loos'd of limits and imaginary lines,/ Going where I list, my own master total and absolute." Certainly there was a strong force of defiance in this—"I nourish active rebellion." But it takes those weirdly self-cancelling Whitmanian forms. On the dominant side we find the "efflux of the soul" with its shapeless conglomerates and mergings. On the rarer defiant side we get the revelations of one who will "know all and expose it," such as "inside those wash'd and trimm'd faces/ Behold a secret silent loathing and despair." Whitman's road-blocks of woozy egomania, quaint prolixities and aggrandizing identifications with everything also belong to the stumblings of many later literary wanders. For, as D. H. Lawrence pointed out, Whitman longed to destroy identity, and so much of his provocative native power lacked deeply passionate individual quality.[4] The Whitmanian indiscriminate voraciousness may find properly poignant expression in Box-Car Bertha. A somewhat literary tramp of the 1930's, she reports in her pleasant account in *Sister of the Road* that when she was asked in the hospital to name the father of her illegitimate child, she replied, "Fifteen hundred lonely men." [5] There's Whitman's love *en masse*. But she was being as accurate as she could; in her very American search for the enlargement of experience she had gone to work in a whorehouse for a few months and kept count of her customers up to her pregnancy. The love-all stance, lacking negative individual center, may finally not be rebellious at all.

Yet how full, and even marked by essential resistance, seems the Whitmanian tradition when compared to the sadly thin moralistic and poetic vagabondage of Vachel Lindsay. His exhilaration on the road—and occasionally tender perception of outcast lives and magic when seen separated from the usual continuities—appears now and then in his slight early tramping sketches, *A Handy Book for Beggars*. He dedicated that work to "heretics" for whom "life is a rebellion with banners." But it was the waving of those banners of sentimental idealism which resulted in ponderous writing and obscured his avowed allegiance to the god of "the perpetual road." [6] He demonstrates all too fully in his further sketches of his travels, *Adventures While Preaching the Gospel of Beauty*, a preachy distaste for tobacco, liquor, sex, most less obviously sensitive souls, and incisive language and awareness. The vital toughness of the contemporary rail-roading hobos in quite lacking in his Victorian "trouba-dour" role-playing. Lindsay's touching exhortations to recreate the dreary midwestern rural villages into earnestly artistic and spiritual communities lacks a hardy sense of social and psychic needs, and ends, as he seems to have known, in quaintness. The heavily sentimental and literary language of his poems about the road result from the same simple and moralistic aestheticism. The way down to the essential experiences of the road—the sense of social alienation, freedom and independence which haunted Lindsay intermittently to his suicide [7]—were not very compatible with genteel uplift.

American vagrancy, in reality and in imagination, gen-erally took harsher forms than the amorphous exaltations of Whitman and the slight troubadorism of Lindsay. The twentieth-century rebellious ur-hero seems to be the hobo. [8] Hobos reached large numbers, perhaps up to several million, only with the full scale expansion of the railroads and the industrial-frontier period in the 1880's. They came most fully to national attention with the economic depression of '93 and the "march" of thousands on Washington in "Coxey's Army" (1894)—a rather loose protest of the dispossesed later repeated in the "Bonus March" of the 1930's and the "integration" marches of the 1960's. (But each generation's type—hobo, unemployed war veteran, oppressed Negro—does not get equally translated into literature or even into the sub-literary communal imagination.) Narrowly defined, hobos were nomadic and seasonal laborers who filled a major economic role for perhaps half a century when timbering and wheat harvesting, railroad building and new industrial recruitment, drew out a large and fluid labor force in a peculiarly non-familial and individualistically atomized way. Far more than with most migratory movements, that individual male separateness was crucial to the hobo ethos.

Usually the hobo has been distinguished from other social outcasts, following Reitman's wry trinity: "The hobo works and wanders, the tramp dreams and wanders and the bum drinks and wanders." [9] The sociologists follow this out with duller versions of the same vocational categories. (Tramps used more elaborate distinctions, such as "blowed-in-the-glass-stiffs" [top tramps], "yeggs" [criminal tramps], "gay cats" [fast moving kids], and many others; some of the jargon—junkie, punk, fag, gun, etc.—keeps a relatively permanent place in the language of marginal experience.) But hobo or tramp may pretty equally cover all of those who moved since many of the tramps, it becomes clear on reading the memoirs, did sometimes work—an opportunity, for obvious social and economic reasons, far more available to American than to European trampdom—while many workers became hobos so as to work more irregularly, or less, as well as to satisfy other longings for adventure, flight, social eccentricity and discontent. Most hobos also spent some time as city bums on "skid row" ("the main stem") and sometime or other practiced begging ("pan handling" on the streets or door to door for "handouts") without joining the elaborately specialized ethos of the professional beggars. Only a small minority seem to have been significantly criminal (robbery, violence), markedly sick (drugs, crippling, psychoses), though drinking and homosexuality were widespread and hostility to authority went beyond any practical need. The largest number of American hobos and tramps seem to have been white native-born Americans of Protestant and northern European extraction, plausibly sane and competent. General intelligence, education and literacy must have been at least average, if not better, and there quite emphatically developed a tradition of the "intellectual hobo." As near as one can tell, these characteristics seem to apply to much of American wandering, though they do not fit into many social-psychological and middle-class moral theories of deviant behavior.

Various changes, such as the disappearance of the industrial frontier, technological complication, the spread of the automobile, the partial switch in the 1930's to family migrancy, and general social embourgeoisement, brought the hobo into decline until now the traditional sort seems vestigial.[10] In the most general senses, the hobo has been reduced by a bureaucratic-technological society to increasingly more menial roles—when any at all are open—and to the less prideful place of pathetic "social-case" migrant and passive city bum. But our interest is less in the social definitions than in certain peculiarities germane to the American imagination. The hobo or work-side of American trampdom seems crucial. The working tramp raised one of the usual American paradoxes: as a tramp outside, as a worker inside. In a society where "the job" ("What do you do?") provides the major way of identity, the hobo had one but frequently shifted and violated it. Thus, imaginatively, the hobo well represented American uncertainty about self-definition since he is neither fully a pariah to the social order not fitted into a fixed place. His justification to others was his work; most often his justification to himself was his flight. The image of the American hobo becomes representative in being both unfixed and righteous. The very fluidity, actual and moral, perhaps provides part of the nostalgic appeal the hobo still seems to have for many Americans.

According to the literature of the American hobo, he was voracious of experience, or, as the song has it,[11] "hard travelin'" (pun included: hard in the senses of difficult, rapid and brave) as well as hard working, hard-drinking and hard-nosed. The frenzy for speed—and the high status given to the "passenger stiff," the fast 'bo riding the blinds or rods, the British "top-cock" and the hitchhiker making it coast-to-coast in four or five days—shows a kind of guilt and hunger in which pure cathartic motion substitutes for traveling. The consumption of space and time, as the accounts make clear, rarely depends on practical purpose, but neither do the Jules Vernish fantasies of millions of American motorists and tourists. The true tramp, whether he works or not, drinks or not, justifies himself or not, is a traveling man who feels a powerful psychic pressure to it, but he is significantly a rebel only if he has reasons and awareness beyond the compulsion to move.

One longing for movement, as almost every tramp memoir reveals, comes from the role of the tramp as a dreamer. A great appeal of life on the road seems at all times to have been what some call its "mindlessness" and Philip O'Connor calls "generalized existence," a regression to diffuse fantasy life—the major activity while riding and waiting. The emotive richness of fantasy intensifies in the very lack of fixed reality and routine confining more solid citizen's dreams. Harsh immediate reality plus the lavishness of free fantasy gives life on the road some of its peculiar tone. For the American to wonder as he wanders, there has been the additional fillip that social reality does not automatically rule out the chance that next week he may not only be far from where he is but also far away from who he now is—the obverse side of the American Dream of opportunity, often inverted into mere acquisitiveness or status jumping. Though a good many tramps evidently ended in the Sargasso ghettos of skid row, many could and did arrive elsewhere. Therefore the American tramp becomes the more positive "hobo" and his optimistic exuberance qualifies the sense of being outcast and defeated. Thus, too, the appeal of breaking away into trampdom remains "open"; taking to the road could be seen as a temporary state, an apprentice phase for the young. It has been so recommended, in effect, from father to son, older brother to younger, bragging young adult to discontented adolescent. The lore of the road seems to have been an important part of the imaginative ethos of three or four generations of American youth. To take to the road thus became a kind of initiation ritual and educational foray as well as rebellion against the given circumstances.

Certainly this applies to the autobiographical sketches of Jack London, *The Road*. These small but cleanly written anecdotes about his early tramping and hoboing from coast to coast show him eagerly becoming a "gay cat" in competition with other road kids. He worked a bit, though usually despising it, moved much, energetically accepted hardship and violence, and exalted in his freedom. The emphasis London puts on the protean qualities of his road existence, the "zest for experience" (and for speed and change and arduous testing) which drive the young tramp on, become typical for the literature. The intensification of rebelliousness that comes from alienation, openness and discomfort provides a heroic cast. London praises the drifter's wisdom of living in the present because of "the futility of telic endeavour." [12] While he also gives other reasons for his hoboing—wanderlust, poverty, rejection of regular labor, camaraderie with virile outcasts—his denial of customary ideals and his pervasive "antagonism to organized authority" seem crucial. Much of his account consists of amusing and tough games against the authority of "shacks" (brakemen), cops, and others in power. London's major point would seem to be that "the hobo defies society" [13] and thus intensely creates a manly and rebellious self.

Jack London, of course, represents one of the more energetic views of the meaning of trampdom, though one curiously casual and limited by the anecdotal and slick form of a commercial writer. The poor poet and later bohemian fixture, Harry Kemp, in his more elaborate *Tramping on Life*, admits that his drifting as a "bindle stiff" with his *Shakespeare* and Latin *Caesar* in his bundle was in part a youthful idealization of the tramp, based on such writers as London, and that he later rejected it. [14] Such idealization ran far and deep, even in those who countered it. Josiah Flynt, one of the earliest of the tramp writers in this tradition and a rather unpleasant type fascinated with criminals, who appropriately became a detective, journalist and sycophant of famous literary men, shows himself driven by the mixture of ideal and guilty longings of an over-mothered minister's son. The feverish dissatisfaction with ordinary reality, which also leads to the self-punishing alcoholism and similar behavior, seems to have as insistent a connection with literary yearnings as with tramping defiance.[15] The English poet W. H. Davies, who bummed in America for five years, shows in his rather modest and uninsightful *Autobiography of a Super-Tramp* [16] that he found only two ways out of his discontent, the road and poetry, with the one leading to the other. Jim Tully, one of the more famous and fluent tramp writers of the 1920's tells, in *Beggars of Life,* of the road initially as an escape for an orphan already feeling trapped in grinding and meaningless labor and puritanic conventions in a midwestern small town. The "man's code" of the road, represented by the sceptical mockeries of a rebellious young 'bo passing through, provided the direct impetus to Tully's initiation. His education on the road taught a fuller sense of liberty, openness to immediate experience and, not least, intellectual awareness. He learned, he said, to contemplate, to read (Dostoevsky in a western public library was one of the high points), and to discover a fuller self separate from conventional social standards and restrictions. Tully's account also briefly explores, in associative writing, some of the free-fantasy which provides a crucial tone to the road and rebellion.[17] As a tramp, he discovers an important symbiosis between outcast wanderer and modern writer. Though now badly obscured by "professionalism," commercial and academic—Tully also became a hack—poetic and radical intelligence would often be improved by turning from professional edification and entertainment to the vocation of internal exile.

The tramping college student and more or less intellectual hobo may partly be the product of the hobo wanderers who went into literature. The hobo writers were quite aware of more ancient literary traditions—Cervantes and Goldsmith and Whitman as well as London and Gorki—and of a nineteenth-century dissident role, partly socialist in origin.[18] Thus the pleasant account of William Edge, *The Main Stem,* describes an ex-college student who spent a year hobo-tramping during World War I and combined a traditional sense of outcast freedom with socialist criticism of "the system" of miserable factories and labor camps. His sense of "superiority" as a wanderer is coupled with an "equalitarian" denial of economic injustice and a self-conscious hostility to restrictive middle-class "obligations" and "hypocrisy." [19] His fairly ordinary, and probably representative, account makes clear that his wanderings served as a personal initiation in which the disillusioning jobs, the companionship with a radical intellectual hobo (who introduced him to the "literature of protest"), and the individualistic freedom of the road gave him a fuller sense of life than he would otherwise have had when he returned to middle-class circumstances at the end of his year. Thus the American road was an intellectual and even literary experience, and, thus too, the intellectual hobos became, as a scholar has noted, "symbols of the unfulfilled dreams, the inward longings of those in sedentary life." [20] The many wandering youths of the 1920's and 1930's were often self-conscious, and "socially conscious," of the role they pursued. Far more than any regular laborers, or other deprived group, they constituted a fluid and reabsorbed but rebellious "class." After all, to have a radical view of society and self usually requires that one at least have undergone at some time a radically separate way of life.

When we turn to recent memoirs of the road we find similar patterns, despite the changed economic and social circumstances. In Clancy Sigal's hopped-up reminiscences, *Going Away*, the key experience of his coast-to-coast trip is the joy of being disconnected:

> Hello, world! . . Gradually, the cold cramped feeling dissolved away; the knot in my stomach unreeled at seventy miles per hour, leaving behind a spoor of vague regrets and new vows. Right out of the blue, that old on-the-road blast of exaltation hit me. I was free again.[21]

Despite his almost invariable bad writing (the heavy triteness, the garbled stomach knot with its spoor and vows), Sigal testifies to the crucial experience. A good many pages and roads further on in his borrowed convertible and style—"*This* was the way to go. On a dusty, moonless wind-filled night. . . . Ah, it was terrific. Slicing through the walls of dark wind, it was almost *creative*." [22] This ecstasy of negative freedom has, as so often in such accounts, a number of distinctive corollaries: a special sense of outcast communion ("we of the road"); an almost apocalyptic hostility to the social order (he rages against "the terrors of America," the horrors of suburban complacency and narrowness, and the whole "deadness" of contemporary life); and, at his occasional best, he reveals a sense of sardonic identity ("traveling on the geography of my temper"; commenting, in a production-sick America, that "the road is my work"). While ostensibly rejecting life "on the bum"—no economic necessity drives him to it—he yet finds on the road a pride-revealing rage against social and emotional falsity and his "fellow citizens who live walled up in their fears." [23]

In *Going Away* these usual rebel motifs take a peculiar cast because of Sigal's contradictory motives. Almost simultaneously, he plays three antithetical roles: he is the ruthlessly aggressive young American "on the make" (the early murky episodes of himself as a Hollywood agent and the mawkish ones, at the other end of the book, about himself as a "writer"—both being so badly done as to deny that he has any insight). Secondly, Sigal was also a former denizen, still nostalgic, of the fantasy land of "progressive" politics (the many episodes about being a blindly energetic Stalinist student leader and about being a left-wing hack in labor union bureaucracy). And last, and often least, he was an individualistic rebel on the road (whose very trips, and perceptions, provide the shape of the narrative). His "fellow-traveling" bombast righteously mixes with his father-longing-and-killing and sexual needs and aggressive ambitions and, more appropriately, with his hungering for a sense of communal activity and purpose which he cannot find in America. The rebel side of this doesn't appear in his nasty union politicing, nor in his fervent and rather forced apostrophes to the dedicated social radicals of the recent past, but in less pretentious episodes and gestures. When Sigal manages to intersperse a tangible scene between rhetoric and voracious catalogues of jobs, girls, places and marginal experiences, the rebel comes through. Working in a demeaning and mechanical job cleaning movie film, he finds more ancient forms of revolt than those sanctioned by "progressivist" mythology; he comically sabotages the films by judicious cutting in a wry twentieth-century version of Ludditism, only thus achieving "purpose, a sense of mastery," [24] in otherwise meaningless work. His friendships with unideological outcasts—on skid row, in an Indian reservation—also call up some apt rebellious qualities. Though he constantly hungers for ideological politics and the sentimentality of "working class" identity, to balance his moral opportunism and give purpose and community, his more natural moments reveal him as a marginal being in revolt against all movements and mechanisms.

Going Away comes out as a jumble of often inadequately presented reminiscences loosely hooked to an automobile drive across the country in 1956, the trip serving as a trope for other trips on the road, mainly hitchhiking, trips up and down the social structure, and the usual mélange of defining experiences with the army, with jobs, with women, and the rest of the energetic and uncertain initiation into America. He also makes a fractured journey into the self, which results in a break with the past by a fuller journey right out of America. The tangible scenes, though usually not well done, do give a sense of an America and self which can't quite be put together. In summarizing his inchoate but energetic longings, and his defiance of the bland contemporary surface America, Sigal does reach for an identity beyond both his revolutionary rhetoric and his personal aggrandizement—the heritage of "the borderer, the outlaw observer, the Proudhonist finger at side of nose, the irrevocably homeless revolutionary." [25] While often confusing this deeply permanent rebellion with bureaucratic revolution, and his drastic discontent with self-flattering artistic sensibility, here he describes the appropriate defiance found on the road. That road all too well reveals, also, the confusing American scene and self whose mixed and fractured shapes makes rebellion both so appealing and so difficult.

For another example of the post-hobo road we might briefly consider some of the writings of Jack Kerouac—whom Sigal, competitively and contemptously, refers to as that "boy." Certainly the way to much of Kerouac's work is to be found in the realm of child responses. For example, on looking out from the road at night he writes: "I wish I was a little child in a crib in a little ranch style sweet house." [26] (This is also a fair example of much of his prose.) Kerouac always pursues his "kid dreams," elaborates juvenile jokes and yearnings, and, as he notes of his gang of middle-aged "boys," "We sorta wander around like children." [27] In this sub-rebellion, the ideal is to return to "the happy life of childhood again." The prose also often moves at a sub-adult level, not just in the inflated run-on sentences but in the "comfy," "heavenly," "raving

great," "dreamy," "glady," or the catatonic "wow!" responses. His insights are often pre-adolescent, it being a
great revelation to Kerouac that everybody walks around
with a "dirty behind," or that grown-ups are "crazy," or
that his friends are "great," or that America is a "nutty"
place, or that a hot-dog is "terrific" when you are hungry,
or that it is cosy "fun" to climb into a sleeping bag. Much
of this is pathetic, but even more so with the somewhat
more adult sections—recurrent paranoid episodes, the
sadly messy and guilty sexual longings, the flights and
returns to mamma, the eager and then disillusioned
identifications with more manly or purposive buddies, the
constant sense of inadequacy and anxiety. Yet, of course,
there appears some charm in childishness, and intermittently Kerouac's kid-world opens into some direct
and suggestive responsiveness of a rebel on the road, junior
division.

The Dharma Bums partly recounts some experiences in
the same year—1956—as Sigal's *Going Away* and ostensibly contrasts with it: where Sigal, on his trip East, thinks
he is profoundly concerned with leftist politics, Kerouac,
on his trip West, thinks he is profoundly concerned with
Buddhistic religion. More actually, both take a youth's
wanderjahr, longing for a freedom and fullness of life more
immediate and intense than that allowed in a banal bureaucratic society. Thus, while we should not take seriously
Kerouac's sententious parroting of Buddhist metaphysical
idealism (anymore than Sigal's sentimental revolution-
ism), that flight into freedom, so indebted to the earlier
hobo pattern, is meaningful. Kerouac's use of the hobo
mode, of course, is sentimental: he rings in a saintly hobo
with a clipping about St. Teresa, another with a Buddhist
quotation, and elaborates indiscriminately on his bumming alter-ego (Japhy, the Zen devotee and wandering
bad poet). A rather older romantic discovery—the city boy
in the out-of-doors—takes a more central role in the author
figure's camping out, mountain climbing and spending
several solitary months as a fire lookout on Desolation
Peak. The searching for a therapeutic self-sufficiency in
nature takes on more importance than the rhetoric of
Buddhistic oneness in the void, the reportorial material on
a rather fatuous bohemian coterie in the Bay Area, and the
post-hobo wanderings. The dream of "rucksack wander-

ers," "Dharma bums," American Don Quixotes of tenderness, who refuse to be imprisoned in a system of pointless work, consumption and electrification "to the Master Switch" [28] is a potentially powerful theme.

But Kerouac cannot create a "Dharma bum" in his own right and we mostly get reportage and rumination on what happened to Jacky-boy and the rest of the kids—symptoms rather than significance. His "aesthetic," ostensibly a rebellion against self-conscious art, merely costumes symptomatic release of free-association, drawing on the similar tradition that runs through much of Walt Whitman and Henry Miller.[29] The inadequacy—except for brief disconnected moments—of this inchoateness appears even more emphatic in the earlier book, *On the Road.* There is no genuine responding self and so, despite the exhilaration of occasional bits, nothing holds together. Dean Moriarity, for example—the central figure of *On the Road*—is variously "a youth tremendously excited with life," a pathetic and psychotic "con-man," a profoundly wild "yea-sayer," a sadly messy classic juvenile case, a "HOLY GOOF," "a rat," and a heroic bum. They all mean the same thing, the same frenzied delinquent who lacks either perception or life style in his excited and compulsive discontent. We may grant Kerouac a serious purpose with the wild kids that he so burblingly hero worships: he longs for a vital and autonomous, lusty and rebellious, picaresque rebel on the road—essentially the same thing Saul Bellow wants with his Augie March and Henderson, Ken Kesey with his McMurphy, J. P. Donleavy with his Sebastian Dangerfield, and Algren, Miller, Heller, and a good many other American writers. The search for the amoral and energetic hero who can contain and humanize the wild energy of the American psyche may be crucial to both our comprehension of ourselves and to the maintenance of rebellious elan. But Kerouac's undiscriminating and associative pictures of Dean and Japhy and the others contravene his announced apotheosis of "the ones who are mad to live, mad to talk, mad to be saved, desirous of everything at the same time, the ones who never yawn or say a commonplace thing, but burn, burn, burn." [30]

A candid kid, Kerouac at times stumbles on some good details about hitchhiking and turns of phrase about his discontents, though much sinks under sophomoric "real straight talk about souls" and the indiscriminate reportage about the gang. While the trip down the road starts in hopefulness, even for Kerouac the revelations are rebellious negations: "Isn't it true that you start your life a sweet child believing everything under your father's roof? Then comes the day of the Laodiceans, when you know you are wretched and miserable and poor and blind and naked." [31] The road is where promise gives way to outcast passion. Like almost every rebel on the road, Kerouac's personal disinheritance leads to a fundamental sympathy with "the great fellahin peoples of the world" and their suffering and immediacy. One recurrent image of this appears in the author's "wishing I were a Negro," or a Mexican, or almost anything other than a "disillusioned" American defeated in direct responsiveness because of "white ambitions." [32] Though only developed in awkward fragments about a pathetic sexual relation with a Mexican girl (or a Negro girl, or the scenes of worship of jazz musicians, etc.), Kerouac here flits around D. H. Lawrence's deep perception of the willful and anxious atomization of "white" consciousness. Kenneth Rexroth's often cited clever remark, that this is "Crow Jimism" (merely reverse prejudice), misses the rebel's point about defying emotional deadness; from Sherwood Anderson's *Dark Laughter* through Norman Mailer's "White Negro" the metaphor remains much the same—the minority sensibility (whether White Negro, Wandering Jew or exotic primitive) *stands for* the defiant longing. The "deliriums" of other-identity which Kerouac seeks are simply exasperated cries for holistic consciousness and life. The more frenzied journeys—especially the ecstatic one down the Mexican road (*On the Road*) where the glimpsed primordial life looks rich and mysterious—attempt to taste a lost innocence and wholeness. Somewhere, Kerouac hopes, exists life as it has eternally been, and will be again after the "Apocalypse" Western man is inevitably creating.

Kerouac's childishness, then, should not be used to deny the confused innocent's perceptions. Despite some of the badness of the writing and the intelligence, his yearning flights reveal much essential awareness of the cold sense of defeat in the American scene, with its elaborately meaningless places and dubious authorities and dissociated young. The "road is life" says Kerouac's narrator, but it is also simultaneously "the ragged and ecstatic joy of pure being" and "a senseless nightmare road" in which even an often inadequate sensibility discovers some of the existential contradictions which are one of the burdens of art.

In John Clellon Holmes' *Go*, a somewhat more analytic fiction about the same material as *On the Road*, the cathartic rebel-delinquents group motive is developed as "an inability to believe in anything . . . and the craving for excess which it inspired." The case is plausibly made, yet the Beat heroes also showed a naive and even frenzied willingness to believe in almost anything, as we see in *The Dharma Bums* and all of the group's notorious mannerisms of ecstatic faith to escape the existential contradictions. Perhaps disenchantment and the religiosity do fit together in that the fanciful nostrums (as also in Henry Miller and the persistent American traditions of the crank-philosopher) provide other forms of excess which go to prove the deepest inability to believe.

Certainly in Kerouac's later travels and autobiographical ruminations, *Big Sur*,[33] where he tries to repeat his earlier Western sagas, the faith as well as the vitality takes on even more of a forced draft. He still travels—in a roomette on the California Zephyr and in a Jeepster on the freeway (where hypnotically following the white center line in the dark gives him a comfy safe feeling). But mostly he renounces the road to report his disintegration, ranging from sick sentimentality about a cat to boozy paranoia. Benign proclamations, as he flees back home again, do not really cover the disappearance of the earlier ecstatic freedom of the road which gave momentary transcendence to the disintegration. As both traveler and writer, Kerouac did his best when least ambitious to find any dramatic shape in his wanderings or any answer to his confusions. In part of the sketches in *Lonesome Traveler* he believes simply in the experiences for themselves, as in the sometimes well-detailed description of working as a railroad brakeman, "The Railroad Earth." Yet underlying this sketch, and providing the subject for the final ruminations ("The Vanishing American Hobo"), is an elegiac sense of a whole crucial order of American experience—of the country which "is the motherland of bumdom." However, in Kerouac's fractured farewells to the searchers after "absolute freedom," the wandering rebels of all times ("Jesus was a strange hobo who walked on water"),[34] he wades in quaintness and bathos. Whimsical bits about skid row, and a final slap at the perpetual cops who want to eliminate free wandering, end the rather pathetic journeyings of an inchoate American boy.

Has the rebel's road also disintegrated? Before turning to some other literary directions in which it leads, we might conclude this summary of several generations of hoboing memoirs with the acknowledgment that as literature they are slight. Yet as a group they have cumulative significance in creating a mode of literary rebellion; and—my major point—they do direct us to a sometimes intrinsically important experience and awareness. While the awareness may be less in the literature than out there on the road, that, after all, demonstrates one of the rebel's points. But looking more generally at this end of the tradition, we may see hoboism as now the flight of bittersweet adolescents. Perhaps the failure of adults to find a notable style of rebellion is what makes the adolescent ones pre-empt the road. Or perhaps the change reveals the end of the tradition and a decadent turn—as in so much of our culture—to professional specialization of clinical and exposé pathos. Thus in John Rechy's *City of Night* we see the young American vagrant mostly confined to the expertise of homosexual "hustler" and the memoir-fiction of the outcast restricted to the male prostitute's narrow anxieties and sentimentalities. The cast of this over-worked reportage of the marginal drifter's sexual business in various American cities is murkily clinical, circling around the plaintive "nothingness" of his childhood experiences and his inability to achieve a rebellious disinterest in himself or an interest in anything else. It seems to assume, partly from the tradition of the road, a character of revolt which it rarely has. Or, as one of the author-narrator's philosophical fairies puts the weary confusion: "Rebellion? Or is there a point where it becomes a surrender to the very rottenness you've rebelled from?" [35]

Certainly the defiant hobo testimony now seems vestigial. A mere century takes us from the yawping foot-tramping Whitman through the cursing railroad hobo to the poetical hitchhiker, ending in the mannered invert tourist. Yet technological-bureaucratic decadence may, in fact, not have entirely eliminated vagrant freedom. The marginal living which the hobo represented is still with us, though the beach-bum, student-bum, tourist-bum, and rather more esoteric vagabonds, take disguised forms. That the vagrant can pass with less recognition and even slip back into conventional places in the society partly reflects a change in circumstances—the desirable general decrease in the overt misery of the outcast—but not the total disappearance of wanderers who still possess some of the traditional wise alienation. Our social order, with its mixture of restrictions, warped specializations, amorphous group powers, etc., does make the marginal role anxious and uncertain. Authorities are still vicious. Traditional charity, as well as the wandering role, is gone. Institutionalized social mobility (whether the set patterns of "horizontal" shifting from bureaucracy to bureaucracy or the set "vertical" pathologies of aggrandizement) obscures more genuine freedom of movement. Current ideologies demand a home identity for everyone. Thus the wanderer in our society may physically exist but he lacks rebellious style and elan; the rebel in America may get by but, in our shrewdly amorphous system of bland ideologies and disguised authoritarianisms, finds it hard to defy. The truly distinctive hobo road exists no more, and with it goes part of the rebel's autonomous identity.

THE IMAGE of the wandering rebel need not be confined to
the memoirs of the hobo, and post-hobo, intellectual on
the road, though since they established much of the
rebellious stance these writers retain a special importance.
Both more folkish and more sophisticated literatures of
the road also exist. For the folkish side, the tramp in
vaudeville and burlesque houses fused with ancient clowns
to produce the comic-pathetic outcast who achieved an
apotheosis in Charlie Chaplin's "little tramp." The type
deeply imbedded itself in the communal imagination.
Pairs of tramps or bums as cartoon figures—from the old
Masses to the *New Yorker*, among others—served as
commentators on current fads of success or anxiety. Some
wit and wisdom can most appropriately be embodied in
images that belong at the edge of the social order.

Such a pair of tramps wander, with relevant anachro-
nism, into the poetic drama in Samuel Beckett's *Waiting
for Godot*. There they combine nihilistic pathos and
buffoonish mockery in one of those peculiarly contemporary attempts to get outside the comic-tragic teleology of
the past. Wherever Beckett may have acquired his two
ex-hobos, they seem comprehensible as a mannerist version
of the vaudeville-Chaplin-cartoon little tramps. Their surreal harlequinade in Beckett's timeless no-man's land
deadly echos "the nineties' " heroic age of bumdom.[1] Even
the Chaplin tramp appears big and brave in comparison;
the anti-genteel gestures of Chaplin (the sniff, the waggled
backside, the mocking walk down the road) becomes in
Estragon and Vladimir stasis and the dead stink of feet
and all human hopes. Beckett's wayfarers to nothing, "tied

down" in a metaphysically empty universe that allows no ties, outrageously burlesque any portentous meanings (such as "the poet" Estragon who has always compared himself to Christ). Their version of the camaraderie of the road becomes the need for someone to await death with or to help commit suicide. Thus, too, the rebels' on-the-road mockeries of authority or compassion for suffering become arbitrary jokes when Beckett endlessly complicates those responses with Pozo (authority) and Lucky (slave) who garble and reverse their roles in a horrendous series of jokes. That sense of reversal pervades the play, including the shape of its actions, its parody-play on all traditional rhetoric of God, and its treatment of the rebel. The wanderer comes full circle [2]—by standing still!—from the man questing for reality to the man waiting only for it to capriciously prove its own nonexistence.[3] As with Melville's Bartleby, revolt has become such a total refusal that it can hardly maintain enough assertion to confirm the void.

Is *Waiting for Godot* truly rebellious? If we grant that rebels question *all* values, certainly; yet in this mockery of a gratuitous universe the rebels from the road have reached its end in static gestures which make them representative of that which they fled from and defied. For Beckett's wanderers not only don't move (the repeated end of act stage directions) and don't say anything (the set patterns of burlesque double-talk) but rebel against the very possibility of rebelling. Even rebellion must have the limit of that which allows, even encourages, further journeys into rebellion.[4]

A note on Beckett seems an appropriate introduction to the more obviously crude and naturalistic materials of hobo literature because it points to the complex and peculiar possibilities just beyond the appearances of what is often taken for simple and social stuff. The folkish and the rarefied meet in the rebel's explorations of extremity. Let us return to some of the folkish materials, such as the song and verse of hobos. The few effective hobo elegies, such as "The Dying Hobo" or "The Hobo's Last Lament,"[5] break sentimentality with the dead 'bo's buddy making off with his clothes. (There are also the noted mythical train elegies—the Ghostly Dutchman theme— such as "The Wabash Cannonball.") Most prevalent among hobos seem to have been the even more satiric verses and songs which, in usual rebel fashion, parodied. Of the take-offs on Protestant hymns and sentimental standards, the best known (though not the best verse) may be Joe Hill's "Pie in the Sky" inversion of "In the Sweet Bye and Bye." Thus we see mockery as a major hobo tone.

In the songs justifying hoboing, fatalism takes a major place, as in the self-explanatory title, "The Dealer Gets It All." The heritage of rambling becomes its own fated justification in a rather effective song like "Wand'rin'." Even in the condemnations of socio-economic injustice, as in Woody Guthrie's fine "Hard Travelin'" and Lawrence Gellert's "Two Hoboes," reform and revolution are not the appropriate responses. (Closely related laments are Guthrie's best, that is least sententious, migrant songs, such as "Goin' Down the Road Feelin' Bad" and the humorous "So Long, It's Been Good to Know You.") Only in the Wobbly songs and verses does bombastic social propaganda dominate.[6] In the political ideologist's view, the best songs and verses of the road can be called "expressions of sublimated protest."[7] More accurately, they contain something similar to the stoic moralizing so favored in hobo writings. The defiant faith that "God is guts" ("The Little Red God") may be a key expression of the American "tough-guy" ethos so often—I think mistakenly—credited to the creation of Hemingway or Hammet or literary naturalism. Such literature may well draw on a more pervasive "hard-boiled" style lived by the hobos. Hoboism could be a major source of the stoic-hedonism now so characteristic of the stylization of modern alienated fiction.

Perhaps best of all of the songs of the road are some of those powerful "blues"—not to be separated from their performance—about railroads and wandering.[8] They display an exceptional fusion of vitality and sadness—an orgiastic lamentation—which makes the "blues" one of the real achievements of American sensibility. A cynical exuberance—as in the refusal to work in the better versions of "Hallelujah, Bum Again"[9] as well as in some of the "Blues"—seems distinctive and appropriate to the best poetry of the road. Sometimes it comes close in defiance to that harshest of all traditional folk songs, "Samuel Hall," and its unrepentant condemned man's refrain of "Damn your eyes!"

The most famous of vivacious mockeries in tramp poetry is "The Big Rock Candy Mountain." Here the "jocker" (professional tramp) tells of the land where cops have wooden legs and bulldogs rubber teeth, where there are lakes of stew and whiskey, and where the only crime is to work. In its most likely tramp versions, the vagrant never-never land fits in a "frame" in which the "Preshun" (apprentice, often homosexual "punked," tramp) mocks the "jocker's" deceitful dream land. Thus the cake-country of the mind, as we might recall from Breughel's painting or the thirteenth-century Irish poem "Land of Cockayne" [10] (where to enter in you must first swim for seven years in pig dung), also provides sardonic comment on all paradisical visions.

If we turn to "literary" poetry about the road—Lindsay, Kemp, Sandburg, etc.—we note an absence of the lively toughness that gives the best folk poems their quality. So far as I can find, the only artistic poet to significantly use the imagery, experiences and meanings of the American on the road was Hart Crane. In "The River" section of *The Bridge* (Part II) [11] he tries to catch the psychic frenzy of America not only in his mythology but in the railroading hobo. The rather uncertain narrative line of this section apparently starts with a young man going West. By the third stanza, when the crack train the Twentieth-Century Limited (also a pun) goes by, three outcasts plod the tracks. They follow the telegraph wires that "Bind town to town and dream to ticking dream" and represent what unity America has. Traveling "blind baggage" (riding the end of the car and—by the pun—sightlessly moved beyond their own volition), they continue the compulsive movement of the American generations. Later, Crane's hobos seem to represent a lyric promise of freedom (in contrast to the prevailing powers: "O Sheriff, Brakeman and Authority"). Their stoic hero is a 'bo knocked dead from a coupling. For Crane, the defiant but defeated hobos touch and transmit the mythic body and song of America. Even deeper, they go "Down, down—born pioneers in time's despite" to the "wayward" awareness which reaches the oldest prophetic-pariah holiness—the "stillness" from "Jordan's brow." Crane fuses the symbolic meanings of the Jordan with the Mississippi River, which his hobos reach going West; thus the Judaic consciousness becomes the American passion—"Tortured with history, its one will—flow!"

In his effort to give transcendence to the ordinary, Crane's fractured condensation loses narrative shape and any actual wanderers. He turns to a more simple and poignant description of the hobo in the most direct passage of this section of *The Bridge*.

> *Behind*
> *My father's cannery work I used to see*
> *Rail-squatters ranged in nomad raillery,*
> *The ancient men—wifeless or runaway*
> *Hobo-trekkers that forever search*
> *An empire wilderness of freight and rails.*
> *Each seemed a child, like me, on a loose perch,*
> *Holding to childhood like some termless play.*
> *John, Jake or Charley, hopping the slow freight*
> *—Memphis to Tallahassee—riding the rods,*
> *Blind fists of nothing, humpty-dumpty clods.*
>
> *Yet they touch something like a key perhaps.*

Perhaps? Crane's uncertainty makes his frenzied myth and his grim details contradict each other. He wanted to raise the pathos of the defeated hobo (and the rebellious child) to a wandering exaltation which opens up an empire of meaning. But his hobos are mere victims and he cannot put the humpty-dumpty of cracked reality back together —any more than he could maintain a coherent style in *The Bridge*. Crane suggests a crucial significance in the man on the American road, intermittently given in images of defiance, but the compelling actuality reduces him to "blind fists of nothing," destroying the myth he is supposed to focus. As Crane writes later in the poem: "Dream cancels dream in this new realm of fact/ From which we wake into the dream of act." The natural facts destroy any possible meaning. Even when the inhuman, machined reality is exalted in the steel bridge, or in the motorized "oil-rinsed circles of blind ecstasy," [12] the flight to freedom turns into the "monotone of motion." The wanderer's defiance becomes mere guilty regression and self-destruction ("The conscience navelled in the plunging wind,/ Umbilical to call—and straightway die!" [13]).

By violating and heightening his fragments in *The Bridge,* Crane wanted to turn the over-powering compulsive actuality of America into affirmative myth. The naturalistic actuality remained stronger. The real "key" to Crane appears later in the title poem of "Key West," [14] one of his most controlled and bitter pieces of invective. Here the wandering rebel finds himself locked out of any hope. The steel and stone that made the cities and the bridge and the mechanical dreams now appear as "apish nightmares" that lead to a "dead conclusion." Accepting the hard self of disillusionment ("my salient faith annealed me") in a universe indifferent to meaning ("skies impartial") he has a more precise illumination ("frugal noon") in which he rejects the Eldorado-Atlantis magic hopes and adventurous winds of the American yearning: "There is no more breath of friends and no more shore/ Where gold has not been sold and conscience tinned." The compulsion and fraud of the American actuality turned dreams to nightmares, golden mythos to machined fake, and left only the rage of the desperately isolated wanderer. If *The Bridge* had been able to discover its own form, that is, had been able to sustainedly follow out the rebel's road to the "Key West," instead of being a contradictory melange of sometimes brilliant but often sentimental and forced lyric fragments, it might have been the first American epic poem of consequence—an epic of vigorous nihilism.

The Bridge suggestively failed to bridge the contradictions between harsh naturalistic facts and lyrical mythic meanings. Most often, American writers—especially those who drew upon the rebel on the road—settled for the harsh naturalistic facts.[15] Physical and social immediacy provides the main relevance of the literary naturalist's images of the hobo; that is also their irrelevance since, except for a sometimes imposed Marxist ideology, they present little else. Where most of the memoirs of the road, from Jack London to Jack Kerouac (despite the dependance of both on some aspects of literary naturalism) show a doctrineless zest, the naturalistic fictions lack all zest. While that may be accurate enough of reality, it is not enough; not reportage but rebelliousness provides the significance of the road. Reduced to its lowest denominators of common reality, wandering displays no more defiance or delight than any other grimly mediocre way of life.

In Edward Dahlberg's *Bottom Dogs* [16] the grittily precise account of the wanderings of his timorous and unintelligent boy are mostly pointless. That would seem to be the point. In the bumming, casual jobs and marginal living, only vague longings for petty pleasure and for the freedom to be somewhere, and something, else, rise to awareness. D. H. Lawrence aptly noted in his preface that Dahlberg refused "any flow of consciousness except that of the barest, most brutal egoistic self-interest." Lawrence relates this lack of deep anger, humor and passion to the dehumanization which resulted from the human defeats and failures—so rarely acknowledged—of American aggrandizement. This type of grimly "pointless" account persists in the American novel about the despairing inability to ever grow up and out, as in the very similar *The Bold Saboteurs* of Chandler Brossard—among others.

Such denuding of sensibility also dominates the "proletarian novels" of the 1930's. In what is apparently one of the more competent ones, Jack Conroy's *The Disinherited*,[17] several bumming sequences provide part of the operatic machinery. The bitter misery of drifting and laboring in factory and field—the one strength of these fictions—submerges in a stylized political actionist ideology as quaint as Medieval allegory, with salvation taking the form of the workers uniting fraternally against their exploiters. While the moral purposes may be kindly, any responsiveness beyond victimage—as with Steinbeck's agitator in *In Dubious Battle* or the preacher in *The Grapes of Wrath*—combines heavy-tongued ideology with mawkish feeling. Even when more intensely written, as in Nelson Algren's *Somebody in Boots*,[18] which initiates its *lumpen* hero on the road, poetic awareness disappears in the ritualism of the proletarian who becomes defeated criminal-victim because he lacks class consciousness. Compassion for the cheated is a fine thing, but political ideology often runs antithetical to it, as rather too much modern history painfully demonstrates.

Pathetic victims on the road probably get better presented in documentary essay, as in George Orwell's *Down and Out in Paris and London*. In his description of enforced pauper tramping in England he refuses to turn the question of minimal decency into political ideology or sentimental allegory. Orwell argues from his examples for the elimination of "silly" (ill-logical) police persecution, of bureaucratic pettiness about charity, of the unnecessary miseries of bad food and lodging, and of the grossly irrelevant righteousness towards the impoverished and outcast. Neither revolutionary ideology nor moral reformism are at all relevant. Admittedly, Orwell at times violates his own emphasis on freedom by slipping into his usual anxious uniformity; he assumes that any other but the common settled life leads to "futility," and therefore hopes that every tramp would be "able to marry and take a respectable place in society." [19] (The Paris account comes out rather better in this respect because there Orwell more often sees the bizarre and eccentric as ways with their own qualities and rights.) Whether tramps take to the road from eccentricity, adventure, pathology, destitution or principle, most societies vent considerable cruelty on them. Part of the intellectual and literary fascination with the peripheries is because those on the outside provide a crucial test of the temper and human values of the society.

But this takes us far from revolutionary and reformist ideologies, few of which make significant allowance for vagrant freedoms. It is curious, then, that more or less Marxist ideologies were taken up by an influential minority of American hobos, despite the political apathy (as Marx noted) of professional tramps and despite the more natural libertarianism of rebels on the road. Intellectual history, from the last quarter of the nineteenth century up to the second World War, accounts for some of it, as do the conditions of embittering industrial exploitation. Where, for historical reasons, Medieval wayfarers called upon Christian charity and salvation, twentieth-century wayfarers called upon ideologies for the the modification of capitalism's organization. (But on the road there were many heretics to both faiths.) The mystagoguery of both Christianity and Marxism tended to obscure the special qualities and experiences of the rebel's road, such as the mock-innocence of the vagabond, the grim humor of trampdom, the voraciousness of American wanderers, the "masterless man" psychology of the hobo, and the nihilistic perceptivity of the outsider.

Perhaps partly because of the contradictions between political ideology and actual experiences, not direct Marxism but the American version of syndicalism, the International Workers of the World, became the most influential and suitable revolutionary movement connected with the hobos.[20] The loose organization of the "Wobblies," the cosmopolitan appeal of "one big union," the direct action approach of the general strike and retaliatory violence, certainly came closer than other political movements to the character of wandering rebels. The Wobbly cast of general antagonism to all authorities (and politics), and its identification with outcasts and unmiddle-class tone, made it both the most romantically appealing and the industrial protest movement least likely to maintain itself. The Wobblies, despite their vulgar revolutionary rhetoric and dogmatisms, showed a much fuller commitment to revolt, and a much smaller capacity for opportunistic and adaptive success, than there seems to be a place for in American institutions.

The outcasts on the road in the fictions of John Dos Passos usually link somewhere with the Wobblies. In *The 42nd Parallel*, Mac, an orphan boy bumming his way around, joins the Wobblies in a Nevada mining strike. For some years he alternates between repressive lower-middle class domesticity and wandering radicalism. In Dos Passos' usual character under-cutting psychology, Mac's Wobbly role is as much flight from domesticity as revolutionary faith. In *1919*, Ben Compton, an obsessive World War I political radical and pacifist, bums his way West and joins in with the Wobblies. He ends as a victim of the vicious "Red Scare" prosecutions with one of those traditionally American and fantastically disproportionate prison sentences. Dos Passos' fervently rhetorical and praising portraits of Big Bill Haywood, Wesley Everest and Joe Hill—cruelly defeated figures from Wobbly hagiography —set much of the historical tone. Since they are not so subject to the author's extended debunking character treatment, they appear as rebel radicals at least partly by compassionate free choice. Dos Passos' later attempt to recapture his rebellious passion, *Midcentury*, presents the related fictional reminiscenes of Blackie Bowman; this hobo, seaman, steel-worker, bohemian bum and Wobbly provides one of the most elaborate images of the socially defeated outsider in America. For in *Midcentury*, despite

the nostalgic-pathetic incantations to the hardy individuality of times past and of lost and soured revolt (and
the sometimes cantankerous anti-liberal moralizing), we
see in Bowman, the dying veteran rebel-victim, not so
much social ideology as a defiant individuality which has
little place in a vast mechanized system.

But Dos Passos' most significant image of the man on
the road as representative of America is the anonymous
youth of the prose-poem entitled "Vag" which caps *The
Big Money*.[21] For this somewhat improbably seedy hitchhiker, the road reveals only defeat and Dos Passos'
repulsion: the worn suitcase of "phony leather," the torn
socks and the underwear with a "crummy feel," a road and
a vagrant reeking of gas, stale flesh and misery. Even with
the balancing dialectical figure of the monied "vagrant"
flying overhead in a transcontinental plane, we are directed
to clouds like "curdling scum," the "eroded hills" and the
landing in "hot air thick with dust and the reek of burnt
prairies." The moon and the sweetgrass and the mixed
realities of the American scene are pretty well over-
whelmed by the stink of repulsion. This dominant tone
becomes unintentionally humorous when the rich vagrant
"sickens and vomits" up his meal and supposedly responds,
"No matter . . . greenbacks in the wallet, drafts, certified
checks . . ."—as if they took the nausea out of retching!

The punch, the slam, the grab, the twist, the snarl—
"the big knee brought up sharp into the crotch"—come
not just from the cop who roughed up the poor vag but
from all of American "history [as] the billion-dollar
speedup." This violent motion without catharsis is the
intellectual theme of Dos Passos, and one which leaves no
individual freedom of experience, on the road or in the sky.
The broad social perception and compassionate anger
presented in the image of the vagrant frenziedly turns
apotheosis to stink and abstraction. The narrowing of
responsiveness—in Dos Passos and more generally in
literary naturalism—reveals a revulsive obsession with
failure which may also be the inversion of the pathological
American insistence on success. Curiously, the hobo as
more victim than rebel, which recurs in so much moralistic American fiction—as a case of social fatality and
stinking pathos without sensibility or elan—denigrates the
impetus to rebel and wander outside.

Partly, then, from literary naturalism, but also deriving from deeper fears and revulsions in the American psyche, we get an archetypal figure whom I suggest calling the "American Joe." His rough pattern might be something like this: he has fled the Protestant ethos of sanctified work, ascetic conscience and respectable ambition; hobo, tramp, hitchhiker, jalopy drifter, a purposeless road beckons him to rapid and guilty circles; he carries out Herculean labors of travel, and intermittently of work, which yet do not give him a sense of accomplishment. His varied labors and voracious appetites reveal a guilty anxiety about finding any genuine self and reality. His vivid moments with booze, whores, crimes, jails and fights prove virility by violence. Despite violence and bitterness, he remains a pathetic innocent with simple yearnings. His wanderings after community in a hostile society may be given justification by that guilty juvenile fantasy of being an orphan, which also expresses our insistent loneliness, and of dubious parentage, which points up our ambiguous heritage. (We are not concerned here with how much the archetype corresponds with literal fact—obviously he partly does—but with his imaginative shape and significance.) Like the anonymous "Joe" of American folk speech—the "good Joe," [22] the "square Joe"—and the pervasive "GI Joe" of World War II, he is strangely viewed as both representative and as a bit degraded. The natural end of the American Joe would seem to be some longed-for castration at the hands of sexual and social contradictions which he never quite comprehends. All he achieves is the "cult of experience"—the awareness of a pathetically over-powering and finally repulsing physical actuality. His defeat, even if given the rhetoric of apotheosis, destroys both self and his rebellious values. The Land of Freedom often achieves a remarkable conformity by making its freedoms compulsive, masochistic, revulsive and destructive.

An illustration of some of this pattern of the American Joe can be found in William Faulkner's best long fiction, *Light in August*. Joe Christmas, orphan of uncertain parentage, becomes a compulsive rebel. Faulkner richly complicates the causes of Joe as self-hating outcast: the children who call him "nigger" because he is different; the fanatical persecutions of a Christian-racist grandfather; the sexual trauma in an orphanage which makes him violently fear women; the rigid and joyless will of his puritanic foster-father; and the southern society full of hatreds, guilt and violence. In the nuclear and best dramatic narrative in the novel, Joe Christmas revolts against the harsh Protestant work ethic and righteous asceticism of his foster-father, strikes him down and flees down the road. He becomes a hobo, working the oil and wheat fields; he enlists in the army only to soon rebel against that and desert; perpetually bumming and hitchhiking, he is "doomed with motion." [23] Faulkner, so obviously drawing on an archetypal pattern, only summarizes, giving brief examples of Joe's violence with prostitutes, booze, flight and self. His "street which ran for thirty years" is a circle of naturalistic fatality ("the ring of what I have already done and can never undo" [24]), finally expressed in a passion-week of flight which ends, suicidally, where he began. To this naturalistic Joe, Faulkner adds metaphors of blood and Christ in a somewhat arbitrary creation of a degraded or tragic-burlesque holy scapegoat who ends as a castrated symbol of the repressive and guilty violence of the South. This is to be finally understood, claims some of Faulkner's more inflated rhetoric, as an apotheosis "soaring in their [the southern townspeople's] memories forever and ever" so that such black anguish will remain "alone triumphant." [25] The allegorizing of the defeated rebellious hobo as Christ (and the hysterical rhetoric of "white" and "black" blood) remain less effective than Faulkner's intensification of physical immediacy with Joe, and his dramatic presentation of the apocalyptic ravages of a Christianity gone insane. Asks the reflective Hightower, Presbyterian minister and historical representative of fraudulent Southern aristocracy, in the process of renouncing his religion, "*And so why should not their religion drive them to crucifixion of themselves and one another?*" [26]

It does. And so does Joe Christmas. For in Faulkner's deeply ambivalent view of rebellion—as also in such works as *The Wild Palms*—he sees the fleeing rebel as at once individually justified and heroic and horribly degraded and destructive. *Light in August,* a powerful work despite its falls into bombast and melodrama, need not be confined to its theme of the ravages of the "Protestant fury" and the American Joe growing and rebelling into his burlesque-tragedy. Faulkner attempts a very large pattern of three tragedies, framed with a satyr play, in which the torturings of American Calvinism do not quite succeed in denying the intense fortitude and joy that come from the earth earthy, given in the lavish heightening of physical immediacy and in the affirmation of the simple folk figure. But the rebel on the road, as violator of the land and himself, remains essential. Attempting to transform the naturalistic image of the all-American outsider into poetic allegory of the fated scapegoat for the righteous ethos may seek to relate the rebel back to the community. But the book properly ends with a comical new rebel, the ex-Christian Everyman (Byron Bunch) following the stoical girl of the earth (Lena Grove), and her new bastard, down the road.

Down that road, especially in various baroque extensions of classical naturalism, will be found a good many other suggestive though peculiar rebels. For example, in James Jones' *From Here to Eternity* the ex-hobo in the army stockade has turned tough-guy defiance of authority into an ornately Jesuitical masochism. In this most central scene and expression of Jones' attitude, self-punishment gets treated as the highest order of rebellion.[27] In a number of other war novels one can find twisted—even patriotic!—versions of the naturalistic rebel as American Joe. Rebellion, being an heroic form, is as open to corruption as many another. But the characteristics of the hobo and the American road become so various that we can no longer simply relate them to the main themes of rebellion. Even the patriarchal Christian moralists, such as Robert Penn Warren, find the road essential to their purposes. Despite his floridly romanticized sagas and the bombast about Time, Guilt, History, etc., each of his main characters must make a simple flight down the road. It is part of the obsessive pattern of Warren's protagonists; fatuous idealists, they rebel, descend into a pit of guilt (a sexual frenzy with a forbidden Jewess, Negro or relative goes with it), try to flee, and finally capitulate to the knowledge that they should have decently defended some richly existent falsity.[28] The road, as with Jack Burden's compulsive drive west in *All the King's Men*, simply prepares them for the trite wisdom of accepting the good-and-evil shoddy reality that they rebelled against. So, of course, the road has been a favorite quasi-quest symbol which can be used in all sorts of pretentious ways.[29] But it can also be used with delight and wit since the road has come, to us, to reflect so much of primal American reality. Even Vladimir Nabokov, with his rococo imagination and dominant concern with artistic gamesmanship, finds his parabolic scenes and lapidary horrors for *Lolita*—essentially an odd-angled fable of the pursuit of the muse—on and along the American highway. For the experiences of the road, historically and artistically, engaged the communal imagination with such effect that we can no longer speak of restricted meanings and types. Perhaps the rebels helped make America sufficiently open so that it not only absorbed millions of actual hobos but, in its discontented movements, its ethos drawing on rebellion and covert nihilism, absorbed the very stuff of the road into the general sensibility.

THE AMERICAN REBEL on the road, and some of the various forms of literature which drew him—and drew upon him—left a considerable legacy to contemporary fiction. In many of these novels since World War II we can see a development of literary naturalism's materials and types, including the American Joe on the road, with a more elaborate artistry. These works combine socially common, emotionally violent and physically sordid subjects—minus the positivistic ideology of earlier naturalism—with metaphoric and idiosyncratic language and complex rhetorical and symbolic organization. The result might be called "poetic-naturalism." The manner is not altogether new since this pervasive poetic-naturalism draws on some deep impulses of American response. For Americans traditionally long for a mythic depth of awareness which they rather helplessly call *experience*: the way-it-really-happened, the truth-of-the-matter, honest-to-god-real-life, and the rest of their hyperbolic insistence on actuality. By some peculiar cross-breeding, the pragmatic, sensible, fact-to-fact flow of sensation has often been joined, for Americans, with salvational fervour and lyric exaltation. Whitman's ecstatic merging with an endless commonplace reality, Thoreau's poignant desire to live "life to the full" when withdrawn in a rather ascetic and alienated contemplation in the woods, Melville's joining the grim facts of cetology and the maritime proletariat with poetic ruminations on the ambiguous evil of the great white American father-God, Sherwood Anderson's religious poeticization of the niggardly lives of small-town midwesterners, Thomas Wolfe's feverish elephantiasis of American names and hungers, Faulkner's fusion of ornate literary melodrama with heightened physicality and harshly modern psychic compulsions, Henry Miller's fanciful surrealism combined with colloquial immediacy—but the list could indeed be long. The strange combinings of raw actuality and lyrical sacramentalism would seem to have a recurrent insistence in American literature that can be found in no other, and such stylizations provide a revolt against both more purely ideal longings and the inadequacy of merely ordinary responses.[1]

The poeticization appears especially striking in those many contemporary urban novelists whose sources and purposes, unlike those of our Southern literary honeys, belong to "realist" and "naturalist" traditions. Many causes may be identified here: the multiple sophistication that followed World War II, the disjunctive styles of an increasingly baroque "civilization," and the poetics of resistance to a mass-technological society. The powers of technology, of mass consumption and its popular arts and propaganda, tend to destroy old ways of distinction and difference, and therefore demand a compensatory self-conscious elaborateness to assert individual sensibility. Even those writers who make much of naivete and simplicity—a favorite American stance from frontier literature through Twain, Hemingway, the Beats and contemporary child-cult writers—show themselves remarkably knowledgeable, allusive, elaborate. Certainly the drastically increasing debasement of ordinary language and feeling in public life and mass culture encourage a defensively ornate, and even mannered, insistence on distinctive responsiveness, or the pretense at it. The impersonality of power in a mass-technological society not only creates the pathetic worship of "personality" (celebritydom) and the pyrrhic idealization of "comfort" (the most persuasive modern ideology) but special codes of "sensitivity." These do not hide the despair about individual feelings and the sense of indifferent fates which makes the scenes of action small, personal, idiosyncratic, and finally involuted and circular. The persons acting in those scenes will not, except obliquely, relate to the faiths of the past. My point here is simply a special extension of the dominant theme of the "modern"—man not being at home in his universe, an alienation quite beyond classical wariness or romantic pathos.

The contemporary literary hero's rebellion, almost every commentator agrees, insists on man's smallness, and so the contemporary protagonist is the bum, the delinquent, the outsider, the victim, the marginal man, the anti-hero. While the threatening universe may be large, his personal world and powers will appear angrily shrunken. Most significant modern novels take a small scope; even the more ambitious contemporary American fictions (such as those by Bourjailly, Porter, Styron, Roth, Mailer, Baldwin, *et al.*) simply multiply or inflate small arenas. We expect defeat and pathos, and they are certainly there, yet the negation also often displays exuberance. The fictions show the energy of American polymorphousness with the discordant profusions, the strange mixtures of sentimentality and efficiency (one no doubt the result of the other), of natural grandeur and machined gracelessness, of candid gestures and huckstering dishonesty, and all the fine and deplorable freedoms of blurred meanings. These poetic-naturalist allegories which involute the "American Joe" insistently perplex the roles and possibilities of rebelliousness.

We might briefly comment on the identity seeking "hero" of Bernard Malamud's main novel, *The Assistant*. Frank Alpine, an orphan, drifter, ex-carnival worker and thief earnestly seeks to improve himself and find a community. This gentile bum becomes an assistant to an impoverished Jewish grocer after robbing him. With the violent gratuities of those without fixed commitments, he alternately cheats the grocer and saves him, adoringly loves and then assaults his only daughter. He rebels against conventional morals, quite reasonably, yet in Malamud's redemptive parable does so only in the search for himself, which must ultimately be to renounce rebellion and commit himself to simple human love-and-misery. To a stylized genre study of an ordinary Jewish-American family in the Depression, Malamud gives a poetic heightening so that his grocer, Morris Bober, becomes the proverbial suffering Jew—honest as ill-fated, his only son dead, his American dreams soured, his health undermined by long hours in a store where business can only get worse, his moral scrupulousness finally the immediate cause of his death. Bum Alpine, whose assistance becomes an outrageous additional burden to this Jewish saint of everyday life, goes to the funeral and clumsily stumbles into the grave—the rebellious son dancing on the surrogate-father's coffin. He then miserably slaves away in the store to support the widow and daughter, who despise him. Having accepted his burden of suffering without reward, he, too, achieves a kind of saintly victimage—his salvation from his rebellion—and converts to the grocer's religion, becoming one of the Chosen People. The irony is repeatedly harsh; the ostensibly pious circumcision of the ex-rapist is supiciously like castration. But he thus renounces his outcast state to become a *mensch* by joining the communion of suffering.

In Malamud's effort to morally commit the rebel from the road, the role of imaginary Jew is crucial. This gentile bum, the irony emphasizes, lacks real suffering in his misery because he has not accepted it and thus given it full meaning. For him to learn what one character (rather improbably) calls "the tragic quality of life" requires the role of suffering communion. Frank Alpine reads a book about the Jews, "about the ghettos, where the half-starved bearded prisoners spent their lives trying to figure out why they were the Chosen People. He [too] tried to figure out why but couldn't." [2] The novice-assistant asks the unpious Jewish grocer why the Jews have suffered so much, and what he, Morris Bober, suffers for. "I suffer for you," Morris calmly replies. In puzzlement, the assistant asks what he means. In one of Malamud's quiet strokes of contemporary Talmudic dialectic, the grocer replies, "I mean you suffer for me." [3] It is the Dostoevskian answer; we all suffer for each other, and only by accepting that do we have the community of men. The archetypal Diaspora Jew carries the pain of that communion. We might almost say of Malamud that to him a Jew is a *goy* who feels and accepts suffering. At the start of the story the gentile bum thinks he does not want to suffer anymore; midway he says, with ghetto humor, to the woman he loves who has just hurt him, "When I don't feel hurt, I hope they bury me"; and at the end he acts as if suffering cannot only enrage but inspire. The author has attempted to answer the denials posed by the representative American outcast by raising them to a religious level. The combination of naturalistic materials—the mean, gritty facts of day to day biological and social reality—with learned poetic stylization and allusiveness—Dostoevsky, Shakespeare, St. Francis, rose symbolism—often becomes morally heavy but it attempts to transvaluate the ordinariness and meaninglessness of American life without losing its tangible reality. The wandering rebel-victim of *The Assistant*, like that of *Light in August*, is the creation of an elaborate poetic-naturalism which seeks to unite the rebel from the road with the society through a religious exaltation of an otherwise unjustified submission to the very order he has rebelled against.

The attempt to poeticize the wandering naturalistic American Joe and give him moralistic resolution takes other forms. In the quite over-written but best novel of Herbert Gold, *The Man Who Was Not With It*, Bud Williams, a young carnival barker and part-orphan, gains his education into moral identity on the road and in the lovingly elaborated underside of life. The wandering, father-defying, drug addiction, sexual voyeurism, crime and varied gross experiences elucidate such aphorisms as "You drink from the cup of wisdom? I fell into it." Hitchhiking, the carnival-world's parody of the business society, and a prolonged nightmarish drive in a jalopy with a demonic father-figure in the back seat, fill the cup. The wisdom, however, is that the ordinary American Joe learns the hard way back to being the urban worker and family man that he originally rebelled against being. Degradation and the road, not convention and culture, provide the truest way to adaption and acceptance. "Down is the long way up." Slanged-over Heraclitean wisdom summarizes the traditional violations and final affirmations of monogamy, loyalty, honesty, filial acceptance, forgiveness and going back home again. The road through extremity provides the leap of faith into ordinary moral life by which the con-man can, once again, become an authentic "mark." "There's a good and with it way to be not with it, too" [4]—which means that you can be a rebel without being rebellious. Acceptance of present day American life seems, in a good many clever writers, to require some such fideistic paradoxes to reconcile the rebelliously intelligent and sensitive to the ostensible social order. The maturity which such rebels reach for eschews the carnival morality of the fast-buck and the con-man's hard-sell to empty success. They also learn to despise the pretty but compulsive and willfully ambitious—and therefore sexually counter-feit—middle-class girl. However, in giving up their larce-nous artistry and longing flights they tend to identify their own contraditions with those of the society, achieving an urbane disenchantment that allows them to be neither vicious nor defiant.

J. D. Salinger's *Catcher in the Rye* belongs in the same line of moral double-play, though it is better written. Here the violent but cut-down colloquialism and physicality of naturalism, and the scenes of flight, booze, prostitutes, physical repulsion, etc., which provide part of the distinc-tive American tone—so different from Gide, Hartley, Alain-Fournier, Vittorini and other European writers about adolescent revolt—has a poetical counter-pointing of refrain-like curses and mockeries of things as they are in the fraudulent adult world. Salinger, of course, borrows from rather than belongs to the explorers of the road. With urbane upper-middle-class pathos, he attenuates the rebellious flight of the adolescent, and taking to the road west remains the great unrealized dream of his child-cult hero. For where Huck Finn could escape to the primordial river or light out for the "territory" in his suspicions of dubious civilizing, Holden Caulfield can only go to the platitudes of the teacher of English and the psy-choanalyst. Salinger's would-be rebel acutely mocks the psuedo-standards—the prep school life-is-a-game trick, the nasty snobbery of well-to-do parents and children, the ex-ploitative pedants and city "service" denizens, the fatuous pop-culture and patriotism, the bland surfaces under which lurk violence and despair—and, in a sometimes mannered injured innocence, sees through the spurious adjustment of passive submission and innocuous identity which prevail. But *Catcher in the Rye*, despite its percep-tiveness—or perhaps because of its refusal to go beyond it—often seems a sentimental indulgence in the illness it mocks. This does not just apply to the conclusion, with Holden's final yearnings for the very phonies he has been so devastating about, nor to the author's Messianic whimsy about adolescent sensitivity. It certainly includes what some take as the "message" section of the book, the advice the admired English teacher gives that he should live humbly for some cause (conveniently unspecified) and in the meantime get a good education so that he can hold his head up with the best people—the snobbery that constitutes the non-technical side of contemporary "higher learning." Oddly, Holden for once has no negative comment on this invidious gamesmanship with which we make the young knuckle down, and his weary silence must also be the author's. Let us also remember that the story of the seventeen-year-old's revolt and flight and collapse are a retrospective confession he makes to a psychoanalyst in a hospital. Thus the rebellious romantic device of the philosopher-child becomes elaborately equivocal in Salinger's hands, and genuine awareness and revolt are merged into the shadows of pathological immaturity. This also comes out in the hero's literally pre-adolescent behavior in many scenes, in contrast to his post-adolescent perceptions. Salinger cleverly plays the pathos of combining the precocious critic with the clinical case, and it is the victim rather than the rebel who dominates in Holden's fearful relation to sex, to his family, to authority, and to all demanding experiences. Holden Caulfield, unlike Huck Finn, frees no one, least of all himself, and never starts the journey westward to self-discovery against the society. He, and his author, utilize elaborately mannered sensitivity without ever achieving the freedom, identity and joy which are its proper ends.[5]

In emphasizing the best known contemporary rebellious work as sentimental—for that is what feelings are when dissociated from freedom—there is no need to deny its merits of poetic-naturalist presentation, so much more immediate and incisive than the archly literary sentimentality of many other novels of wise-child sensitivity, such as those of John Knowles, James Purdy, Truman Capote and James Leo Herlihy. But the discrimination with which Salinger's rebel sees through all the "phonies," and the directness of response which ostensibly distinguishes him from them, just serve to prove his sensitivity amidst his ordinariness. For change and rebellion, all the modern sages assure him, leads to bitterness and madness, which are neither mature nor practical. For him, and apparently for much of his fervent audience, the longing for the rebellious road and the impotent imitation of the extremities of the outcast merely provide a purgative code of ersatz-rebellion.

Where the dogged rebels on the road of Dos Passos, or

the sententious ones of Steinbeck, were accusers of society, many of their descendants are self-accusers reconciling themselves to society. The involuted treatment of the naturalistic rebel often must strike the reader as a meta-phorization of the over-powering mundanity, the nihilistic force, of the American scene, rather than the lyric exalta-tions and ironic confrontations which the authors seem to claim. Thus, when Saul Bellow, an intelligent writer who started as a dryly sardonic social realist concerned with the meaning of the marginal man, self-consciously adapts an urban rebel to a mythic and poetic-picaresque heightening, rebellion becomes even more circumstantial and wryly self-defeating. The artful author of *The Adventures of Augie March* glorifies, in an intellectual Whitmanianism, the plenitude of American reality around the peregrina-tions of his naive Jewish boy from Chicago during the early 1920's to the middle 1940's. A duplicitous enthusiast, Augie carries strange burdens: tremendously varied wan-derings, some from the naturalistic road but others from noted rebels such as D. H. Lawrence, which a fancy rhetoric insists on relating to Greek heroes and Roman emperors and Biblical prophets and Elizabethan villains and manifold artists and explorers. The author attempts to give a cultural density to the naturalistic restrictions of his ordinary, and rather femininely passive and ethnic, semi-rouge and Sammy of small success in his skittish embrace-ment of what is. True, Augie does announce his essential "opposition" and nay-saying,[6] but he rarely shows it with any incisiveness. Augie, and his author, cannot engage defiance because of a skittish admiration for Machivellian manipulators (a series of sagacious successful men who dominate much of the narrative and contain a mystique of power for which there is no corresponding rebellion) and a rather inappropriate, essentially feminine, sensibility. We are only told of the superior profundity of the confused and loving experiential hero in his somewhat portentous comic wanderings towards his mediocre "fate." His wise-ness supposedly comes from the effort to accept *all* experience while yet becoming "what I am." The imposed ironic intellectuality and amoral immediacy, which cer-tainly do not fit the character, merely delay Bellow's "Columbus" in discovering the comfortable ordinariness that his origins, time and place would have made him anyway. Similarly with the inflated comic rebel and yea-sayer of Bellow's later synthetic (though sometimes funny) fantasy of a discontented American millionaire who wanders through a Reichian Africa, *Henderson the Rain King*, the hero is so busy musing on "becoming" that he quite fails to *be* anything. Indeed, Bellow's elaborate *discursus* on "being" and "becoming" and love and death, along with his ponderous explorer and animal symbolism, are far more verbal than vital, more ruminative than rebellious. What we get turns out to be a suggestive but not very intense mock-rebel.

In another direction of the mock-rebel, Nelson Algren's *A Walk on the Wild Side*, the manner goes into more brutal parody of the sterling young American on the road to success. (Is it really so hard for Americans to *dis*believe in the success story that wild imaginings and violence are the only way to give it form?) Partly a poetical re-doing of his earlier naturalistic novel, *Somebody in Boots*, it takes his Texas boy, fleeing his religious-fanatic father and the small town, down the road to New Orleans Storyville where he becomes a professional performer in a whorehouse. Algren carries his rogue's mixture of cupidity and innocence through jail, a vicious fight with a cripple, then back, blinded and crippled, to the same small town road down which he fled. In part this plays savage parody on the young man on the make: initiated by rebellion and the road, proving himself by gross manliness, defeated and going back home again. But the satire contradictorily serves as a vehicle for sentimentalizing, in lavish loving detail, the underdog and outcast. Algren stands out as much of a nostalgic buff for the prostitution and destitution of the Depression thirties as others are for the ante-bellum South or the make-believe England of gentlemen and drawing room finesse. A righteous undertow runs through the swirl of comic grossity, an anger against the "Do-right Daddies" who denounce and demand and exploit the bums and whores and pimps. The author's sympathy, even in the nastiest episodes, goes out to the "tricked, the maimed, the tortured and the sly" from the margins, those who "hid out in that littered hinterland behind the billboards' promises, evading the rat-race for fortune and fame." [7] Yet the dramatization reverses this since his bums, pariahs and defeated often simply parody

the successful and powerful. His gross-innocent hero
concludes:

> All I found was that those with hardest ways of all to go
> were quicker to help others than those with the easiest ways.
> All I found was two kinds of people. Them that would
> rather live on the loser's side of the street with the other
> losers than to win off by themselves; and them who want to
> be one of the winners even though the only way left for
> them to win was over them who have already been
> whipped.[8]

The "loser's side of the street" provides, certainly, the
proper place for the aware and rebellious. But Algren's way
to it is merely sentimental assertion; we are told but not
shown that the whole class of bummies and tarts "were the
real salt of the earth." In such cliche, now denuded of
ideology and discrimination, rests the recent American
rebel's desperate claim for a class (or declassed congeries)
of authenticity in an amorphously embourgeoised society.
Instead of taking his rebels where he finds them, Algren
has started down the American road, turned it into gross
and comic burlesque of the "greater" America, and then
announced that he has also discovered the really real
people who touch and transmit life.

Now where is the rebellion in this decade of poetic-
naturalist "quest" fictions? Certainly it seems a subordinate element in this representative handful of sometimes
powerful writers (and not just because of my truncated
commentaries). Yet the violent road to the affirmation of
what is does show that the rebellious inheritance provides
the raw materials for some ironic transformations. The
poetically insistent effort to embrace as many as possible of
the harshest American sensations still reveals the rebellious
longing for fuller experience. The refusal to simply moral-
ize the common wandering anti-heroes, the staunch refusal, too, to remove the puritan-American sense of
repulsive actuality (the sweat-and-pimples delineation of a
face; the angry and bitter commentary on American
success and power; the discontented and violent underside
of our social life) remain central. While the journey of
degradation provides the therapy that allows guiltily
unmanned mediocrity as the concluding state, ecstatic and
rebellious wandering still remains the way to identity. It is

not so much the bum as hero, though he pretty clearly
lurks behind most of these figures, as that the novelists
almost ritualistically draw upon his kind of experience, his
outsider's confrontation of extreme contradictions, disaf-
filiations and denials.

These especially limited worlds and heroes may, if you
wish, be seen not only as reflecting the special perplexities
of contemporary literature but as the contradictory
idealization-degradation of the stranger and his extremity.
That would, then, serve as an exorcism of the "diabolism"
beneath the surface blandness which so forcefully struck
D. H. Lawrence on reading the classics of American
literature. While polite moralists may bemoan that rebellious flight and harsh sensations become the initiatory
experiences, rather than refined cultural and communal
activities, they quite miss the point. Even affirmation of
the society and self as given cannot be produced by
middle-class education and manners and goals; any real
commitment requires some enlarging rebellion. The excess, the heightened compassion, the amoral knowledge,
the violation of the given, may be the deepest part of our
ordinariness. The search for a larger freedom and the tense
need for defiance may also run deeper, become an expiation for even belonging at all to modern civilization.

There is of course some irony in self-chosen alienation in
a society which, despite its affability, is shot through with
the compulsions of lonely and guilty outsiders. Perhaps the
poeticization of them seeks an *amor fati* in the despair
about identity in a mass-functionalist society. Thus the
continuing efforts to yoke poetic art and natural extremity
around the rebel from the road may be one of the major
directions of our literary vitality. For despite the limitations of these works, their ideal longings and rebellious
energy and obscure penance reveal a fundamental power.
They also suggest that our glittering blandness only partly
obscures violent and guilty and defiant impulses. Pursuing
them, the contemporary unhero often finds a fluid society
but a closed world in which his rebellion leads to an
exhaustion of being rather than to new adventures. His
affirmative hyperbole announces a sense of defeat about
the world we live in which seems bounded by elaborately
circular roads.

The rebel from the road in current fiction need not be

confined to the purgative wisdom that we have just emphasized, for in touching earth and a variousness of human response he can also affirm a more defiant identity. Two partly different, and promising, contemporary American rebellious fictions—first novels—will make the point. Ken Kesey's *One Flew Over the Cuckoo's Nest* shows some obvious defects, such as the derivative literary mannerisms of portentous Christological analogies and a forced Conradian narrative technique, which are almost parody. But the energy of its conceptions goes beyond its literary techniques. Placing the main action in a modern "mental hospital" puts the rebel, appropriately, up against an over-powering bureaucratic institution. Here the spurious claims of the "Therapeutic Community," the phony rhetoric of "adjustment," the bureaucratic ethic (*"everyone . . .* must follow the rules"), and the vicious technology (used to "tranquilize us all completely out of existence" [9]) well represent the larger struggle of the rebel and the power society. The narrating Indian Chief—a sometimes awkward device since he must, in his paranoid awareness, tell more than he knows—is a crippled legendary giant. He is also a patient who plays deaf because "white" men in authority can never seem to "hear" the Indian, especially when they want, in the name of progress, to take his way of life from him. The Chief's "paranoid" fantasy that a machine based on fear and hatred, "the Combine," works everywhere with most people wired up to it, structures much of the story. The Combine aims at "adjusting everything," eliminating eccentricity and individuality, carrying out for the social good the mad dream of "a world of precision, efficiency and tidiness." [10] Larger than any single hospital or bureaucracy, the "nation-wide Combine" and its complementary devices, such as "the fog machine" (run by Public Relations to obscure things), seems to be recognized only by those with some madly anachronistic sense of freedom.

The Combine's unbeatable power in the mental hospital is "Big Nurse"—breasts tightly bound beneath her starched front—implacable enemy of anyone who is "free enough to foul things up." This matriarchal "ball-cutter" of sexual-denying and man-destroying psychiatric authoritarianism uses petty restrictions, guilt, shame, innuendo and the latest psychological techniques; she is one of theose myriad "people who try to make you weak so that they can get you to toe the line, to follow their rules . . . to knuckle under." [11] As with the most up-to-date society, behind her sophisticated tranquilizing and castrating drugs and ideas, lies brute force: endless confinement, electric shock, lobotomy.

The rebel against this is a red-headed Irishman, R. P. McMurphy, "a wanderer and logging bum," ex-soldier (both decorated and dishonorably discharged), fighter, boozer, gambler, drifter, who faked his way into the hospital to get out of a workhouse sentence. In the psychologist's jargon, this perennially insubordinate wild westerner is a "case" because he shows "repeated outbreaks of passion," which defines to the pedestrian mind "the psychopath." [12] Or as McMurphy puts it, he has the true rebel syndrome of too much fighting and fucking. "Maybe," muses the admiring Indian Chief, rebellious McMurphy "growed up so wild all over the country, batting around from one place to another . . . traveling lightfooted and fast, keeping on the move so much that the Combine never had a chance to get anything [the conforming 'apparatus'] installed." [13]

This rebel from the road (also the traditional brawling Irishman and, rather more arbitrarily, a latter-day cowboy hero) goes to work battling the Combine—his vocation—and Big Nurse as its local manifestation. He hilariously mocks the bureaucracy, Schweikishly over-playing the rules, denying the categories of intimidation and vitalizing the victims. He "accidentally" breaks the glass wall behind which Big Nurse reigns; he organizes the inmates in various protests, especially against their own passivity and the pseudo-democracy of the therapeutic group; he arranges a hilarious fishing trip; he slugs it out with the sadistic orderlies; and he slips booze, whores and laughter into the all too organized ward of boredom, guilt and fear. He sings, he fights, he shouts, he laughs, and he refuses. The usual charge against the rebel is made: he "acted out his hostilities against authority figures." [14] Since Kesey's rebel is, quite clearly, not caught in compulsive acting out, this could very well be a definition of individual sanity.

Big Nurse has the combined power of human anxiety and institutional forces on her side, and McMurphy's rebellion is not simply a splayed series of satiric jokes. Big Nurse damages the fraternity between the rebel and the other inmates by playing upon the usual fears that the rebel acts out of sickness (modern psychology being particularly vicious this way) and out of selfishness (talented McMurphy does win when he gambles and has the ambiguities of the con-man sage). Rebellion, of course, is for the strong, and some of McMurphy's implicit demands do connect with the suicides of two inmates, though authority (Big Nurse) is rather more to blame than the rebel. In good rebellious spirit, the novel has some fine comic episodes, some acute pathos which engages and traps the defiant one, and a quite plausible blandly vicious bureaucracy. But Kesey also draws a more portentous direction in heightening the rebel to Christ, and a Christ who will pay the tragic price for defiantly freeing the others from their guilts and fears and submissions. McMurphy becomes the con-man as saint, and the lusty rebel rather too quickly switches into the frantic martyred lover of mankind who refuses to flee the hospital (he could) and demands punishment in his effort to free the others from themselves and compliance to the Combine. The "Shock Shop," where McMurphy is sent for punishment, disguised as electro-therapy, has a table shaped like a cross "with a crown of electric sparks instead of thorns." To cure his rebelliousness, the hero is lobotomized. The devoted Indian Chief smothers the half-dead and quite meaningless body of the defeated rebel giant and consubstantially gains sufficient belief in himself to rebel and flee from the hospital. The Christ-apotheosis of the all-American con-man rebel seems rather forced. Certainly it is, as with most modern theological resolutions, imposed melodrama. Lusty lovers don't canonize well. While the ultimate defeat of the rebel, the man without power other than defiance, may be wise, his standarized sanctification seems too artistically manipulated and rebelliously dubious. But Kesey's perceptive and frequently apt novel does end with the fugitive Indian, another giant of refusal, hitchhiking up the open American road.

One of the better subjects of our literature is the lower-didacticism of how the lively individual can exist and exalt against the collective institutions, whether in simplicity in the woods or down and out in Paris, in the hobo jungles or on the California margins, and especially in the armies, schools, factories, jails and madhouses. Kesey, hearing Thoreau's drummer (to whom he refers twice), also attempts, with a mixture of satire and melodrama, one of those imaginative handbooks of resistance. These how-not-to-do manuals, for resisting authority, have an obvious artistic roughness. But they should not be examined by, say, the canons of the Jamesian novel—they lack both its finesse and its compulsive renunciation of life. Moral, neo-Aristotelian, symbolist, and other such forms of aesthetic musing also lack relevance. The canons applied to essentially rebellious works should be essentially rebellious.

Let us take a final example of the rebel from the American road. In the wanderings of one of the most delightful of contemporary novels, J. P. Donleavy's *The Ginger Man*, we have what may be the best poetic-prose rogue adventures at least in the quarter century since *Tropic of Cancer*. Donleavy uses one of the oldest of rebel stances, though you would never know it from most of the comments on the book: the usual order of life is a farce, and the best way to present that is by outrageous burlesque. Donleavy's Sebastian Dangerfield does not want to rebel; he longs for conventional comfort, peace, security and luxury. Though clearly "incorrigible and a ruffian," his constant longings are to be an American businessman, a rich Irish attorney, an English snob—any and every form of stock success, including his favortie dream of domestic suburban bliss, slippers on beside the fire.[15] Actually, a down-and-out student living on the GI Bill in Dublin, then on nothing in London, he exists on seductions, brawls, farcial flights, comic fantasies and the mocking reflections of a rebel in-spite-of-himself. The furthest extension of the road puts the not-so-innocent American abroad in an inverted success story. Dangerfield is waiting for his rich American father to die, but is tricked out of his inheritance even when he does. In the meantime he struggles to get ahead, going regularly to his "broker" (actually a pawnshop) where he disposes of everything his landlord owns, plus a mirror from a public toilet. As he laconically notes, one must, like a good American frontiersman, "live off the environment."[16] A pious man, and great admirer of the social utility of religion, he prays: "the Lord is my shepherd as I am one of his sheared sheep." [17] True, life abroad dirtied up some of his American ideals; he has now given up bathing for fear it may wash off some of his personality. But he remains the great American optimist; after all, things "are so damned bad that you have to cheer up or die." [18] Besides, he's a philosophical fellow. "Rare," says this pragmatist of the street, "that I ever make these dogmatic statements but I cannot help feeling that, when other things are gone, carnal knowledge is here to stay." [19] Serious? Of course; he believes, he says, in every fine cliche since it is so much work making up new cliches, especially when there may be nothing else.

Our hero's cheering up in his down and out world comes less from principle than natural rebelliousness. Nagging wife, squalling kid, pompous father-in-law, avaricious landlord, righteous father, genteel morality, proper ambition, can't compete with a voracious delight in the fundamentals—food, drink, laughter, anger, sex—no matter how hard our earnest lad tries to rise. Propriety always loses out when the "mystic maniac" discovers himself, or when, "bled of his seed, rid of his mind," he sharply observes the sensate world. The bawdy scenes curiously fuse naturalistic fact with poetic delight. And since much of it is presented in the fractured ruminations and sensations of inner dialogue it achieves a subjective stress rare in portraits of rebels. The mock-innocent is naturally far enough outside to register, intensely, the contradictory qualities of himself and the world. "One night I was walking behind a lonely young girl with long golden hair and my heart beating with desire. She turned around and I saw her face . . . an old toothless hag." So on to the next woman!

Beneath all the wise-cracks, puns, bawdy and tense prose of physical sensation and broad mockery of conventional sentiments is the precise awareness that "life is a matter of resistance." And that means resistance to any order, for "How small we make our worlds. Gather them in, tighten them up into little castles of fear. Must get out." [20] Except that one never can quite get out. As one of his wry little ditties goes: "There was a man / Who made a Boat / To sail away / And it sank." [21]

While some of the farce gets pushed too hard in a topsy-turvy Christmas party, an animal masquerade in the

London streets, and in the parodies of success in which Dangerfield's Irish lass turns into a movie star and his oldest drunkard friend strikes it rich, this is not mere bedlam. Like all good jokes, underneath it is a desperate awareness of the capriciousness of life, of some mad comic universe making all morals and manners fantastically irrelevant. Much is funny just because life threatens to be meaningless as well as miserable, starting and ending, Dangerfield sardonically notes, with the smell of antiseptic—and so you better get a bit dirty with reality between times. Existence grows intensified by nihilistic awareness, as the sharply alternating prose—sensation and mockery, sentiment and joke—insists. With disinterested compassion, Donleavy notes that many don't get enough to eat; of those who do, many don't get enough loving; and of those who do, many don't get enough life; and of those who do. . . . So what can you do but resist and hunger for more? Especially when you are awake enough to see the bottom side of everything—"a cloacal grip on life"—you can hardly have enough. Each escape becomes all the more necessary, and all the worse, as Kenneth, the self-styled Duke of Serutan (natures spelled backwards, from a famous patent-medicine advertisement), always fleeing into greater disenchantment, notes bitterly. Hold tight to the simplest of human needs, such as freedom ("I don't want to be caught by anybody. Nor imprisoned or put down"), and you will always be running outside. In such a sardonic compassion the revolt is not local but total, against anything that would destroy the ginger of life and the defiance of inevitable sinking into dullity and nullity.

The concluding image of Dangerfield, natural American rebel of mocking tongue and avaricious penis, is of a lonely young man walking down an alien cold road on Christmas day, "a straight dark figure and stranger" with the apt and discontented eye for the sordid, humorous, odd, intensified and honest awareness. In his final reflections he has a vision of death: "a winter night . . . horses on a country road, beating sparks out of the stones. I knew they were running away and would be crossing the fields where the pounding would come up into my ears. And I said they are running out to death which is with some soul and their eyes are mad and teeth out." [22] The counterpoint of this, from the same paragraph, is the purely human paradisical vision of the place where one finds "the sea high and the winds soft and moist and warm, sometimes stained with sun, with peace so wild for wishing where all is told and telling." The lonely road, the harsh awareness, the passion for more life, the sardonic responses and restless lively defiances—they are the American individualist abroad in life and the ancient rebel on the road. We need no further moral.

IN A NUMBER of recent literary commentaries, American rebellious fictions have, somewhat reluctantly, been more acknowledged. For example, a variety of strident poetic-naturalist and angry-parodistic novels (Blechman, Freidman, Stern, Southern, *et al.*) are linked—sometimes quite dubiously—with the black humor and defiant art of the major rebel modes. (Some pseudo-rebellious fashions provide the themes for discussion in the next section of this study.) Can the rebellious minority now be the intellectual majority in contemporary American literature? That would be logically contradictory. It would also be factually improbable, given the stupid and vicious nature of most of our literary "establishment" and the anxious ambitiousness of so many of our cultural power-personalities. The rebel ways are crucial to our literature and awareness, and far more central and influential than often admitted, but hardly dominant. The adequate and authentic rebel remains—and no doubt will continue to remain—a singular figure on a far road.

SOME PROBLEMS OF RECENT REBELS

SOME PECULARITIES of literary rebellion seem especially contemporary. For example, several recent writers point out with asperity that rebels have become cheaply fashionable [1]—as with the publicity in the late fifties about the Beat Generation, the adoption in the past decade of various stylizations of anti-painting and anti-drama, the increased tolerance of adolescent revolt, and the sophisticated hunger for a literature of dissent. A curious stage of current culture may lie behind this *apparent* acceptance of rebellion. In the arts, rebels for some time seem to have set styles and responses. The "modern" becomes so equated with revolt in literature, art and speculative thought that the old fashioned or the muted or the decorous contrarily seem daring, for a moment. Certainly what is sometimes rather strangely called "literary culture" in contrast to "scientific culture" (as if science's methodologies and technologies could possibly produce the styles of gesture and communion) has been disruptive for at least several generations. [2] A large part of our better art and thought draw on seemingly rebellious qualities of refusal, rage, disgust, bemusement, perversity and chaos so that we have come to expect, if not accept, the angers and negations as the very colors of contemporaneousness. Since much of recent cultivated sensibility—though not recent living—seems shaded by rebelliousness, any particular rebel appears limited; any specific defiance sounds restrictive. Has rebellion lost its force and meaning by winning out?

First, we should emphasize the obvious point that a great deal of what passes for contemporary rebellion lacks genuine denial and defiance. Almost everyone agrees that the angry young men of recent literature are not really very angry. Apparently defiant "Hipsters" merely provide a style of sophistication for institutionalized personalities. "Writers in revolt" often means, in Paul Goodman's apt naming, producers of "*Avant-Kitsch*." [3] Many of the more "daring" artists maintain tried and truly weary "experimentalism," which is mostly verbal pedantry, or mawkish "self-expression" (the "mind-flow" style) rather than rebellious counter-expression. Pseudo-rebellion may be the result of the apparent acceptance of revolt as an esthetic phenomena, as fashion of sensibility, which turns out to be a neutering of rebellion as a fuller commitment and life-style. Our increasingly clever tolerance and sophisticated separation of sensibility and activity achieves such completeness that, in effect, we define "maturity" (or "education" and "cultivation") as the ability to contain a rebellious awareness in an unrebellious life.

Nearly two centuries of various romantic exaltations of rebels, the partial institutionalization of artistic avant-gardism, and the openness of a supposedly pluralistic and luxurious culture make some rebel gestures not only modish but competitive in the market places. Thus cultural purveyors search out, albeit for their own purposes, a new rebellious generation, a striking piece of eccentricity or a titillating violation. Rebellion, too, becomes a commodity. A way of defiance serves as a disposable package for an inversion of a convention that serves to reinforce conventionality because it only provides a brief (and rigidly confined) indulgence. In America, the generations' styles of rebellion go out of fashion as rapidly and arbitrarily as they are offered for consumption. Indeed, that may be part of the inherent reason they are offered for vicarious titillation in the first place. The rubrics of the Lost (disenchanted) Generation of the twenties, the Social (leftist) Protest of the thirties, the Anxious (war weary) Age of the forties, and the Beat (disaffiliated) Generation of the fifties soon lost their shock effects and revolted and turned into nostalgic institutions. Not only do generations and movements get neatly telescoped into decades, and less, but to a mechanical and fatuous periodicity. Ortega y Gasset, in his "Concept of the Generation," argued the conservative view that the morphology of change took a rhythm of senescence and rejuvenation, age and youth, order and revolt. Our generations tend to be all young and rebellious, in an aged and orderly way. The American pattern of the generation—really of recurrent minority revolts against the majoritarian culture—come out simultaneously immature and senile. The literate public shows an eager exhilaration in a half-grown defiance, which thus need not be taken seriously, and then quickly assimilates its manifestations into quaint history. The contemporary aesthetic revolts seem largely inoculatory, creating a quick immunity to any fuller disillusion, anger and defiance.

Or, to change the figure, one of contemporary America's distinguishing modes as a civilization may be its intellectual "protective coloration." Almost any attitude or gesture, and especially the threatening, can be taken over, organized and adulterated, and put into full scale production, distribution, export and satiation. They used to selectively punish rebels; now they indiscriminately peddle them. Nothing can bring down an attitude more rapidly than mediocre reproduction. The honesty of straightforward hostility, resulting in concern, argument, anathema and exile, might have superior virtue. Our ingenious adaptiveness turns some manifestations of revolt into bland conversation pieces instead of intense confrontations. Other defiances seem to be taken like mixed doses of barbituates and stimulants; one's responses can have gone drastically up and down without having gone in any clear direction. Rebellion gets promoted only in restrictive forms of consumption—the arts, the young, set fashions—which means that the tougher, continuing and autonomous criticism and negation have almost no place at all. Mocking jesters may, on suitable minor occasions, be better treated and paid than in the past but no longer have a permanent place in the court. Rebellion, or its imitations, becomes a popular game but, to my knowledge, no powerful institution—no governmental or private bureaucracy, no entertainment or education industry—allows a place for drastic criticism or shows any willingness to openly meet and confront its defiers. Disagreement must be either bland or peripheral; even then it gets cleverly adapted and ameliorated so that it loses all excitement and independence. Authenticity as a rebel becomes increasingly perplexed and difficult.[4]

The apparent acceptance of rebellion as even an aesthetic phenomena rises another order of contradictions. Art is Rebellion—such is the dubious principle of a number of "rebel" spokesmen (some of whom will be discussed later) and popularly results in ersatz faiths. For example, there is that gross belief that the appurtenances of art (vast arrays of "good" inexpensive books, records and prints; displays of art, music and culture heroes; massed statistics on the millions who write, paint and play) indicate a transformed public consciousness.[5] If the practice and appreciation of art constitute rebellious acts, then revolt is currently endemic. However, the endlessly flexible collections of such evidence can be left to unrebellious administrators who know how to organize the material for usefully specious ends. The land may seethe with rebels, though their slyness in behaving pretty much like everyone else (and in ways which can best be explained without any reference to art or rebellion at all) seems truly astonishing. Are the millions of would-be "creative" ones really even potential artists and/or rebels? [6] A multitude of lonely and longing individuals, with sufficient sensitivity to feel misplaced and unappreciated, long to play "creative" artists and thus comfortably defy the "system" of indifference and meaninglessness. Since "artist," "writer," and similar honorific terms, still suggest unconventionality, enlarged personal freedom, sincerity, bohemianism, individuality—and quite a few rather more luxurious goodies—we have legions of pseudo-rebellious litterateurs.[7] Tell the lovelorn, "be an artist or writer," says the diabolical Shrike in *Miss Lonelyhearts*. There's a "way out." Out of what? Out of more genuine rebellion.

The pathetic sophistication of art as personal and social therapy, as hobby and time-off defense against boredom, as commercial entertainment and production, as academic and intellectual specialization, as polite resentment and covert superiority—in short, "creativity" as the American addenda to *bovarysme*—relates neither to significant art nor to genuine rebellion. Surrogate culture and defiance surely serve practical purposes, and some imperatives of those in power: they inhibit and falsify deeper and fuller discoveries of discontent. The millions of Americans who practice, or vicariously partake of, self-expression and nonconformity only in the arts have found a convenient way of not doing them in their institutions and the streets. The categories reveal the trick: "art" but not ordinary work is "creative." "Imaginative writing" is something to take a course in, not something to do in public statements, letters, and all that dark wood of printed matter constantly growing around us. Pictures and poems, but not our cities and people, reveal "form" and "feeling." "Style" is proper in art, irrelevant in life. Our public ceremonies, festivals and poetry (that is, television, institutional gatherings and advertising) are of course mostly fraudulent art. But should not the "artistic" also be condemned for systematically insisting that "imagination," "awareness," "insight," "passion," and most of the other superlatives attributed to the processes and objects of art, do not belong in more tangible life? Can these qualities, then, actually be in the art? That so many wish to direct their thought and intensity and discontent away from their daily rounds to a formalized and removed activity uniquely defined as "creative" provides millions of sad comments on the qualities, and the lack of freedom, of our daily living.

But in sketching the background to some of the difficulties of the contemporary literary rebel—the imitated rebellion that makes the rebel's identity so uncertain, and thus his work so exasperated—the points should not be left at the level of social polemic. The large claims, implicit as well as explicit, of literary rebels defeat their own particularity. For instance, the traditions of literary rebellion I have been defending—Blake's extremity, Melville's labyrinthine denials, Corbière's exacerbated sensibility (or whatever equal figures one wishes to add) provide inappropriate cynosures for simpler souls. The fullest styles of defiance are demanding vocations for exceptional figures. There must be lesser traditions of both defiance and art than those practiced by the great rebels. (The experiences and literature of "the road," I implicitly argued in the preceding section, provide some lesser traditions.) And for literary rebellion to be meaningful, it must not be confused with the totality of art, as some claiming to be rebels do. Art may be the song, dance and tale of a communal festival, the collective enactment of ritual and mythos (the type usually exalted in an organic society). Or art may be the mastery of a talent, the perfection of a form and style, for an audience of connoisseurs

(the type exalted in polished class societies). Or art may
be the loving concern with the crafts and actions of daily
living (the aesthetic exalted by utopians for the "good
society"). Communal ritual, connoisseurship, and crafts-
manship do not exhaust the possibilities we lump under
art but they at least suggest that much does and should
exist which is not primarily rebellious. The rebel, a peculiar
and limited fellow, may best find his suitable role when
other patterns of art exist for him to pit himself against.
A disproportionate number of our artists and audiences
pursue versions of the defiant anguish of the rebel, thus
producing cut-down and imitated rebellion. By viewing
art as rebellious, and by confining rebellion to the artistic,
we distort both. Our technologies, commerce, entertainment and authorities contain very little art and very little
rebellion. The synthetic relations we maintain between
art and rebellion and the rest of life—including critical
blandness, neutered doses of dissent and art in the mass
media, smug institutionalization of pole-climbing dis-
senters and artists, and diabolically efficient mis-packaging
and mislabeling of the troublesome—tend to confuse
things the more. Our society is wrong even for the rebels
who wish to defy it; they cannot see their way, nor each
other, in the amorphous displacements of values. Thus
there seems to be a good bit of rebellion around, but it
also seems uncertain, confused, ineffective, lacking genuine excitement, lucidity, vigor and place.

Similar perplexities permeate contemporary bohemianism. A few comments on this large, and over-romanticized
and yet under-allowed, marginal living might be appropriate here. Some individualistic rebels—Cynics, hobos,
Beats—provided, as was noted, patterns for minority
living. Are bohemias, then, communities of literary rebels?
That would assume that artists as such are rebellious and
that bohemias are conclaves of artists. Neither will stand
up. Small groups usually make drastic demands for conformity, in understandable defensive solidarity, and the
artistic would appear to be no exception. The "jollity" of
the traditional image of *La Vie Bohème*, in its century of
fashionable variations from Murgerism to current
"upper-bohemianism," includes little revolt.[8] Partying and
aestheticism are not very defiant in themselves, though
they may appear so in puritanic and provincial places.

As for literary professionalism, that is exceptionally un-rebellious; one can probably find less sychophantism and more free social behavior among skilled migrant laborers, for example, than among writers. The image of bohemia as a locus of radical discontent and drastically different living goes back to much deeper sources than sentimental bohemianism—much older, too, than the influence of revolutionary political doctrines, which have usually had a quite minor role in bohemia. For in its most serious senses bohemia consisted of over-lapping "undergrounds" of social, ideological, ethnic and personal deviants. Often the socio-economic structure of urbanization, going back to ancient times, put vagrants, painters, foreigners, students, sodomists, utopians, alcoholics, reformers, confidence men, writers, beggars, and the more *outre* pleasure seekers in curious proximities, physical and intellectual. The uncertain roles of artists, perhaps especially in the extreme periods of mass-technological change and romantic doctrines, led to alliances with other malcontents and outsiders. Alienated artists certainly identified themselves with the social undergrounds—and some of the outcast justified themselves with art—so that many modern literary styles show particular qualities derived from homosexuality, Jewishness, drug addiction, Negro jazz, and so on.[9] The sentimental and arty senses of bohemianism, largely the product of publicity movements for middle-brow titillation, quite miss the underground and outcast ways which the more serious art drew upon, and which usually reveals utopian longings. The self-conscious contemporary person existing in a minority life-style is more likely to think coolly of his way as "marginal" than as "bohemian."

The histories of the traditional American bohemias might properly emphasize the ethical as more important than the artistic.[10] The communal and programmatic aspects of bohemia showed much moral reformism and social utopianism, frequently activated by the same, or same sort, of people who engaged in nonurban utopian experiments in America. A number of the rebels from the road also settled, for a time, in various bohemias.[11] And, of course, by both taste and necessity, bohemias attracted all sorts of eccentrics, especially the kind that should be called the "ghetto-type." Only the naive and the righteous ever pretended that Greenwich Village, Chicago's near North Side, the Quarter in New Orleans, San Francisco's North Beach, Los Angeles' Venice, New York's Lower East Side, Big Sur, and all the similar semi-communities in marginal urban areas, near universities and in some off-beat resort places were full of artists. The loose sub-cultures of disaffiliated individuals included only a minority of artists, and of rebels.[12]

While minority-group conformity is probably no more encouraging to thought and art than one would expect, it may, because of the established image of the bohemian and because some deviants need to pretend honorific justifications, encourage certain gestures which can be called "art." For example, the poetry of Beat-bohemias is not poetry in the usual literary senses but language as oral ritual and group celebration-therapy. Much the same may be said of the other arts—and thought—of such bohemian coteries. This "art," so obviously simple and repetitious (as its oral or other spontaneous "acting out" would necessarily make it), has little significance or merit outside of its immediate communal display. Even its communal development into established and rich forms is not possible because contemporary bohemianism is transitory: we allow only the general uncommunal social order. Giving such group ritual-therapy to the larger public, under the guise of rebellious literature, confuses both the public and the producer.[13]

Most of the knowledgeable discussions of Beat-bohemianism also insist that in its own terms it is not primarily a literary movement. Even Lawrence Lipton (*The Holy Barbarians*), though quite lacking in critical acumen about Beat "literature," insists that Beat-bohemians primarily choose a way of life rather than create art.[14] Their justification is religious rather than aesthetic (though too many of his cases reveal more pathology than theology). Some of the most earnest studies of current bohemianism demonstrate, even if unintentionally, that merely existing as a bohemian takes up all the "creativity" such rebel-victims can afford.[15] One of the more astute sociological commentaries on Beat-bohemianism notes that upward of ninety percent make no literary claims, and for most of the remainder the major form is the "wise-crack." [16] The insistence on a literary identity for bo-

hemians is the work of a mere few litterateurs in bohemia
—and of a great many litterateurs outside who, again,
confuse dissent with art, whether righteously or apolo-
getically.[17] Expectations for literature from bohemia would
seem generally unreasonable, especially in America where
most exceptional works come not from literary movements, not from any public elite, not from any communal
expression but from isolated and even grotesque singular
individuals. If Beat-bohemianism does contribute to a
major writer—or if it has to one not yet generally recognized—all odds are that his relation to the peripheral
group will be peripheral.

Most Beats draw indirectly upon literature for their
cluster of values: the anti-work ideology, the post-hobo
wandering, the pacifism, the anti-authoritarianism, the
holy poverty, the communal ecstasy (including non-
addictive drugs and jazz), the bisexuality, and the political
and moral disaffiliation from the majoritarian culture.
These views are defensible—and I think often meritorious
—in their own right, without any artistic role playing.
While I have earlier argued that the Beat-bohemian style
belongs basically to the most ancient heritages of Cynic-
heretic-rebel modes (leaving aside the specifically contemporary details) it must be granted that some tone and
force seems to be missing. What is wrong with the
contemporary personifications of rebellious values?

This again brings us up against the perplexities of
rebellion in an amorphous society. Even the sympathetic
commentators sense drastic limitations to the Beat—a
mawkish, pathetic, fragmented, unrigorous and not very
defiant cast which seems true of so many contemporary
rebels. There is no simple answer, but we can eliminate
the nostalgic political actionism of some commentators
(harking back to an earlier day) and the outraged moralizing of public relations paranoids as simply irrelevant.
Contemporary bohemians reflect much of the general culture, with its uncertainty and sentimentality, and the general sense of oppression by an over-ripe world in which
power, bureaucratic mechanization, and fatuousness are
dominant and diffused. The hopelessness of our rebels
tends to the woozy way down and out—drugs instead of
self-created ecstacy, hip-passivity in place of angry denials,
the gang-huddle in preference to tough solitude, confession

instead of mockery, prolix artiness instead of sardonic anti-literature, synthetic religiosity instead of the impassioned recognition of nothingness, etc. Our adolescent flights from loneliness, our "positive" sloganizing, our naïve opportunism, and our egotistical pretentiousness were not invented by current bohemian rebels, though they obviously suffer from and exhibit them.

Why hasn't our bohemianism, literary or not, "matured" into a tougher tone and richer style? America, after all, is the oldest home of continuous modern discontent and our rebelliousness has been going on for some generations. Yet, of course, most things in America—building cities, writing poetry, becoming disillusioned, discovering evil—are done over and over as if each time were the first time. So with our bohemians. Pragmatic as well as psychic causes must be acknowledged here. One clever commentator on our bohemian history suggests that "in the basically conservative American character there is room for Bohemia only as a way station" [18] (more accurately, a social and political conservatism). The transitoriness of rebellion inhibits full growth, and allows the partially accurate public image of revolt as adolescent. Usually the positive side gets emphasized: our adaptive society allows —encourages—the bohemians back inside the majoritarian forms. Only the real victims, the "cases," tend to stay bohemian. The skilled and energetic rebels, perhaps unfortunately, make bohemianism just a "phase," and carry vestigial elements of it elsewhere. (Thus the word "bohemian" is now probably more used for slightly eccentric social and familial behavior than for the denizen of a bohemia.) Consequently, a certain bohemianism—as most Europeans fail to recognize—is fairly widespread, if weakeningly disguised and isolated, in America, rather than concentrated in the small, enfeebled hard-core and transitory bohemias. The diffusion—as someone said of Hellenistic culture—may equally denature poets and barbarians. It is my impression that the contemporary denaturing accelerates, partly for reasons of the "protective coloration" of the society at large, partly because the rebellious have less and less genuine place.

The "lack of place" for the bohemian should be understood also in a quite literal sense. Since World War II, as such commentators as Isaac Rosenfeld and Paul

Goodman have noted, it becomes less and less feasible to be intelligently poor. Societies geared for affluence and inflation destroy casual and holy poverty. Economically and socially it becomes exceptionally arduous to live a decent marginal life: occasional jobs, lowly sinecures, hoboing possibilities, living off the land—all such ways of independence rapidly disappear. The accelerating stand-ardless "standard of living" disproportionately punishes those not on some economic escalator, or well up in the social elevator. When it is easier to get a "professional" job (with all its personal demands) than to get "casual labor" (with all its personal indifference), then "making out" and "getting by" are a "rough go." And any more or less bohemian housing, such as a group of low-priced rentals in cultural purlieus where repressive forces (police, puritanic landlords, petit bourgeois neighbors) are unusuallly tol-erant, turns out to be an archaic stop-over awaiting the progressive work of the bulldozer.

Socially, of course, the premium goes so heavily to the manipulative personality that the expectations for that type become universal, and the intransigent are more and more penalized. Liberal politicians and benevolent moral-ists worry about suitable housing, work and entertainment for the low- and the middle-; several more wry moralists worry about a place for the upper-; but all pretty much manage to systematically eliminate the places for the bohemian, the odd and the rebellious. (Probably the same is true with the intellectual landlords: editors, publishers, etc.) John Stuart Mill's conception of liberty included the imperative that "people should be eccentric." [19] But nec-essary for that is a literal economic and social place for the eccentric to be; the special dynamism of mass-bureaucratic societies eliminates, practically as well as psychically, free eccentric possibilities and autonomous smaller societies. No economic determinist seems yet to have written the history of American sensitivity as the endless search for a plausible independent way of living—in the woods, in utopian communalism, in hoboism, in bohemianism, in expatriation—but even non-determinists can recognize its power as one of the failed dreams of America.

Another side of marginal life's difficulties are literary adaption and adoption. Though rarely noted, much con-temporary literature constitutes what in past times would have been considered bohemian reportage. Almost endless random examples can be taken from well-known and praised non-coterie, non-Beat, contemporary "realist" novelists: William Styron, *Set This House on Fire*; James Baldwin, *Another Country*; Herbert Gold, *Salt*—to mention only three ambitious, inflated works whose primary subject matter is bohemianism.[20] But note that each of these works, and the many others like them, harshly attack bohemianism. Unambitious living, insist Baldwin's aggrandizing Negroes as well as whites, is terribly destructive. Such works, though drawing on rebellion, take insistently anti-rebellious postures. Much bohemian living, of course, is self-destructive—partly for reasons we have been discussing—but whether significantly more destructive and less genuine than other ways of life is not a real issue treated by these literary moralists. An almost endless list of works of some skill exploiting marginal living could be made from contemporary fiction; their pervasive failure at significance, I would suggest, comes from their twisting the marginal material to serve moral and aesthetic patterns alien to that material. Since serious contemporary literature lacks many traditional subjects—religious myths, heroic figures, a meaningful social order—marginal living tends to be the central subject but one forced into religious and heroic and social-moral ends. Also, in such works, the long "modernist" development of artistic narcissism holds sway; the artist writing about art in the social texture of the novel becomes the artist writing about artists, or, rather, producing a literature of the folkways of aspirants to professional cultural roles. This tedious egotism is reinforced by the exposé legacy of naturalism, the reactive imperatives to explore sexual varieties in America, the inadequacy of the bland and blurred material of most more "normative" lives, and the congratulatory role of playing at artist-rebel. But when everyone pretends to be marginal, no distinctive marginality remains; and when rebellion is everybody's profession, no rebel vocation remains. Such imitation is anti-rebellion.

Literary rebellion, I argued, gets generally adapted and denatured, especially in current American culture; voluntary rebellious living, I suggested, is not allowed much independence and vigor; add, also, that the natural "underground" subject matter of the rebel becomes moralized and mannered, as we see in many "bohemian manque" rococo satires of underground life, such as those by Thomas Pynchon, William Gaddis and Bernard Wolfe.[21] The older form-violating-forms of literary rebels—the impetus for such personal, eccentric poetic documentaries as *Walden, The Enormous Room, Tropic of Cancer, Let Us Now Praise Famous Men*—now necessarily become exacerbated and despairingly willful.[22] So withdrawn and abstracted does the recent rebel impulse seem to be, as in the "novels" of Samuel Beckett and other arcane nihilists, that no particular world remains to be revolted about. Pity the poor rebel: simultaneously put down and plagiarized, he turns to labyrinthine art and involuted symptomology as the testimony of his futile rage, ending in unviable desperation where he must rebel against his own rebellion.

Let us comment on an obvious recent example whose extremity seems mostly representative: William Burroughs, *Naked Lunch*.[23] Loosely, the book is yet another poetic-prose documentary of intensified awareness—a drug addict's consciousness. The author insists, alternately, that the chaotic shape of the account is the way things are, and that he willfully eliminates plot, character and the other usual signs of order to separate his work from that of the mere "entertainer." [24] Certainly his "cut-up method" of accidental and gratuitous mis-sequences of fragments perversely denies any order and defies any other than its own special schizophrenic disorder. Drug addiction (somewhat faddish in would-be rebellious literature) itself provides a near total, and destructive, rebellion against the limits of ordinary consciousness. (The disorder of the narrative, however, only reflects the addict's dream consciousness by a conscious author's willful abeyance of will.) But where the rebel traditionally moves away from anxiety—his great justification—the addict, and especially one as paranoid as Burroughs, gets his intensification by accelerating anxiety. The homeopathic potion, whether as drug or literature, turns out more horrendous than the original poison.

Burroughs shouts, in a prefatory moral, for the renunciation of drugs—as anomalous as if a heretic were to deny any interest in religion.[25] In context, the morals come out as jokes. For in tone, much of *Naked Lunch* is humor gone to bilious disintegration—the comic schizophrenia of

Miller and the outraged disgust of Céline (writers to whom he may be indebted) turned to compulsion in which many of the wise-cracks and verbal twists are not just fragmented but repeated and repeated. The apparent materials of this violent pastiche include paranoid fantasies, "soured utopianism," [26] addict underground reportage and poetic-pornographic meditations. They may only fall together. Amidst sadistic pederasty dreams, naturalistic descriptions of terminal addiction, and exacting catalogues of physical nausea, the positive elements become the most outrageous: the defense of cooperatives, the hortatory demands for spirituality, the simple human loneliness ("Last night I woke up with someone squeezing my hand. It was my other hand." [27]). Between monotonous rendings of the flesh, the merely human seems fantastic, the decent almost embarrassingly obscene.

But Burroughs' truly fractured account does not stay with this or with any other shocking reversal to break through the already exploited limits of rebel subject and strategy. Most essentially, he records the loss of all rebellious possibilities. The traditional images and gestures rise to view just to submerge in a hopeless repulsion which is only intermittently angry. The account starts down the American road, but with a sense of futility ("there is no drag like the U. S. drag" [28]), and actually moves only within compulsion, from sick need to sick need, "junk" to "junk." Both the fragments of travel and the exotic-satiric bits of underground documentation (New York, Tangier, Mexico) serve to deny any enlarging experience. Except for the briefest moments, the material supports the author's insistent conclusion that nothing at all happens in the addict's underground world. Any significant rebellion, therefore, must be away from addiction, but the whole world is a junk habit, and addiction provides the only world and only rebellious awareness.

Burroughs' apparently libertarian attacks on cancerous bureaucracy take form in a horrendous (though weakeningly chopped-up) fantasy of a vast, nearly omnipotent, sodomist-sadistic apparatus, a police state hospital. Actually, this supports the sense of weakness and destructive longings of the authorial consciousness, and the most vicious of the anti-utopian details display a lavishness of affectionate self-hatred. Burroughs' major insight, on the analogy of addiction, is that *control* of people by power *"can never be a means to anything but more control."* [29] Addiction itself, rather than the fantasy fiction, confirms the more-and-more of power for its own sake.

Some of the ingeniously nasty fantasies of scientistic destruction aim at fairly specific satire of doctors, modern gadgetry, cops indistinguishable from criminals and the willful American character: "Americans have a special horror of giving up control, of letting things happen in their own way. . . . They would like to jump down into their stomachs and digest the food and shovel the shit out." But since, in his far-out consciousness, Burroughs cannot and will not take an even mildly consistent satiric view, such statements serve mainly as a rebellious gloss for the book's primary commitment to self-destruction and human revulsion. Burroughs obviously delights in the willful shoveling from the gut. Despite claims to exposing himself because he wishes to expose universal self-hatred and the suppurating flesh that underlies civilized pretense, in his "prophetic mutterings," he identifies with the destructive process. The victim demands the torturer in his insistence on his own disorder and helplessness. The author, too, is one of the citizens of a world threatened with endless controls—"Citizens who want to be utterly humiliated and degraded—so many people do nowadays, hoping to jump the gun." [30] Such self-excusing asides, rather arch to be convincing, may provide incantatory purges of his own rebellious awareness which has been caught in compulsive nausea and violence.

Burroughs is less a nihilistic utopian than a destructive excremental visionary. He exploits his dissociations and inversions in the attempted way down to illumination. The Buddha becomes a metabolic drug problem, anal rending opens up a greater reality, bodily discharges provide the ecstatic colorations, until "we see God through our assholes." [31] The method, even at its mystical reaches, is reductive, despite poetic pretenses to a more elaborate consciousness. The bottom-side feast of the soul, and the pain of automated ravishment, leave this devotee of resentful derangement in a post-nausea receptivity. He nakedly settles for a rebellious snack now and then.

Actually, I think, Burroughs' best writing comes out in his bits of comic rhetoric ("mail order whorehouse," "osteopaths of the spirit," etc.), in some of the fragmentary caricatures (junkie and police types), and in intermittent burlesque splaying of ordinary claims to order and sense. But the homo-erotic (yet hating) obsessions, the rather tiresome pedantry of addict information and jargon, and the search for mystical "connections" (which contradict his main positivistic bent), leave the whole an hysterical overdoing. Burroughs is too busy being the artist in some of his ornate fracturings, horrifyings and strident claims. He is also a moralist. None of the pleased withdrawal of the addict, not much of the pleasure of drug and erotic longings, are allowed by Burroughs' obsessive sense of sin. His distinctly modern wickedness takes the form of melodramatic power and compulsive action— "The face of 'evil' is always the face of total need"—which quite misses the banality of evil. He documents, rather than revolts against, that need. That he incongruously thinks of *Naked Lunch* as a rejection of drug addiction, a satire on capital punishment, and a libertarian defense of individual freedom provides moralistic claims for a destroyed character. Burroughs is more mannered moralist than rebel. The odd bits of defiant brilliance cannot be digested because arbitrary and overdone assertions against a quite opposite context. Such works lack a world, except that of fantasy, and a point of view, except moral-literary self-indulgence. Quite absent is the rebel's sense of other possibilities, and of refusal as the most meaningful choice. Anxieties get horrendously enlarged instead of contemptuously put aside. Compulsions become total, and even desired as visions of evil, instead of being human failings. Freedom, independence, individuality, vigor, refusal, exist by their mystic absence. If this be taken as rebellion, the modern literary rebel has been defeated in trying to confront blandly disguised powers, trapped in an anxiously amorphous society, absorbed into pseudo-rebellious destructiveness, perplexed into a frenzy of mannerism and exasperated weakness, totally rejecting the outside ways which are his main subject and meaning. Such characteristics too well reflect rather than defy the world we live in. Some rebels, then, lead the anti-rebellion.

ONE OF THE MORE likely rebel limitations is defiant posturing. Impelled by his self-definition to go beyond artistic propriety and self-interest to denounce, complain, demand, confess and defy, the literary rebel—especially in an amorphous and depersonal society—reaches for involuted and exasperated forms of assertion. Such rebel ways take on a further perplexity in that some not-very-rebellious litterateurs, properly impressed by the strength of rebel identity, may employ similar forms of assertion for unrebellious ends. Not all that sounds troublesome is troublesome, unfortunately, and more than one sycophant of sophisticated powers-that-be has profitably played at rebellion to give authority a flattering sense of tolerance and freedom and individuality.

A mild way for the rebellious, and their imitators, to express identity and display their commitments is to make pronouncements on rebellion. They prove themselves as literary rebels by talking about literary rebels. Such contemporary gestures of denial and defiance often require a bit of sceptical probing. Even when authentic, the intellectual narcissism of rebel-on-rebel reveals a pathetic lack of communal place in which revolt could be directed more fully outward. The embarrassing "second-hand" qualities of the intellectual broker at one or more removes from the direct experience apply, of course, to other than rebellious literary critics. In general, the wide-ranging intelligence and sensibility—the Man of Letters—gets excluded in contemporary society by bureaucratic specialization and technological ideologies from any broadly significant role and engagement. Independent literary intellectuals, of whatever persuasion, would seem likely guides and performers of education, entertainment, public festivals and moral dialectics—of the general intellectual, cultural and religious activities of the ·community. Or so they believe. Obviously, the literary intellectual gets allowed no such role in a world of educationists, public-relations technicians, culture salesmen, scientistic experts, clerics of administration, and other anti-intellectual professionals who control intellectual activities in Western-style societies, and perhaps most grossly in America. We do not suffer the vices of a mandarin civilization, nor the virtues of intelligence in public.

Yet we also do not have an "intelligentsia" of any proportions which stands outside the official order as a rebellious group or class. Our mass-technological-bureaucratic societies reveal shrewd self-preservative instincts; other societies threw intellectuals into the streets where they became troublemakers. Our way is to give the literate and intellectual great opportunities to forego those traits and take up, in proper disguise, commercial and technical roles. Or they can keep a modicum of their devotion to the life of letters and arguments and become specialists, properly institutionalized and insulated, practicing their expertise. The contemporary effulgence of literary criticism becomes one such form of institutionalization, apparently providing a specialist refuge for moralists and theologians and philosophers and artists as well as rebels. Replete with some of the appropriate learning, techniques and issues of professional literary study, quite an odd variety of intellectual passions find an outlet, however limiting, in "criticism." [1]

The forced linkage of art and rebellion, discussed earlier, may particularly attract some rebellious spirits to literary criticism. Yet criticism with its heavy traditions of pedagogy and uplift, may also appear restrictive. In literary criticism, too, the rebel strains at the limits and twists erudition and appreciation to peculiar purposes. Three somewhat dubious and perplexing figures—one each for American, British and French contemporary literature—may represent a much larger field. To start with one previously cited: Leslie A. Fiedler, a well-known belligerent American writer, occasionally turns out verse and fiction of not very substantial merit, but most effectively functions as a polemical "literary critic." More exactly, he is a literary critic of non-literature. Using the left-handed strategy that the modern methods of literary criticism provide revelatory techniques in themselves, he writes about criminals, politics, social fads, religion, popular entertainment, bohemian ideologies, sex, and cultural power politics—his real interests—as if he were dealing with particularly obscure literary texts. Perhaps Fiedler displays his inverse best on a subject like "comic books." [2] Playing an Aristotle of sub-literary popular culture, he uses mock-erudition to categorize comic book forms and types as significant allegories of good and evil and mythic expressions of urban folk consciousness. The argument claims more than it should, often gaining suggestiveness at the price of tangential forcing. (As in the analogy of comic books with jazz music, which ignores that jazz is not only of much different quality but, unlike comic-books, has always had a life separate from its mass-technical reproduction on records.) Fiedler does not take his burlesque scholar-criticism of comic books altogether seriously. For he makes much of the more pertinent point that the artifact of mass entertainment acquires most of its meaning as a reduction of expression to a "commodity" rather than as individual art or collective symbolism. His inversion of comic books into richer signficance serves as a defiance of those who righteously attack them. Fiedler's main purpose in "The Middle Against Both Ends" comes out in the assault on the banality of standardized middle-class taste and morals because the "middle-brow" who denies the vulgar also denies the intellectual. From his opening assertion of reading comic books "with some pleasure," through his defense of all arts—elitist and popular—which concern the "instinctual and dark" (death, sex and guilt), to his final insistence on a hierarchy of intellectual values, he strikes at the "drive for conformity on the level of the timid, sentimental, mindless-bodiless genteel." [3]

Some of the strength of Fiedler's polemic derives from his awareness that some past literary rebels' intellectual egalitarianism and cultural democracy results in both comic books and the righteousness of those that attack them. The weaknesses of the argument reveal not only the forced posture of defending comic books but a self-indulgent eagerness to win against fools—the minds inspired by the more mawkish best-selling novels and the charms of resentfully easy virtue. Why so vehemently fight cripples about toy dragons? Fiedler is not alone in using such quaint strategy. The angry Man of Letters wants to do battle with social monsters but his identity and justification drive him defensively to his literary expertise —thus the apparatus of symbol and myth and cultural standards on the incongruous battlefields of sub-literature and psuedo-literature. It takes a covert pun for the "cultured" to claim any right to enter the large social arena of "mass culture." Mostly excluded, at least on their own merits, from the fields of popular thought and entertainment those of intellectual temper and talents must fight the "middle-brow" where ever they can. It's a lonely life to talk only about real things.

The outrageous ways of trying to assert low-down humanity and high-handed intellectuality to the vast bland powers that dominate modern culture also reveals other defensive peculiarities. Critics like Fiedler rather lack individualistic qualities—always so skittishly and anxiously *au courant*—and do not like to get caught in either too old-fashioned or too idiosyncratic intellectual dress, despite the desire to stand out. Thus the anti-fashionable way of wearing a fashionable subject matter. Despite the off-beat strategies, the preoccupation with big battalions —"high-brows" and patronized "low-brows" versus "middle-brows"; comic books and serious art versus popular novels and magazines—represent old ideological class warfare (no less when defined by literacy than by economics). In such hands, hypostatized entities like low-middle-high culture serve as yet another up-dating of tired neo-Hegelian dialectics. Severed from the now bankrupt revolutionary ends, the partly disguised style of radical social criticism remains. Outrageous enough to focus attention but also conventional enough in underlying form to receive a traditional minority audience, the neo-radical critic finds his place.

In a society which protectively submerges the rebellious free speech it more or less permits in near-sighted indifference and blatant noise, position-taking on comic books and the like does provide an "image" with a loud sound-track. Over-elaborating crypto-homosexuality in a classic boy's tale such as Huck Finn ("Come Back to the

Raft Again, Huck Honey"), or exposing man's-man Hemingway just before his suicide as a tired oldster trembling before a literary critic, or inverting the titillation of bohemian reportage into archly sordid games (many of the stories in *Pull Down Vanity*), or turning literary psychoanalysis into ornate pedantry (*Love and Death in the American Novel*—an unadmitted burlesque of the more tiresome form of literary history [4]), serve similar rebellious display. The usual charge of "bad taste" thrown at such defiances shows a self-congratulatory obtuseness. Whether or not Fiedler's sometimes nasty posturing is a compulsion and shrewd self-aggrandizement, many contemporary literary rebels seem impelled to use rather similar ways to get a hearing.

The rebel's inverted vanity should not be used to dismiss his arguments. Fiedler's main issue is simple, if not always apt. In *No! in Thunder*, for example, he holds that the best literature shows us the "Modern Muse" as "Demonic, terrible and negative." [5] Literature which does not call upon that muse is suspect. This, of course, confuses literature and defiance, falsifying both. Thus Fiedler prefers easy enemies where the confusion does not stand out, and so rightly attacks the "pseudo-no" of the sentimental "protest novel," moralistic righteous art, and the essentially unrebellious, "progressive and optimistic, rational and kindly dogma of liberal humanism." In adapting Melville's famous phrase of cosmic defiance to a purely ideological scope, Fiedler assaults bland dissent and holds up the principle that *"to fulfill its essential moral obligation fiction must be negative."* [6] Our dominant form of literature must be rebellious, at least in manners, to provide the counter-dialectic for a society dominated by the superficial and complacent and for a culture ridden with a pseudo-rebelliousness which falsifies criticism and awareness.

As cultural politics, the point may be well taken, though as a broad prescription for art it suggests an authoritarian dosage. Fiedler best supports the argument in those essays in which he holds up the mendacious and fatuous in "middle-brow" culture. Granted that his anger might achieve more if it could be separated from the pontifications of a Brigadier General of Critical Rebellion (Ret., apparently, since he speaks for no army except in fantasy), who insists on pompously mapping out the cultural terrain in every essay. He also speaks for very little literature when his points are examined outside of cultural politics, for he becomes loosely eloquent about mediocre and unrebellious writers (R. P. Warren, Henry Roth, John Hawkes, etc.) or a pedant about the standard works of the academy. His predominant taste for Gothic moralism and his commitment to a self-defensive and manipulatively abstract aestheticism ("form," "myth," "symbolic ornateness," "coherence," "archetypes") as ultimate values rather eliminates most literary rebels, past and present. Leaving aside the self-aggrandizement, what is Fiedler being rebellious about (and not just towards)? He shows little interest in rebellious ideas, actions or ways of life, and patronizes the few he even comes near. So energetic is his concern with cultural politics that the reader may not note that there is hardly anything else. The range of thought and literature, though knowingly and sometimes provocatively handled, is just a narrow rehandling (all the books, names, terms, positions, can be found in a small group of literary-social periodicals). Since he attacks pseudo-rebellion, the vulgarization of intellectual standards and hierarchies, the absence of artistic complexity, failures at social and sexual maturity, middle-class mediocrity, and similar traditional American vices, his manners rather than his matter constitute his rebelliousness. A professional "rebel" only within the terms of the quasi-establishment of American literary business, he offers very little that is truly defiant or independent. In such academic rebellion, Fiedler's suggestive manners often seem to serve outraged moral and aesthetic conservatism; his own cries as mock-rebel support his useful arguments about "pseudo-rebellion" in American culture since he, too, is mistaken by his liberal audience as a literary rebel.[7] His weakness in individualistic and radical awareness may, however, have its social uses, not least in reminding us of a basic American amorphousness and provincialism in which any drastic gesture (by a sly adolescent, a reactionary politician, or an underdog fraud) can fulfill our standard role of "maverick."

Such is the uncertainty of, as well as about, the literary rebel in contemporary discussions that the appearance rather than the substance represents denial and defiance.

Let us turn to a symptomatic British example, Colin Wilson. This popularizing British essayist also attempts fiction. (His autobiographical novel, *Adrift in Soho*,[8] gives us flat detailing and petering out anecdotes about a rather smug, even genteel, young, bookish man who quite lacks passion and peculiarity.) But literary essays, sometimes partly disguised, provide Wilson's main efforts. His first, *The Outsider*, appears to be a rebellious demand for missing values. It takes an interesting subject matter—the modern intellectual in revolt—and mishandles it. A hodge-podge of quotations, simple-minded summaries and thin deductions about such a mixed lot of writers as Shaw, Gurdjieff, Kierkegaard, Newman, Niebuhr, Berdyaev, Lawrence, Hulme, Camus, Eliot, it argues—in a parody of some of his sources—for a sensitive and prophetic alien-ated elite searching for meaning, a religious exaltation of life and purposive freedom. Wilson's assumption that his melange of writers "held basically the same beliefs"[9] is ludicrous. Many of his assertions—such as that the same intellectual outsiders insist on a new "intensity" of life and also "lack appetitie for life"[10]—turn out to be unrecognized simple contradictions. His specific com-ments—such as that D. H. Lawrence's revolt was "sim-ple" and a "back to the animal" attitude—are both ill-informed and incompetent reading.[11] In sum, his out-siders merely support Wilson in finding most things chaotic, and this they rebel against.

Wilson's *Religion and the Rebel*, a continuation but also revision of the admittedly sloppy *Outsider*, shows some possibilities. In the "Autobiographical Introduction" he summarizes his adolescent nihilism and his disgust with futile and petty jobs. Unfortunately, his possibly rebellious perceptions around this one real subject remain unde-veloped: witness the intriguing comment that he had a "delighted recognition that one's salvation can lie in proceeding to extremes of indiscretion and ignoring the consequences."[12] Nor does he at all present his wander-ings, which he says were based on a "vision of freedom" in "otherness" but ended in "perpetual anxiety."[13] The awareness is quickly submerged because he insists on rolling around portentous and stock abstract themes, such as complaining about "the *lack of spiritual tension* in a materially prosperous civilization." On the positive side, he finds that the rebel's sense of futility leads to the search for *"increased intensity of mind,"* [14] which also serves as Wilson's vague definition of religion. His partly repeated, partly new, roster of "rebels"—Arnold Toynbee, F. Scott Fitzgerald, Blake, Newman, Rimbaud, Whitehead, Pascal, Rilke, Wittgenstein, Boehme, Spengler—lacks coherence and analysis, though there is nothing especially wrong with the elementary summaries borrowed from standard reference works. Wilson's view of the "craving for meaning" now strikes some authoritarian tones; the author shows no sense of compassion or social justice, and flatly agrees with what he takes to be the outsider's desire to make *"a whole civilization think the same way."* [15] (While there is not much shape to the arguments, the author's frequent italics are accurate in establishing his points.) "Will" and "discipline" become exalted terms in the hunger to change a petty and boring world, to revolt (as Wilson assures us most great men did) "against inanity" by combining "new consciousness" with applied power. Such contempt more naturally leads to a demand for authoritarian order than for rebellious freedom.

Not very insightful, however, Wilson translated his own new consciousness and power to publish any opinion into slightly slicked-up old-fashioned moralizing. In such essays as *The Stature of Man* he weakly imitated American literary journalism by summarizing popular sociology and minor symptomatic fictions (quite without the rhetorical sophistication and sneering energy of a Fiedler) on the theme of individual insignificance, of which he quite disapproves. A bit better, if still unanalytically, informed —he now recognizes a quite different D. H. Lawrence as a better existentialist than Sartre or Camus [16]—Wilson finds the modern "spirit of defeat" rather disturbing. Thus he recommends more "inner direction," positive freedom, moral assertion and traditional heroism. This is to be known as "affirmative existentialism." Even at his best, there is a rotund smugness ("Heroism, in its purest definition, is an appetite for freedom, a desire to live more intensely." [17]) which suggests the displaced schoolteacher. The more fanciful side comes out in his not very shocking shockers, the ruminations somewhat awkwardly disguised as fictions, such as *The Sex Diary of Gerard Sorme.* Here Wilson attempts to pursue traditional rebel themes: how the exceptional/outcast man can live and find meaning; the "existential" (i.e. extreme) search for new forms of feeling and expanded sexual orgasm; and how to change the world by changing individual consciousness. But the vantage point is that of the slumming pedagogue—the type of protagonist in his three novels—whose search for new realms of experience comes out just as a sceptical but fascinated voyeurism around a charlatanic magician-occultist and rapist. While occasional notions are interesting, though derivative, there is no dramatic or dialectical acuteness. For example, fascinated with sexual violence and diabolic violations, the smugly obtuse narrator-author argues that men who are not sado-masochists are "weaklings and dupes"; two pages later he declares, with equal certainty, that all great men have an "inability to hurt anyone." [18] His heuristic declarations about supermen, primarily literary, admit little sense of actual men (he claims more knowledge about women, though mostly exploitative while his protagonist is exploited by women). The confusions at least save the Wilsonian view from following vanity into viciousness. While such work lacks stylistic and analytic power, it may have some descriptive significance as the reports of an earnestly eccentric autodidact yearning for heroic literary and religious postures in an age of their absence.

Coming from "outside" (in conventional social and psychological senses in a snobbish society), Wilson had the misfortune to be published and praised for the process of his somewhat uncertain, somewhat resentful, slightly rebellious, intellectual education. But he was only a literary outsider, with a literary message, and no other commitments or other intensity of origin, experience or attitude (in contrast to a William Blake, a John Clare, or even his hedgingly idolized criminals). Literature-as-philosophy just isn't enough to make a real rebel. But the rich traditions of British eccentricity tolerate much, and in England a Wilson may merit a decent minor place "inside." That he should be taken for a rebel (or a writer or a thinker!), by himself and others, simply expresses the blurred role of the rebel in modern culture.

Essentially similar points, but at a higher level of talent and concern, should be noted about the growing-up-from-rebellion of that humanist moralist, Albert Camus.

He, too, took to broad literary discussion in *The Rebel*. When he there defends the rebel, the result is more than ambiguous. Camus avows that art *is* rebellion "in its pure state." [19] This equation requires some exceedingly abstract analogies—of the sort few Anglo-Saxon writers would attempt to stretch out—such as that rebellion and literature both remake the world and affirm human significance. Camus must also vaporize both art and rebellion to "rational freedom" in order to give them moral restraint, though this seems the least likely term for most particular artists and rebels, including those cited by Camus. In collateral pronouncements he reduces specifically "modern art" to the work of "tyrants and slaves" and denies any literary merit to "negation" and "despair." [20] Thus few contemporary writers and even fewer rebels could fit into his meta-rhetorical formulas. No wonder that so many of the commentators spend less time on Camus' actual arguments in *The Rebel* than on his moral significance, which turns out to be a parochial polemic against his Marxist and existentialist opponents who turned rebellion and art to the service of totalitarian politics. [21] In sum, Camus holds that art and rebellion which are not reasonable and decent are not art and rebellion.

We need not leave the argument of *The Rebel* in such a naked state. The literary and historical commentaries aim to drastically revise artistic and political nihilism, including the author's own intellectual education in rebellious "absurdist" philosophies. The examples, largely confined to the post-Enlightenment rebels who defied moral rationality, include De Sade, the Dandies, Dostoevsky, Stirner, Nietzsche, Lautréamont, Rimbaud and some of the surrealists. In Camus' treatment, each of these rebellions of sensibility degenerated to nihilism, which led to unrebellious destructiveness, the extreme reaffirmation of conformity, or other anti-rebellion against human solidarity and decency. That rebels against injustice could become warped and cruel, that Dandies reacting against conventional dullness could become bourgeois pattern-setters, and that surrealists committed to absolute revolt of consciousness could (in France) become Stalinists, support his mixed feelings towards literary rebels. These contradictions, and parallel ones in social rebels, are certainly true and provide proper warning both that discrimination about rebels is necessary and that our times are inherently corrupting.

But these last points do not come from Camus. He wants to find within rebellion itself (at the most thoughtful places in his argument) the logic of affirmation and restraint. Thus: "rebellion is one of the essential dimensions of man." [22] Rebels make an ultimate, metaphysical defiance, beyond social and intellectual protest, against the very order of the universe and human mortality ("the universal death penalty" [23]). Therefore the true rebel recognizes "that freedom has its limits everywhere that a human being is to be found—the limit being precisely the human being's power to rebel." Rebellion is the absolute. And Camus several ways highlights its life-affirming side: rebel negation is not to be equated with renunciation of the tangible world and its opportunities; "the rebel defies more than he denies" [24]; even isolated rebellion asserts compassion and human solidarity; rebellion, too often equated with mere destructiveness and emotional outpouring, reveals inherent limits and shapes.

Yet Camus turns to the intellectual and political terrorism since the French Revolution as the logical culmination of rebellion. Despite an "ineradicable opposition between the movement of rebellion and the attainments of revolution," he sees revolution as belonging to "the spirit of rebellion." [25] However, even his own arguments cast doubt on this logic since most of the rebels he cites were antagonists of the official revolutions. No doubt the French political tradition makes it difficult for Camus to adequately separate anarchic rebel from authoritarian revolutionary. While he recognizes, at least abstractly, the great difference between individual nihilism and state nihilism, he too anxiously allows that futility forces rebels into revolution, which also overlooks that the rebel reaches his metaphysical defiance by recognizing the ultimate futility of all claims to order and permanency. Camus affirms that "rebellion is, by nature, limited in scope," [26] but his decent fear of tyranny makes him treat this as prescription rather than description.

As a humanistic moralist, he generally finds extremity in any direction distasteful. *The Rebel* ends with a rhetorical and dubious pean to a supposed Mediterranean temper of unrebellious moderation. Would that this had been true for Classical Greeks, Romans, Philistines, Hebrews, or could be found in modern Greeks, Cypriots, Spaniards, or his own Algerians! He more specifically denied the rebel attitude in saying that "it is not rebellion itself that is noble, but its aims." [27] As with traditional moralists, experiences are not allowed as values in themselves (so the aim of sex is procreation, the aim of punishment is correction, the aim of art is fame, the aim of life is immortality). For if the aim of rebellion is not rebellion, and a value in itself, then it becomes a merely temporary (and very often unsuccessful) means deserving of only the rarest circumstantial justification. With characteristic confusion, Camus also reaffirms revolt as permanent and ultimate; given the evils of existence, the rebel is necessary to express human compassion and awareness, and "rebellion will only die with the last man." [28]

Camus' later works, self-conscious pronouncements and allegories for the public good of a successful ex-rebel, show little spirit of revolt. Though we can find admirable moral intentions in the essays collected in *Resistance, Rebellion, and Death*, especially in the arguments against capital punishment and political terrorism, they lack resistance and rebellion. For example, "The Artist and His Time: Create Dangerously," might initially suggest a Nietzschean demand for an art of defiance. However, its main point is that we have too much literary rebellion. From the moment middle-class society achieved power, he says, "a literature of revolt developed" and "official values were negated," but this has gone on too long and "hardened into a presumption that one can be a great artist only against the society of one's time." [29] He indiscriminately concludes that this results in the sterile and hostile egotism of the modern literary intellectual who denies equilibrium and social unity and lucid affirmation. Camus thus ends by moderating his own romantic legacy of rebellion into neo-classical prescriptions. He only affirms rebellion as part of the process of his own education into restraint. Even in the rebellious part of that process, when Camus felt "outside," as in the essays in *The Myth of Sisyphus*, he longed for limits, unity and clarity. Those values were then seen as rebellious since "revolt gives life its value," [30] and Camus ticks off coherence, awareness, freedom, passion, diversity, art, and fullness. By revolting against the dubious limits and confronting absurdity, like rebel Sisyphus rolling his stone back up the hill against the gods, one achieves stoic defiance. "There is no fate that cannot be surmounted by scorn." [31] The main moderation comes from "playing it cool" while rebelling, in maintaining a sardonic negative awareness and tough individual consciousness within the spirit of revolt.

But Camus took too much as revolt; if rebellion includes everything—all social and metaphysical revolution, even all art and consciousness—it becomes nothing. No wonder that he must finally revolt, in the name of restraint, against revolt. Confining the problem to literature, it takes only the smallest of surveys to see that neither all art, nor great art, shows any necessary connection with the particular qualities of revolt. The reversal is already implicit: if all is revolt, then no specific literature, no tangible acts, no distinctive tone, style, arguments, of rebellion are needed or desirable. Thus a moralistic universalizing shades an explicit defense of the rebel into an implicit denial of rebellion.

Camus' initial failure to recognize the limits of rebellion (even rebellion as an absolute must be limited) led to his later rejection. Some of the impetus apparently came from repulsion to the more exacerbated style of modern rebels, from De Sade to Genet, which was often dubious rebellion. Some came from a longing for positive and compassionate communal values, whose lack makes revolt endemic and arbitrary. While Camus' morality aims against the terrible extremity of violent power, his rebellious awareness drew on a quite different extremity: the defiant solitary's attempt to find a way to rebel against human isolation in a counterfeit society and an indifferent universe. Camus' inflated claims for art and revolt (and art as revolt) often obscured this, though he did make the connections in his few significant works. Surely the best of these is *The Stranger*,[32] and some analytic commentary on that novella might adumbrate the marginal and ambiguous case of a contemporary rebel. For his stranger, Mersault, the clerk in Algiers leading a petty and anomic life with stoic-hedonist honesty, ends as what has elsewhere been called the rebel-without-a-cause—more accurately, the rebel-in-spite-of-himself.

The first half of the short tale raises apathy to revolt.

The stranger to ordinary illusions "couldn't be bothered" about most things; he "didn't care one way or the other" about love, ambition, friendship, moral judgment; he nihilistically accepted all given points of view because other people appeared equally absurd, pathetic "robots" of whom it was "hard to believe they really existed." [33] Highly responsive to immediate sensations—all that honestly remains in a grotesque and atomized existence—he commits a homicide because of the malign pressure of nature (the glare and heat of the sun), fortuitous circumstances (a chance "friend" and an hostile encounter), the gratuities of unconscious assertion (the breakthrough of rage which pushes him to shoot, and keep shooting) and because his author is doing a parabolic literary exercise in the traditions of literary revolt (Gidean gratuities, Hemingwavesque stoicism, anti-bourgeois mockeries and existential confrontations). In brief, his honest indifference to all conventional claims ends in fated revolt against the accumulation of meaninglessness.

Having asserted himself by a gratuitous act of destruction, his imprisonment, arraignment, trial and condemnation reveal a finally rebellious stance. He gradually learns to make his rebellion conscious. "I'd rather lost the habit of noting my feelings," [34] says the dry clerk confronted with the histrionic claims of the prosecutor. With only implicit mockery, he feels himself "quite an ordinary person," [35] though candidly aware of the absurdities around him, and so repeatedly has "nothing to say" [36] against the rhetorical charges and motives thrown at him. Like a Stendhal rebel, the negative freedom of confinement brings him to full awareness of self. In his grotesquely ordinary trial he is condemned because he claims no standard sentiment, moral evasion or public guilt—condemned for the lack of conventional responses and ideologies. To all portentous claims, he reacts with nausea: "The futility of what was happening here seemed to take me by the throat, I felt like vomiting, and I had only one idea: to get it over with, to go back to my cell." [37] His refusal to play the common frauds provides prosecutor, jury, judge—and some readers—with the idea that he is a monster, a mother-and-father-killer, a total violater of the pretended community. Only against the awareness of such total condemnation does the stranger finally recognize freedom, "with a wild, absurd exaltation." [38]

Now he is the rebel, intensely rather than passively refusing any palliative, escape, immortality, guilt, God. For the first time, he consciously asserts himself, angrily denying the priest and any certitudes other than tangible experience and death. In spite of his previous passivity, indifference and nausea, he argues, shouts, defies, and asserts that he had been "right" and was "still right." Not penance and abasement but wrath and denial purify him—the "great rush of anger had washed me clean"—and he is ready, even joyous, in an indifferent universe to go to his execution. Condemned for values he did not, and would not, have, he hopes only for a final defiance of the false crowd—for their howls of execration—as he walks proudly to his death.

In making the honest mocker into a defiant rebel, Camus oddly presented him in the guise of ordinary marginal clerk, which took a drastic attenuation of consciousness and responsiveness. Mersault's history—his education, past disenchantment and circumstances of withdrawal—are hardly hinted at. This reversed Julien Sorel shows a perceptivity reduced to such a narrow scope by his parabolic author that no demands on society and no defiances appear until the *denouement* of melodramatic violence. His passivity is so great that his jailer must suggest masturbation to him! *The Stranger*, romantic literary rebellion in archly neo-classical restraints, drastically thins out character, development, milieu—and thus rebellion. Behind Camus' introversion of rebellious energy, we may see some of the same exasperation at the excesses and falsifications and futilities in our sort of world of rebellion which appear in his literary commentary in *The Rebel*. While revolt against pretentious claims for revolt still retains an essential defiance, especially in a world where individual rebellion seems almost incomprehensible, it also testifies to the despair of the literary rebel.

Fiedler, Wilson and Camus—some of the most influential post-World War II "literary rebels"—may be far from being the most significant rebels but seem even more representative than I have suggested in discussing their work. (That the American example should be self-insistently Jewish and a professor of English, the British type lower middle-class and self-educated bohemian, and the French cynosure Algerian and anti-Communist leftist, and so on, might lead us into the sociology of national dissent.) Granted that their roles as well as qualities are partly different—though all somewhat uncongenially attempted to write novels while primarily doing didactic literary essays about literary rebellion—with the American focus on cultural sociology, the British focus on eccentric self-education, and the French focus on moral-political exemplums. Yet, I suggest, a certain common ground also deserves attention. Their subjects, experiences and values are mostly literary, as are their rebellions. Discontented with the role of literary man in our literate cultures, they emphatically end with a literature mostly of literary discontent. The thinness of their work and the ambiguousness of their rebellious gestures provides an insufficient defiance. No doubt worthy in their intentions, critically useful in attempting to define a tradition, poignant in not fulfilling a more incisive opposition, perhaps victims of a decadence beyond their possibilities, they must be read in their commentaries as inadequate rebels.

REBELLION, I have argued in several different contexts, is both ultimate and limited. It should not be equated with either art or revolution. The rebel, as rebel, most essentially chooses his extremity to exalt those values and gestures which deny and defy the inevitable false fixities of society and the cosmos. Rebellion thus remains as restricted as it is crucial, and so many rebels seek to go beyond it. A new religion or a new society may be urged as the teleology of revolt. Is the rebel who kills God still a rebel when he worships a greater mystery? Is the rebel who fights social institutions still a rebel when he promulgates new social institutions? The answers, I believe, must remain rather perplexed since pure rebellion rarely exists; most actual rebels seem to be basically mystical and/or utopian. But attempts to create religious acceptance and social morality must also conflict with the engagement to rebellion. The rebel's gravest limitations may be the refusal to accept his own rebellious limits.

It might be appropriate to take as examples of the perennial mystical and moralizing tendencies a pair of often unsatisfactory but suggestive contemporary American literary rebels: Norman Mailer and Paul Goodman. Despite obvious contrasts, they link together because both depend on, and get marred by, the same parochial ambiance—avant garde literature and socialism-cum-psychoanalysis, carried in the responsive energies of a secularized Jewish heritage. The "New York intellectual" literary localism may not be easily mapable but is nonetheless easily recognizable with its grandiloquent political mannerisms, aggressive intellectuality and sophisticated awareness, however synthetic and self-aggrandizing at times. Its more rebellious spirits, such as Mailer and Goodman, employ a post-Marxist social and a Reichian psychoanalytic rhetoric in the service of a more ancient and alienated prophetic fervor. Self-identified "libertarians," they bring to the gentiles an angry demand for a revolutionary change of sensibility. Both also display comically inflated egos, defensive uncertainty and an anxious ambitiousness which result in considerable posturing. Both attempt varied literary crafts, each being an ambitious novelist, a casual versifier, a sometime literary and art critic, an insistent sexual polemicist, a time-or-two dramatist, an occasional short-story writer, a quasi-political speech maker, and—most significantly—a propounder of a style of rebellion for the young against the contemporary social and psychic order. Viewed from literary standards, neither Goodman nor Mailer write well, and often they write very badly: Mailer's verbosity and arch-sensationalism; Goodman's grossly synthetic language and sloppy dissociations of sensibility. Neither has produced a single poem, story, play, study, novel or essay which could bear attention as a major or masterful work. Realizing this, some readers dismiss them out of hand, quite missing the point that it is not as primarily aesthetic phenomena but as protean and rebellious men-of-letters that they merit attention. (But Mailer and Goodman also fall into the higher piety of impersonal objects, and sometimes pretend that they are primarily "artists.") Their ambitious blatance adds some American poignance to their uncertan performances. Drawing on similar sources and angers, they suggest contrary directions— mystical yearning and programmatic utopianism—which may also be complementary. At their best, both speak out with some provocative effectiveness in opposition to the counterfeit society and its falsities of convention and viciousness of power. *As public spokesmen,* Mailer and Goodman may be as good literary rebels as we have around.

Norman Mailer's initial fame and curse, and thus his still would-be definition, was, with *The Naked and the Dead,* as a popular fictional writer, which he interprets as "major novelist." Whether or not he ever writes the "big one" he longs for in his baroque dream of being the Great

American Novelist of Rebellion, one may doubt that Mailer should primarily be considered as a fiction writer. Even leaving aside the very considerable prolix writing and trite conception and stock craft in all his novels, they should be recognized as serving a special and limited function: moral assault. The energetically negative purpose-controlled his Anti-War Novel, his disillusioned Ideological Fiction (*Barbary Shore*), his Hollywood Satire (*The Deer Park*) and his Poetic-Obscene Shocker ("outlaw from the underground" published in excerpts). All of these are well-worked rebel sub-genres. Style, character, dramatization, aesthetic re-creation—and most other such traditional qualities of the novel—take secondary place to the desire to strike blows. Neither distinctively accomplished nor original, indeed often imitative, conventional and ragged, as a novelist Mailer is most interesting as a social and moral rebel.

Similarly with Mailer's makeshifts—his search for a viable rebel role—as versifier, dramatist, newspaper columnist, public debater, journalist of the margins, theological commentator, intellectual exhibitionist in the mass media, and uncertain celebrity. He does not practice these crafts and roles in their own right—at least not with deep competence and commitment—but as that special figure, Mailer-the-Rebel. Thus shock effects, flamboyant identifications, belligerent stances for their own sake, combine with great earnestness (this is what shocks clever intellectual snobs) to produce the insistent self-advertising that dominates Mailer's "occasional" writings.[1] It could be said that Mailer's talents run shallower than his angers, or, better, that his central role of provocateur and defier, sometimes put in awkward novels, sometimes in other literary and sub-literary forms, provides his one talent. However, Mailer often spoils his taste for trouble-making by cloying it with adolescent sweets or aggrandizing popular goodies. For example, the self-reported pathos of Mailer's going to pieces because his Hollywood satire was only a moderate best seller (and even that due to the carry-over from the partly fortuitous popularity of his war novel, the air of censorship-scandal and the obvious efforts at titillating subject and treatment) provides sad comedy.[2] This rebel wants not only to be grand art but big business. He yearns, contradictorily, to be a celebrity and to be taken seriously, to run as a middle-aged *enfant terrible* and to stand as a Public Voice, to be both wildly "disruptive" and conventionally "powerful," [3] to be respected as an artist-sage while making noises and faces. Mailer's obsessive and devouring fear of failure—of not being Mr. Big in sex, in literature, in dissident political Americana, in public personality—often undercuts his authenticity as rebel. Sometimes the fundamental antithesis in Mailer, who is not always the fool he exposes himself to be, gets wryly expressed: "You can't grow up in America without thinking once in a while of becoming president. But since I'm an anarchist, I try not to think about that too much." [4] When, in the prologue to his most ambitious piece of literary defiance, he announces with usual bravado that he wishes "to destroy innocence" we may also recognize the internecine strife between Angry Despair Mailer and Horatio Alger Mailer.

Only in America, I suppose, could resentful megalomania take such ingenious candor as in the confessional asides in *Advertisements for Myself* or in the gross identifications with the moderately glamorous but rather empty political style of John Kennedy in *The Presidential Papers.* His assumptions that he should be treated with high seriousness in the press and on television, like his playing the prophet at a prize-fighter's press conference (Sonny Liston) or sexually hungering for a "lady" identified with power and "class" (Mrs. John Kennedy), neither reveal nor embarrass so much as they dramatize the pathetic displacements of the American rebel.

Rebels, of course, often tend to self-advertising, not only because the "unappreciated" ego swells in frustration but also because they serve as cynosures of resistance and rediscovery. As with Peregrinos and Whitman and Nietzsche, the self-hyperbole and exposure helps to break the isolation and hopes to provoke. Mailer's mixture of the defiant and aggrandizing in *Advertisements* produces a characteristic rebel product, a potpourri of confessions, polemics, poetry, didactic anecdotes, philosophizings and outrageous pronouncements. It may well be his most essential writing. As an American document, it also deserves attention for its display of our endless capacity for disillusionment. While Mailer can be exceedingly obtuse in his conventional ambitions and parochially tiresome

when ruminating on such subjects as literature, he angers
well against war, politics (including "official liberalism"),
New York literary racketeering, the mass media, middle-
class sexuality, and himself. With American charm, he
brings to every disenchantment the optimistic faith that
his rage will somehow realize something truer and fuller.
His cumulative angers give his limited talents larger
purpose, and so he announces he will "settle for nothing
less than making a revolution in the consciousness of our
time." [5]

Yet Mailer's effective rages take small and fractured
directions, from the neo-scholastic rhetoric of political
radicalism (apparently an incurable training), which he
properly uses in accusation against the liberal ideologues of
sociology and psychoanalysis, to the demi-poetry of street
curses ("the shits are killing us"). His arguments achieve
significant order only in odd-shaped pieces. Once again we
see that rebels more effectively deploy their efforts in
"marginal" rather than in "major" literary forms. Thus
Mailer's most perceptive story telling may be "The Man
Who Studied Yoga," [6] a loose and intentionally cater-
cornered novella not quite autonomous because of an
obscurely pontificating narrator. Though heavily discursive (on such topics as the horrifying blandness of modern-
power-for-power's-sake, psychiatric self-consciousness as
self-defeat, and the mystical-orgiastic destruction of mortal
time) it does effectively portray its representative of urban
frustration, a literary *manque* who "thinks himself a
rebel." Mailer's sympathetic mockeries of the familial
orgies of a self-despising comic-book hack and would-
be artist take form in curious meditations and bizarre
jokes, including the showing of a pornographic movie. The
story ends in a tone of sad anger at mediocre discontent.
The pornographic twist produces a burlesque of the rebel's
traditional longing to break through ordinary consciousness. The joke about a "mystic," which provides the title,
parodies the same sad limitation. The superior tone of the
narrator does not quite hide certain broader parallels to the
ingeniously candid author. Here, sardonically inverted, is
the tangible side of Mailer's defiant desire to "mate the
absurd with the apocalyptic" so to enter into "the mysteries of murder, suicide, incest, orgy, orgasm, and
Time." [7]

The disproportions between Mailer's pronouncements on apocalyptic revolution of consciousness and the petty orgies of his stories and sketches demonstrates, yet again, the conflict between his common-sense angers at a meretricious society and his overweening ambitions to make the largest possible statement. This may come from the recurring desperation of the rebel to be simultaneously within and without, to get "outside" the restrictive role and yet back "inside" power and significance. (The fusion of negation and over-affirmation in many rebels no doubt starts from a very personal need, though it hardly need take such gross forms as with Mailer wanting to be mayor of New York—without being a politician—or buddy to presidents and dictators—without accepting their ideologies—or well-loved and a celebrity—without paying the inevitable restrictive prices.) The "doubling" of response applies also to Mailer's specific gestures of defiance. For example, as a wager, Mailer made a public pronouncement that the white Southerner's racial hatred was based on his fear of sexual adequacy in comparison to the Negro.[8] About this apt, though not sufficently developed, point, Mailer became unduly anxious and defensive because the statement got little attention and approval. His concern with being fatly accepted while thinly negating makes his rebel shape uncertain. And why hasn't Mailer done essays and fictions developing his announced truths, such as "the totalitarianism of totally pleasant personality" (the vicious American geniality), or against the reigning literary bureaucracy "which uses the language of taste in the service of repression" (most American editors and critics), or more fully at the castrating "adjustment ethic" of contemporary psychiatry, or about our ornate institutional order as the "petrification of the over-extended American will"?[9] Good rebel points, all. Mailer could well have gone further and deeper in Schweikish mockery than careless anecdote ("The Patron Saint of Macdougal Alley"),[10] or done something with his passing sarcasms on power viciously disguised as liberalism and culture. His apparent answer (and most repeated excuse) is the quasi-mystical one that he is saving, protecting and furthering his "talent." But he should know better, he whose best talent comes out in his rebellious commitment, since "one loses a bit of manhood with every stale compromise to the authority of any power in which he does not believe."[11]

While Mailer would appear to have the contumaciousness to savage many of the falsities of a "vast, powerful and
hypocritical" society, he seems to want something other
than the healthy virility of the rebel. His anxiety, not just
about his talent and public role but about his manhood,
may forbid it, as we see in his obsessive and often punchy
over-indentification with "manly" posturers (from Hemingway to James Jones in literature, with Kennedy and
various other "golden goys" in public life, in the slick-
stud protagonists in such of his fictions as "The Time of
Her Time," *Deer Park* and *An American Dream*) and in
his bravura self-testing in foxholes and foxy wenches.
Mailer yearns for the compensatory fever of a "mysticism
of the flesh," for states of exalting and aggrandizing
possession which are, finally, a "lust for power." [12] The
large denunciations of power tend to reverse-worship.

His rebellious philosophizing in "The White Negro" on
the "destructive, the liberating, the creative nihilism of the
Hip" posits an ideal virility figure of revolt.[13] A rather
suspect combination of Negro with bohemian and delinquent, the Hipster supposedly contains a force to supersede all weakness, impotence and emptiness—or at least
such a façade. Mystical dispossession of the self, through
detachment ("cooling it"), violence and superlative impersonal orgasm, provides the mysterious force which will
conquer lesser powers. To insist on the pattern of the
American Negro sophisticate here seems a displaced
literalizing of a metaphor for demonic powers. With a
heavy "neo-Marxian calculus" Mailer theorizes a socially
revolutionary class, the Negro, and an active type, the
psychopath, as the vanguard for militant change. (But
more actually, such psychopathic hatreds might well turn
to ambitious conformities and authoritarian compulsions.) What once was the virility of the proletarian in
radical social mythos now becomes the explosive orgasm of
the declassed Hipster. Though Mailer tends to "revolutionary" claims, the declassing and re-coloring of the social
material exalt rebel marginality. While we might grant
Mailer's point that individual barbarism is "always to be
preferred to the collective violence of the state," not least
because of the state's inhuman technology, the imitated
Negro psychopath may not be an adequate image of the
rebel barbarian.

In his defiant glorification of the outlaw and an ethic of

extremity, Mailer sometimes tumbles around in the rhetoric of stock social types. The Marxist-psychoanalytic metaphors weight down his more individualistic vision of demonic energy. For Mailer's Hipster also personifies—if somewhat dubiously—a demand for special knowledge, "extreme awareness," and heroic potence in his "cool" withdrawal, esoteric responses (drugs, jazz, etc.), and armoured character. While Hip violence aptly comments on the blandness of modern power which specializes in depersonalized "orderly" repression and destruction, it remains gratuitous destruction. While the black imagery demonically reverses the white-willed denaturing of the flesh and emotion, Hipsterism retains an inadequate responsiveness. This apocalyptic and orgiastic mode defies the rationalist's religion of "science, factology and committee" [14] but does not suggest an independent life style. The provocativeness of Mailer's beyond-good-and-evil mythology also runs aground on the tangible material—from the New York ghettos—for the passivity, the probable spastic orgasm and the certainly incoherent withdrawal and violence of the Hipster contradict the visionary ends he is supposed to serve. Mailer's ambitious mystic rebellion against the dominant manipulators—the free re-creation of God in intense and direct individual experience—manipulatively glorifies the Hipster, who often turns out to be a manipulator in darkface. Such bows to power again cripple a style of upright defiance.

The disillusioned social radical finds a special difficulty in recognizing any vehicle for the rebellious elan he so intensely demands. The "classes" of revolutionary ideology, especially in America, make no sense, as Mailer knows from his own "progressive" experiences. The Beats, as he rightly notes (though also with some old revolutionary disdain for middle-class "fellow-travelers") refurbish bohemianism but lack vital independence. Liberalism provides variant rationalizations of bureaucracy, mass culture, and all the rest. Traditional religions—and thus also traditional heresies—hold no more (nor less) significance for Mailer than for most of his contemporaries. Therefore the rebellious quest for new intensities makes up its own mysteries of apocalyptic orgasm, Hip saints—and the mysterious "talents" which can perceive them. In the war of adaption and adoption which the sophisticated "regulators" wage upon the rebels in contemporary America, anything less could be taken over—and even this is! The disguised and bland shapes of contemporary powers (rationalized), authority ("democratized"), repression ("liberalized"), and destruction (technologically moralized), force the rebel into a peculiarly synthetic worship. It is as hard as ever for the rebel to be truly heard and seen—perhaps harder because of the amorphous order and rebellious imitations—and terribly difficult for him to find his authentic place and appropriately defiant style.

The mixture of defiance and worship often leads Mailer to peculiar gestures, such as the more or less Reichian argument that false values (repression, narcissism and boredom) produce the real diseases of cancer.[15] This magical belief in a *quid pro quo* of the spiritual and physical worlds suffers, as with so many primitive heresies, from a gross displacement away from the tangible. Sexual intensity and defiant passion might have some more direct benefits than dissolving malignant tumors. Similarly with Mailer's displaced magical role as kingmaker—his suggestions that he may have significantly helped elect Kennedy president (by a long-winded article in a popular magazine[16]) or failed to help Floyd Patterson win the heavyweight championship (by not wishing hard enough[17])—which have nothing to do with his more genuine commitment to tyrannicide. Magical gestures, of course, even to longing for a traditional heaven-and-hell to intensify moral choice—when all the more intelligent Christians have pretty well given it up—provide "leaps" out of his existential despair.[18] Mailer more coherently pursues the demonic religiousness of the rebel, as in such ruminative fragments as "Truth and Being; Nothing and Time" and "Advertisement for Myself on the Way Out." In the latter, he makes mystical claims for the demonic; his "satanic" coloration and "search for the devil" in fractured time are to lead to an expanded, orgiastic, immortalizing present intensity of feeling and power. The down-going mysteries of the flesh and the illicit (but antique values sometimes threaten to be the most illicit these days) promise the enlargement of consciousness, the post-primitive way of returning to the mysterious sources of existence.

Yet in his fictions the effect comes out less demonic and

primordial than ruminative and exacerbated. For example, he wants "the extreme, the obscene and the unsayable," [19] in religious longing, but the demonstration—in one of his better though somewhat posturing fictions, "The Time of Her Time"—provides an old mocking theme with modern explicitness: the willful Don Juanism of a "messiah of the one-night stand" and an ornate commentary on sexual power-plays.[20] Or he asserts strange realms of time and feeling but actually presents an old Gothic and upper-bohemian cosmogony of philosophical pimps and poetic prostitutes and satanic literary masqueraders ("Prologue to a Long Novel"). Or, in *An American Dream,* the inconclusive melodrama of orgasm and murder aims to show that an existential "God is not love but courage." [21] But, for his professor-celebrity-playboy, moon magic, Reichian orgasm with a nightclub singer, cancer as the product of a disintegrated soul, the hysterical nausea of bedrock existence, and a sloppily "perfect crime," only produce the pyrrhic mysteries and braveries of drunkenly walking a balcony railing and winning a pile at a dice table. Such demonic religiousness looks suspiciously like indulgent literary bedeviling.

As in most mystical patterns, Mailer's purging or destruction of the ordinary self and consciousness—by excremental insults, violence, orgy, demonism, frenzy and bravado—rests on the salvational teleology that the above or the below, the cosmos or the unconscious, will salvage all. Under the terrorist, Rousseau; above the immoralist, trancendental mysteries. Short of the mystery itself, all should be "creative rage." At the individual level, apparently, that means "acting out"; at the literary level it means, from the evidence, ornately frenzied art. Thus, in our amorphous rationalized society, the rebel asserts himself as a religiously sanctioned exemption from organized blandness and technological decorum.

Some of Mailer's difficulties in declaring that identity stand out if one holds up *The Presidential Papers*—a much weaker miscellany than *Advertisements*—against his declarations. Dismissing the large part which is self-sentimental gesturing politics—Mailer claims to be a "court wit" when he is an unemployed buffoon—we can see the faltering of his existential engagement. Committed to fighting our psychic totalitarianism of "deadening reality by smothering it with lies" and of speaking out in the "vast guerrilla war going on for the mind of man," [22] he, however, cannot find a subject that at all fits these purposes. He justifies "existential" thought (in this context that means "extreme," in much the sense Blake meant "excess") : "The logic in searching for extreme situations, in searching for one's authenticity, is that one burns out the filament of old dull habit and turns the conscious mind back upon its natural subservience to the instinct." [23] But Mailer finds no genuine extreme situations, within or without, which could be the locus for heroic elan, enlarged consciousness and defiant intensity. His "face to face confrontations" mirror the silly, as when Mailer attempts to play the prophet at a press conference, commits petty acts of violence, elaborates fantasies about demi-monde "living it up" (as in *An American Dream*), or writes coyly belligerent speculations such as "Metaphysics of the Belly" in which he argues for analyzing excrement to determine the spiritual values of the producers, and holds that manly men will eat "bulls' balls." [24] In this unadmitted burlesque of American "he-man" gestures, and also in his demonic-fecal prayers ("Truth and Being; Nothing and Time") he becomes a literalist of the excremental vision and a mannerist of the rebel's defiant announcement of the news from down under, posturing a mysticism.

Rather better are a few fragmented attempts to pose an existential ethic. Thus Mailer attacks modern war (and our permanent war structured economy, politics and public psyche) by rejecting "*inhuman* violence." [25] Unlike the ideal faith in universal love of the Ghandian pacifist (or the grotesquely hygenic-abstract rationalist faith of the war-game theorists) this remains individual-centered—not non-violence but non-impersonal violence—which would not deny complex possibilities of love and hate and the human freedom to contain them within a responsive being. Similar is Mailer's passing gesture about judicial murder. Albert Camus, in his long tract against "capital punishment," argued that proponents of the death penalty should favor public executions by their own logic of deterrence. Awareness of the individual death agony, which modern societies attempt to cover up, would make society really confront the issue. Mailer, characteristically, "goes one better" than the liberal moralist by demanding that death sentences be personal hand to hand combat, by which the audience would experience some sense of dramatic tragedy, the winner would personally carry the feel of the other man's death in his psyche, and American society would have to honestly confront its covert sadism.[26] It is a very American noble savagery.

But apparently Mailer has become increasingly desperate in the paradoxical attempt to enlarge consciousness so as to return to primordial human values. Often in the *Papers*, the "far out" turns to the old "in," and revolt comes close to anti-revolt. Thus his commitment to sexual release, intensity and orgasm are twisted to a new found fervency against birth control, masturbation and, even, in favor of chastity![27] Revolution and social defiance come out as earnest liberal disagreement with American "conservatism" (which, of course, is no such thing because of its commitment to social resentments, any profitable technological "progress" and a totalitarian war process)[28] and as pious longings for some sort of renewed political heroism. The existential quest for a living god of immanence produces petty bravado, dabbling in minor magics, even yearnings for "a life after death"[29] to give morality more force. Taking himself too seriously in minor scrapes, leaping out of existentialism into mystifications, swinging wildly (in a few minutes in an interview he first pronounces for sophisticated "complexity," then denounces it in favor of simple responsiveness; he rages against false roles, then advises one to counterfeit so that he can "bore from within" in the mass media;[30] etc.), Mailer seems unable to break through the "mediocritization of psyches" and the "limbo" of meaningless existence which he wants to defy. Certainly Mailer is committed to a rebel faith— "life seems to come out of the meeting of opposites"[31]— that he only fumblingly practices. Perhaps too large a claim—political, aesthetic and cosmic—allows no room for an ecstatic outlaw vision. While we may still intermittently see a rebel, despite Mailer's inverted power worship and adolescent ambitions and anxious skittishness, the freedom and intensity and confrontations he longs for increasingly exist only in realms of unachieved otherness: the rebel as lost soul.

A partial alternative, though lacking Mailer's woozy

charm, pathos and promise of excitement (which makes
him "everybody's rebel"), is the programmatic moralizing
of Paul Goodman. Like many literary rebels, Goodman is
one of those curious anomalies—a significant writer who
cannot write well. Though much preoccupied with his role
as a "cultivated artist" (his self-description), he weirdly
mangles what, with usual quaintness, he calls "our dear
English tongue." His early stories, *The Facts of Life*,[32]
provided some rather stilted reportage of literary-class
Jewish life and some truncated sententious parables. The
mixture of garbled colloquialisms, literary archaicisms and
jargonish abstractions of his later writings may be a
rebellious attempt to find a fuller style, but often result in
the almost uniquely clichéd and emotionally fractured
stories in *Our Visit to Niagara*.[33] The stock characters also
do not engage each other in the five novels collected in
The Empire City,[34] where the authorial pontifications
about abstract metaphors (the more obvious choices from
Marx, Freud, Reich, James, etc.) also appear in tone-
deaf slang and whimsical disjointed musings. The arty
additions of allegorical bits of sociology, muddled "GI"
and "shaggy dog" jokes, private allusions and pedantic
burlesque truly achieve "an almanac of alienation." The
solipsism reminds us of the perils of literary rebellion,
especially in a time when there is little community of rich
speech, and the writer with no intuitive sense of language
and drama can assert arbitrariness as individual innovation. Goodman does better in his "novel" *Making Do*
since he sometimes imitates the language of his intermittent subject matter—the underground life of an intelligent
bisexual schizophrenic "drop-out" from our meretricious
social forms and a miscellany of related underground
adolescents. The desire to present this rather shapeless
underground does allow some tangible description, dialogue and schematic analysis of the actual. But synthetic
writing and stance frequently take over, especially the
author's often coy and ponderous descriptions of an aging
homosexual social philosopher—"the man," "our tired
friend"—who is full of self-pity and dubiously relevant
editorials and idiosyncrasies which are presented earnestly
but unthinkingly in his paradoxical effort to be a pater-
nalistic rebel. Thus a grossly sentimental scene about his
dog's death, an unexamined bias against heterosexuality,

tired traveling salesman type details on a Goodman-like sociological lecturer, and similar flat irrelevances drastically misfocus the narrative. (*This* material could be the subject of a burlesque fiction itself, in the hands of a witty writer, and he could also use unchanged Goodman's earnestly dissociated chapter titles, such as "banning the cars from New York," "shit," and "Plato's ladder." The crux might be that somebody gives the good man a job as super-chief social worker to get him off the literary streets.) The theme of *Making Do* seems to be pathetic boasting about how the author—so "generous and citizenly and over-worked" [35]—makes do in a bad society. The better subordinate theme condemns the society for its lack of place for those who attempt to "contract out" of a competitive and meretricious order. Goodman aptly makes his points about the independent young lacking any viable alternatives—meaningful work, community and a warm style of dissent and response—and sympathetically shows that as a result they become "terrible fuckups." [36] However, his analysis is also often grossly out of balance because of his impatiently asserted ideological commitments. Thus he somewhat spitefully attacks Mailer-style defiance—wisdom for rebellious youth is to learn that there "finally is little difference between a hipster and a cop." [37] Or he drowns the human in political polemic: "It takes a lot of bad education, a venal economy, and a really insane foreign policy to achieve that hoodlum strut, that junkie slouch, that hipster cool." [38] There is truth in both points, but neither Norman Mailer nor the State Department provide an adequate dramatic or intellectual focus for dealing with his sometimes tangible adolescents. No matter how rebellious, ideology does not portray authentic life.

The alienation from most literary merit as well as incisive human context marks most of the poetry collected in *The Lordly Hudson*. From the title on, the scenes and forms are quaintly synthetic and this Goodman cannot, in contrast to some of his contemporaries, wittily play with because he lacks "natural" talent: a dead ear ("poetical" often), lack of sensory responses, taste for the flat generality, earnest sentimentality, and no redeeming concreteness. Only a few idiosyncrasies manage to find their own shape: the middle-aged bitterness around a sentimental

image ("Birthday Cake"), the gross and therefore sometimes effective flatness about self-importance (several of
the "Sentences for Mathew Ready"), and the reversal of
poetic pretension in an apostrophe to his penis ("Dis-
honored Sex").[39] The love poems, the narratives of things
never seen, and the prayers to something or other may
have some private therapeutic significance. The fantastic
self-conceit—the major subject of his verse—makes Goodman deserve the insult he unironically asks for: finally my
countrymen/ will make of me a statue in the park." [40]
Often as a writer (as well as for this characteristically
garbled syntax) he deserves to be stuck alive into a
concrete pedestal.

Yet his very weirdness makes Goodman a suggestive
voice, despite the absurd literary pretensions. As he rightly
notes of himself, his "words and behavior [sometimes
have] a random freedom that unsettles people" in a
provocative way.[41] Social "edification" (his word) from
the fanciful perspective of a dissociated utopian rough-
jack of letters can be, like a drunk giving a demonstration
of first-aid, both unintentionally comic and didactically
salutary. In endless angry moral ruminations, from the
anarchist theorizing in rather academic terms of *Art and
Social Nature* [42] through the cranky-perceptive letters to
editors and officials collected in *The Society I Live In Is
Mine* [43] (with righteous footnotes added), Goodman
hectors all ways of the villainous "Organized System." In
the main, the monster is damned for being too unimagi-
natively organized and too much of a system, i.e., not a
confrontable and responsive human entity.

For an example of Dr. Goodman's quaint mixture of
almost pedantic radical earnestness and of angrily whimsical eccentricity, we might note several of the motifs of *The
Community of Scholars*. This academic critique charges
after the "phony" ideology and bureaucratization of
American higher education, and effectively cuts down a
good many academic spokesmen. In an earlier (and
excellent) piece on the modern academic man and his
"freedom," Goodman held to view the university schizophrenia which so often submerges the rebellious intellectual in the organizational bureaucrat.[44] In his longer study,
he elaborates the theme in a programmatic assault on the
replacement of intellectual communion, especially of

students and teachers, by "a community of administrators and scholars with administrative mentalities, company men and time-servers." [45] Outside the usual institutional loyalties and ambitions, he can be devastatingly apt on the pseudo-democracy of higher education with its administered concensus and ideologies which encourage mediocre teaching and intellectual vapidity. He raises the obvious, but usually ignored, drastic criticisms of officials, hierarchies, grades, credits, academic gamesmanship, and other authoritarian formalizations, which tend to devalue content, skill and responsiveness.[46] Conclusion: do away with them: no more ornate programs, ranks, big buildings, staffs, credits, grades, administrators and psuedo-intellectuals. An admirable extremity!

But Goodman is opposed to destructive criticism; as he announces elsewhere, "negative criticism insults and disheartens." [47] So he offers a "constructive" program — "secession." The pacifistic academic civil war can be waged by dedicated teachers and their protégés going away from the organized schools (but staying close enough to use the libraries) to form new, unadministered, "communities of scholars." Rebellious in its extreme refusal but oddly archaic in actual form, Goodman's proposal up-dates romantic notions of the Medieval university. Such a movement might have a refreshing openness to it, and could serve as an impetus to several small liberal arts colleges, though of course it would make only the most peripheral marks on the vast technician factories, research ranches, bureaucratic apprenticeship programs, cultural rest homes, genteel spectacles, class institutes — and occasional teaching and thought — which comprise the higher learning in America.

For those who would with equal earnestness reply to this unwitty Veblen that "No doubt much of this should be changed, but that really means a social revolution," his probable answer would be, "Of course. Let's get communally started." A utopian revolutionary demand thus gets lightly disguised as a practical pedagogical proposal. Such is Goodman's strategy. Actually, a report on a real educational situation might be rather more to the point, and have less over-insistent mannerisms of practicality in his mish-mash presentation, but Goodman aims at less revolutionary practice and utopian thought than rebellious irritant in the thickly hypocritical rhetoric of current higher education.

Another deceptively simple rebel motif appears in *The Community of Scholars*. Goodman really seeks to bring into community the alienated intellectuals, and rightly polemicizes against the organizers and imitations who are much the cause of the alienation. His major twist to his arguments on almost everything—and he argues about almost everything—is an individualistic anti-individualism. Ideas of community, whether about poetry or about stores, provide his persistent answer—partly a reaction against his own fractured consciousness, partly the Jewish sense of the community as the deepest entity, partly the legacy of the radical social ideologies' attacks on atomization by industrialist-capitalist-modernist forces. His educational example comes in arguing that "veteran" masters of professions should be teachers of communities of followers. (He must strangely pretend that philosophical, artistic and religious passions constitute recognizable professions in our society.) And he adds: "it is importantly because they are not on the faculty that artists and writers are so individualistic and fragmented as to be almost treasonable in co-operation with *l'infame*." [48] For the moment, he has amusingly forgotten that academic faculties belong to the infamous Organized System. (A present plethora of writer-artist academics also does not substantiate his point.) And then that curious equation of the "individualistic" and "treasonable."

To counter the Organized System, Goodman demands his smaller organized systems, euphemistically known as communities, run by egotistical master "professionals" instead of bland administrators. Rather than debate which system, in practice, would be nastier to individual freedom—one could sometimes prefer the large, educationally irrelevant, and bumbling educationists since their confusions, willy-nilly, allow some pedagogical and personal freedom—we should grant that Goodman yearns for something else. Once again, a literary rebel dreams of a religious caste of dedicated ones with independent identity and communal place and power. The historical-minded sceptic will note that Goodman never explores the tragic qualities of social change—not only the often disproportionate human price, but the transformation of utopias into anti-utopias. Even the large and shifty Organized System allows certain freedoms almost never permitted in small, and probably inherently self-tightening, communities. His anti-individualistic and anti-rebellious side comes out, for just one example, when Goodman talks about actual rather than ideal academies. He recommends "taking stupid rules whence they come, refraining anger." More specifically, he urges biting on a pipe to keep quiet. His natural obstreperousness, however, also leads him to admitting that this is "craven advice," and "spirit-breaking and probably even unhealthy." [49] Ruins a lot of pipes, too.

But the willingness, in his unbuttoned ruminations, to expose all sorts of dangling and striking and far-fetched notions should not be lightly dismissed. Here the rebel carries out a major "social utility"—to use Goodman's favorite standard—by bringing to view eccentric insights and perplexities which are repressed by more conventional or more rigorous minds. We can see these qualities in varied areas in *Utopian Essays and Practical Proposals*. In introducing them, he defends the social-moral function of the "Man of Letters"—he means the literary rebel—as defier of acquiescence, especially in America, where he should confront our compulsiveness, conformity, meaningless work, and standardized and polite failures to be imaginative. In "Utopian Thinking" he warns of the powerful forces of anxiety that rush to fill every opening in rigidly set thought and response. The purpose of "utopian" thinking—or as he more aptly called it in earlier essays, "millenarian" speech [50]—is to counter this anxiety by raising "rebellious hopes." [51] And he proceeds to suggest breaking stock responses and fears and passivity by direct actions (no pipe biting here). Direct action for community, including the release of anger which allows true affection, provides Goodman's major psycho-therapy for the victims of the Organized System.

One of the forces victimizing us all is technological authoritarianism, the subject of " 'Applied Science' and Superstition." Why isn't our technology subordinated to choices which "foster the quality of life"? [52] And why don't more people rebel against the impositions of modern technology when they violate taste, feeling, comfort and sense? Actually, the deepest explanation cannot be found in the scientistic superstitions Goodman dissects but in a deeper religious awe for technology which Goodman himself demonstrates, elsewhere, when he writes: "Certainly the most thrilling and romantic happening of these years is the adventure in space. . . . This adventure makes life worth the trouble again." [53] That "grand" displacement of human concern to rockets (our Egyptian monuments) and of human dreams to the impersonal realms of lunar pathology, shows Goodman worshipping in a way which can hardly be modified by his practical proposals.

In "Pornography and the Sexual Revolution," Goodman defends the main libertarian principle of modern times. "When excellent human power [such as sexuality] is inhibited and condemned, it will reappear ugly and dangerous." [54] While his discussion of censorship is not well-informed,[55] and Goodman ignores the manifold complexities of eroticism, his demand for more direct pornography makes rebellious sense in the context of American advertising and entertainment. Following the usual "absolutist" argument against all censorship, he holds that even bad pornography raises less danger than repression. He summarizes an analogous argument for pacifism, defending the "natural violence that diminishes war, e.g. the explosion of passion, the fist fight that clears the air. . . . War feeds on the inhibition of moral aggression." [56] While a nice restatement of William James' classic demand for a moral substitute for war, Goodman's usual psychologizing may partly distort the issue. For Goodman's Rousseauist Freudianism poses a terribly simple psychic economy in which "unblocking" meets most demands. Modern warfare in the West, after all, depends less on direct hostile feelings than on their displacement into the communal longings and technological piety which Goodman himself displays. Similarly, the low-level pornography of American advertising and entertainment provide special forms of communal gratification, such as ritualistic fetishism and commodity consubstantiality, which would not be confronted by more direct pornography. But these limitations of Goodman's utopian logic would not appear so strongly if it were taken as a form of defiance rather than as a program. Also, Goodman might, if pressed, grant that the release of anger and eroticism should not be reduced to utilitarian social amelioration since these contain ultimate meaning for self and awareness. In "Some Remarks on the War Spirit," he again simply reduces the "sexual revolution" to answering the "war spirit." However, if we ignore his analytic and polemical moral claims, it provides a touching demand for the human dimension. "An occasional fist fight, a better orgasm, a job of useful work, friendly games, initiating enterprises, deciding real issues in manageable meetings, and being moved by things that are beautiful, curious or wonderful—these diminish the spirit of war because they attach people to life." [57]

Goodman may be at his best when discussing paradigmatic situations, as in "Seating Arrangements; An Elementary Lecture on Functional Planning," where he visualizes metapsychological qualities to various physical ways of arranging people. Like Fourier's discussion of work, or Thoreau's meditations on housing, the fusion of concrete imagery and ideal meaning achieves a lyrical mode of independent contemplation rather than a practical program for perverse reality. This prime quality appears in what may be Goodman's best book (coauthored with Percival Goodman), *Communitas*, "Means of Livelihood and Ways of Life." [58] Much of this discussion of community planning (in the largest senses) suggestively combines the aesthetic and the speculative with the social image. The merits of *Communitas* do not reside in the historical plans discussed (often dubious in ignoring such things as the intellectual fatuousness and chauvinistic role of the *kibbutz*, in blandly assuming that New York City could be anything other than a vast anti-community, etc.). Rather, the virtues may be found in the defiant metaphors: the satiric plan of American society as one superdepartment store, or the rebellious ideal plan of a subsistence society (alongside the "affluent" one) where a universal hoboism of part-time work provides the exchange values. Though sometimes merely quaint, the Goodmans' mixture of physical concreteness and philosophical fancy provides a liberating form of literature. (One of Goodman's major problems—and an old one for rebels—is in his usual inability to find suitable literary form; novel, verse, fable, literary criticism and discursive essay are essentially antithetical to his fractured and self-indulgent cast of mind.) And what better defiance of our dull society and mechanical social thought than a wild rationality which combines eccentric insight, communal literalness and other-worldly order?

How disappointing when we turn, then, to Goodman's discussions of literary rebels only to find him bogged in an egotistical lack of the concrete. In "Advance-Guard Writing in America: 1900–1950," for instance, he apparently argues that the rebellious artist provides an underground identity and defies the society by asserting "the marginal as the central and to prove its justification, thereby demolishing the norm." [59] Just what literature of bohemian life mocks conventional living is rather difficult to determine since Goodman's only reference to his specified subject consists of a wisecrack at Hemingway. [60] The obtuse prose does not quite hide the blatant vanity of generalizing without being held to account. "Good Interim Writing" also avoids any specific reference, which makes it easy to speciously deny any ironic defiance in contemporary literature. "Underground Writing, 1960" ignorantly assumes that there has not been much such writing in the past. Goodman does appropriately attack the Mailer style of defiance by noting that "hipster" literature is not really "rebellious" because of "spite, conceit, fantasies of power." [61] His uncomprehending sarcasms about better writers, such as Nathanael West, or (elsewhere) his excessive praise of a maudlin shouter such as Kenneth Patchen [62] suggests his basic incapacity for discussing literary rebels. In *Growing Up Absurd*, Goodman's passing comments on Beat literature show more relevance, perhaps less because of literary perception than because of personal acquaintance from which he realizes the coterie role and fatalistic passivity and adolescent murkiness found in many Beats. This leads them to an indifferent substitution of therapy for art and, as Goodman notes, to works "likely to be personal or parochial." But though much Beat work is "ignorant and thin," Goodman holds, for homiletic reasons, that the Beats emphasize "live response" and make a worthy, if confused, withdrawal from the Organized System into anarchic free sub-communities. He quaintly recommends Balinese dancing and his eccentric version of Taoist theology for their edification. [63] As a self-elected master of protest, he concludes by praising any "rebellious group" in these desperate times, for he is "heartened by the crazy young allies" against a dubious social order. But too often, Goodman's remarks on literary rebels reveal spite, conceit and fantasies of self-importance.

Thus Goodman's literary excursions into criticism, as well as fiction and poetry, undermine his communitarian radicalism, though they provide him with an identity as a rebellious Man of Letters. As we can see in *The Structure of Literature*—a neo-Aristotelian academic exercise on standard works—Goodman has a general emotional deadness and absence of existential intellectual engagement in literary matters. Outside of his social preoccupations, his literary comments tend to loose pedantry and truistic interpretations unless, as in *Kafka's Prayer*, he can find the scared child watching his stern father on top of his mother or, in "Some Problems of Interpretation," speculate on Beethoven's masturbating.[64] Quite possibly, these could be points of understanding, but they seem to serve Goodman simply as mock-serious gestures to emphasize the distinctiveness of his learned-*outré* belligerency.

A strange, and often comical, war goes on in most of Goodman's work between defiant gestures and portentous moralizings. In *Growing Up Absurd*—awkwardly done ruminations on varied social problems, loosely hooked to the theme that "lads" in our society need "manly" work, "Honor" and "Community"—he alternates as wild rebel and cornball sage. In the latter role, he reverses his pertinent assaults on public rhetoricians ("phony" and "hypocritical" on "youth problems") to quote George Washington's patriotic placebo that everyone in these States is "free and happy." Goodman tells us that such sentiment from the good old days brings tears of joy to his eyes.[65] Similarly, his Boy Scoutish rhetoric that the young need "knightly leaders" and a "flag to salute"[66] displays the pathetically shoddy public style, instead of searching for a genuine leadership and patriotism (which would have to be communal and personal instead of archaic and nationalistic). His trite, and often laughably garbled, discussion of the "rat race" of current organizational life reveals the same verbal and intellectual deadness.[67] Though his major moral club is a demand for more significant work—in proper contrast to our dominant emphasis on status, "role-playing," covert power aggrandizement and other forms of self-alienation—he says very little about actual work. At the theoretical level, he finds the Protestant "work ethic" a "saving grace," thus illustrating his drastic incomprehension of its willful harshness and of the tortuous revolt from the Protestant ethos in current pseudo-work patterns.[68] Moralistic triteness reaches its apogee in a bold type-face catalogue of exhortations to complete the good work of the past years in URBANISM, LIBERALISM, FREEDOM OF SPEECH, FRATERNITY, ENLIGHTENMENT, HONESTY, etc. Goodman pretty much ignores that some of the tired old moral rhetoric may itself have helped to destroy, or missed the cruxes of, meaningful work, a viable role for the young, a pertinent culture, and all the other too obviously "good" things he favors. After all, the villanious Organized System grew partly out of those moral demands—and their limitations. Thus the good society which Goodman sometimes pregnantly projects merely becomes weary programmatic moralizing which does not help bring to birth a new truth and life style. As a scornfully intelligent man, Goodman does rather better in mocking the fraudulence of official claims. He does better yet in his asides on a more indigenous subject, a place for minority communities and eccentric and rebellious individuals who are getting eliminated in our majoritarian society and culture.[69] On this subject, Goodman points deeper than most commentators because of his extremity; thus he recognizes that there is little economic place for the dissident since "the chief reason for [American] economic activity is to keep the economic machine in operation"—the system now serves its own continuance rather more than any genuine meanings or satisfactions. Goodman even illustrates, with himself, his point, alternating between no-place and a spurious place in that mechanism, having leaped out of eccentric "neglect" to play the Big Moralist's game, though he does snap at the public rhetoric he feeds on. For Goodman sometimes subordinates his genuine rebelliousness—his belief in "Drawing the Line," resisting our "relentless" organizations and maintaining the "free spirit"—to neo-official style concerns. His theme of providing a viable way to grow into liveliness and integrity might be better answered in the ancient traditions of individualistic rebels than in "practical" programs for the inevitably pseudo-communities of the Organized System. Perhaps because of his uncertain New York communal background, his anxious ambitiousness, and his unlimited literary and social claims, Goodman fails to achieve more than a fitful suggestiveness, though such utopian thought as his may remain a necessary vehicle for any full and defiant awareness.

The contemporary literary rebel desperately needs a more incisive style and commitment. In emphasising some of the large weaknesses of Mailer and Goodman, I am not denying that both *are* rebels, and both are sometimes nicely provocative—more than some rather neater sensibilities and polished writers. Since their main talents seem to be as rebels (despite some claims they make to the contrary) they deserve criticism as rebels. Mailer's choice of destructive mystagoguery and Goodman's of programmatic moralizing represent central rebel weaknesses, not to be glossed over in men who take self-proclaimed public roles as spokesmen for "our generation" (Mailer) and to "young people" (Goodman). In rebels we may also get the amorphous and aggrandizing and arbitrary shapes we deserve. Goodman is right: most of us lack "love, style, excitement"—and the true anger which purifies them. Perhaps both these angry men often do so badly, muddying so much fine passion (Mailer) and thoughtfulness (Goodman), because of the painful perplexity of defining and being the rebel in contemporary America. If that is so, it provides yet another harsh indictment of our time and place.

13   CONCLUSION:
THE LIMITS OF THE REBEL

DOSTOEVSKY SUMMARIZES a persistent and paradoxical problem of the modern intellectual rebel when he has Ivan Karamazov reply to his saintly brother, "Rebellion? I'm sorry to hear you say that. . . . One can't go on living in a state of rebellion, and I want to live." While one might be tempted to retort that there is no unrebellious life worth living, still, the terrible weakness of men must be granted; including that of most rebels who reveal a strong desire to cut-off or go beyond rebellion. I have argued that rebellion is its own justification and, since man is never free enough, the social order never fair enough, and the cosmos never meaningful enough, the rebel remains permanently desirable and necessary. Yet rebellion also remains dangerous. In Dostoevsky's extreme dramatizations, the logic of the rebel leads him to desperate acts of withdrawal or destruction which destroy the living self. More practically, to deny those conditions and powers which would deny fully human life can become such a limiting obsession that much of responsive life gets denied. Yet, in literary fact, not even a Dostoevsky really shows that the most possessed rebels, as rebels, limit life and destroy human meaning more than many of the unrebellious. We can further qualify Dostoevsky's stance by noting that most of his arguments "cut both ways" in metapsychological regress, and so virtue, order, authority and God can also provide a way to the destruction of the fully living self. Dostoevsky really holds that all logic is finally destructive of the illogical richness of life. Thus the logic of rebellion may be destructive, but is it really more limiting than many another commitment?

My examples should certainly suggest that rebel oppositions cannot be confined within a narrow logic and rigid
goals. Then, too, rebel failures seem quite obvious and
self-limiting, making authentic rebellion less duplicitous
and fraudulent than other modes. Since no refusal or
change can be adequate to the spirit of revolt, the rebel's
limitations certainly are evident. He simply and permanently cannot acquiesce in the order, power and success
that other men accept. While this appears to be a rejection
of much of life, it can also be equally seen as a demand for
more life. To the degree that rebellion won't do for a full
life, neither will the refusal of rebellion provide a full life.
A cause for despair can also be a cause for affirmation. One
defies the destructiveness of rebellion by the wisdom of
still more rebellion.

If Dostoevsky's Ivan could not live in rebellion, it must
have been because he would not accept the limits of
rebellion, and affirm further rebellion. Dostoevsky's men
in revolt, of course, partly suffer from the desperation of
not finding adequate way and place because of the
monstrously oppressive social and psychological order they
live in, which drives them away from rebellious living into
madly destructive revolution or nihilistic mysticism. That
lack of place seems to be one of the major and recurrent
senses of rebel limitation which produces the alienated
sickness that ends by denying all rebellion. If there is not
a fundamental, and fundamentally rebellious, place for the
rebel, he indeed may deny the life that he is denied. With
this despair, and with his particular form of the obsessive
Dostoevskian self-punishment, Ivan mistook rebellion for
the totality of meaning in life (or lack of meaning) and
wished to renounce his truth. Put another way, Ivan makes
the nihilistic rebel's point that much of life *is* unlivable,
but refuses to make the rebel commitment that the way to
bear with it is to deny and defy the unlivable ordering of
life. Ivan does not, and cannot bear, to lead the life his
awareness has carried him to: everything may be permitted
but he permits himself almost nothing. (Or put it this
way: inevitably one cannot permit himself everything; that
is the failure to choose and to be—quite the opposite of
rebellious choosing and being against! So all Ivan permits
himself is not to choose against, after he has revolted, and
so does not permit himself further rebellion or life.) For

rebels, too, must have faith—faith in rebellion. To remain rebels, and live the life, they must really believe in denial and defiance, in the ultimate drama of opposition, in the role and significance of the rebel.

Most of the rebels discussed sometimes exemplify the renunciation of rebellion in their inflation of individuality into an eccentric phantasmagoria, or in their mutilation of rebellion into egotistical posturing and power, or in their deflation of living into merely grim despair. We may also grant commonplace cynicism about rebelliousness its truths: "life is hard enough without making it harder"; "live and let live"; "get your kicks and forget the pricks"; "trouble everybody's got enough of"; and "what's it get you in the end? what's it get anybody?" In other words, rebellion is bound to fail and trouble is trouble—as what isn't? But refusing the arbitrary patterns imposed on life also constitutes meaningful and pleasurable living. Or, to randomly cite three rebels: "Life is a matter of resistance"; "Anything that *triumphs*, perishes"; and "The rebel is nearer to God than the saint."

No human saint manages to love all, no rebel to resist all in the endless corruptibility of human concerns. But the vocation of each is clear. (Though the two may cross, the rebel has an advantage over the saint: few triumphant institutions are founded in the name of the rebel.) The inadequacy and falsity of any and every ordering does not mean that there won't be, as there must, some order. But the unrebellious will take care of that. Not everyone should be the custodian of moderation, decency, reasonableness and ameliorative faiths, or the authorities and lies they end up serving. The solid citizens will build their inevitable boxes. Many always busy themselves at such ordering, which should not be mistaken for the City of Man, much less the City of God. Human communities seem necessary, as barbarians demonstrate, though much of modern life manages to keep going by "social relations" and quite an array of manipulative techniques in place of human communion. The positive role of the rebel may deserve more emphasis: individual resistance to dubious institutions—that is, all institutions—cries out for the good society. Denial and defiance posit the possibility of something different, and it takes something like the rebellious extremities to educate even the few who can achieve another style and consciousness. Those who make no demands are the real nihilists of human freedom. The rebel can both be defined and tested by his refusal to accept a static view of truth, any successful society as the Good Society, any institution or style at its own claims, any established circumstances as appropriate to human possibilities.

Some perplexed limits of recent rebels partly derive from the fraudulent groupings they pit themselves against: pseudo-communities in which communion is replaced by ideologies of comfort and manipulation, and where, consequently, individual separateness turns into despairing isolation and intense opposition becomes exasperated flamboyance. But that is less condemnation of the rebel than of the world he tries to resist. The quality of its rebellions are also tests of a civilization and a culture. The rebel contributes most to community, even in its absence or counterfeit, by remaining a rebel against what parochially and viciously passes for the community of men, even if he be an inadequate rebel.

Opting out, the black mock, nihilistic utopianism and outrageous individuality also help create a fully human ordering. The presumptiousness of those who know that a moderate and expedient "good" leads to the good, when very often it does just the opposite, is not for the rebellious temper. In effect, I think the rebel says: If I tear down what others build up, we just might between us get a bearable shape and color of things, whether it be an idea, a style of art, an institution, a society, or a vision of the cosmos. However, if the rebel worries too much about the hopeful "up" rather than the defiant "down," he does not persist in his true vocation, and all may be the poorer for it.

The legitimacy of the rebel's negation, even unto perversity, should not be confused with the more optimistic and restricted dialectics of rational humanism. The "liberal tradition," as much by temperament as on principle, allows dissent (when it is "constructive"), and divergence (when it accepts the official "consensus") and opposition (when it is moderate, decorous and "reasonable"), but most essentially only if these plausibly contribute to a benign, enlightened and progressive view. So far as I can define them, most rebels do not believe in such progress, and such restrictions; instead, they see denials, defiances and extreme oppositions as fundamental to the truths of human existence, without regard to other ends. This "otherness" of the rebel values may be viewed as religious. But, then, religious thought and response must be distinguished from religious institutions and acceptance — from salvation and non-existential faiths — for the spiritual otherness of the rebel is to be found in other ways of doing and perceiving and living. And rebels find the sacred only in the strangest atheistic places. Rebel thought may, perhaps, be aptly perceived in religious perspectives because the rebel foolishly and bravely insists on confronting the very basis of existence, nothingness or God, the most extreme possibilities. At bottom — in several senses — the rebel is not likely to restrict himself to being a very "liberal" fellow. He is equally not a "conservative" about things moral, social and aesthetic because his greatest exasperation is at the inevitable self-satisfied and defensive nature of any social and cultural order. Both "liberal" and "conservative" tempers would deny the rebel's insistence on a drastically different consciousness and life. For the usual responses suffer — even at their rare best — from attempts to meet particular rebel criticisms without meeting the main rebel demand: that there be at all levels a place for the rebellious and their rebellions. Denial and defiance must be a central and continuing part of life everywhere. The rebel, I am arguing, is a thing himself, neither a junior version of revolution, since revolution usurps and rejects him, nor an exacerbated liberal or conservative. The rebel is not part of the two-headed axe so many use to hew a trail through morals, history, art, social discontents, etc. This third party to all pairings does not primarily ask for tolerance or for a position in the hierarchy — for a liberal considerateness for the ill-liberal or for a conservative patronage of the outrageous — but for extreme and oppositional awareness and confrontations. The rebel dramatizes dissatisfaction at its own ultimate truth.

Nice people, that is, those who accommodatingly lack either a positive or negative faith, do not so much have a "practical" dispute with the rebellious about politics, institutions, and all the rest, as a deeper antagonism which they have difficulty in recognizing. What could be more infuriating to nice people, they who do not even believe in their own rebellious wrath and despair about the world, than those horrible rebels who believe that nothing at all (and especially not the "nice"!) is good enough? While I have mostly avoided psychological portraiture of the rebel, I will grant that they range only from difficult to impossible—in terms of niceness. Pick your order of description: lean and hungry types; self-consuming (even to being literally "consumptive") complainers; manic-depressives and anal-explosives; capriciously indulged children who never quite "grew up"; perennial and perfectionist malcontents; "misfits" and "loners"; and angry and perverse souls. Or, viewed from the other direction, from the character results of being married to rebellion, we can see that almost every one reveals an insistent egotism of self-display, self-pity and self-exaggeration. Such may be the price as well as the cause of separateness and opposition. The self-grandiloquence of the rebel seems as much a defining trait as the waywardness. Note, too, that rebels seem to characteristically shove other rebels—often all other rebels—among the objects of their angers and mockeries. Rebels are hardly more loving and loveable than they are affable and agreeing. Even a taste for rebels usually seems to be a rebellious taste, a willful taste if not (as all too often) a bad taste. The issue, however, goes beyond sentiment and taste to the fundamental denial and defiance and despair of all men. For however good it may be, it also *is* a bad world. All men know it, says the rebel, but only a few stick to the truth and try to live with it. Perhaps that is because only a few can—and even they only irregularly—which makes the rebel all the more important.

In insisting on the value of the rebel as rebel, we should not, of course, deny the importance of their "messages," which usually take such directions as the power and pleasure of the instinctual life, the endless falsity and corruptibility of all institutions, the inadequacy and viciousness of all ideologies (and not least, the prevalent ideologies which smugly disguise themselves as anti-ideologies), the value and rightness of the individual against the collectivity—and even against himself. Granted that rebels have some susceptibility to their own negative ideologies and utopian institutions and rebellious stylizations of art and living. But those aren't quite the same thing. The rebel's allegiances belong only to the "otherness." In announcing the news—not always just bad news—from contrary realms, the rebel sometimes breaks into deep and immediate truths. Sometimes even very practical truths—for that manual sub-titled "How to Beat the System" which so many rebels seem to be rewriting— that are much more widely absorbed and utilized than is generally admitted. Agreed that the rebel's personal motives may include a strong desire to get "within" (he must be partly within the established order of sense and acceptance to even be able to communicate his "otherness"—a dialectical balancing and drastic self-limiting which some rebels lose control of). But the rebel is the wise one who can't get very far back in because he knows, perhaps despite himself, that "within" is an illusion, and that we all stand sadly "without." Even if, like Dostoevsky's Ivan, he attempts to renounce rebellion, once he has been there he cannot pretend very fully to be back in a certainty, comfort, order and acceptance which were not true in the first place. Dostoevsky, then, was partly right: rebellion is terribly limited, a near impossibility leading to a great despair. But to know that truly, you have to be a rebel. The rebel is he who reveals, as he resists, the limits not only of rebellion but of all, and the pervasive desperateness which can only be accepted by rebelling against it while yet remaining open to some equally desperate possibility of a richer life.

Perhaps these remarks are too broad an attempt to suggest the general nature of the rebel. Yet it does seem crucial to oppose the widespread subsuming of rebels under such categories as revolutionaries (or irritable liberals and violent conservatives), or avant garde artists, or saints and moral adventurers, or particular historical, social and psychological syndromes. Let the rebel be viewed as less protean, as limited, and he may be seen in a more particular significance. My proper subject, the literary rebel, may show up as even more perculiarly limited than the rebel in general. Especially these days, things and people desperately need a distinctive shape, and not least rebels.

Surely not all rebels belong to literature any more than all literature belongs to rebels. There seems cause to suspect that the literary role—in the very nature of literature—blocks up and drains off denials and defiances which could possibly take more direct forms. The rebel who goes too insistently literary may be of the lesser quality of rebels. Who would be more likely than the placeless and despairing rebel to use art as a compensatory way? And in the practice of art rebel against it. Evident in many of the examples of rebellious writings are nagging discrepancies between the rebellious and literary motives. Some consequent literary imperfections and limitations appear basic to rebels, who must necessarily be at odds with many of the given forms and responses and be generally perplexed in finding appropriate artistic shapes and styles for their resistance. Thus I have repeatedly argued that though rebellion is of major significance it usually takes minor literary forms. The rebel tendency to parody, burlesque, diatribe, the idiosyncratic potpourri, the individualistic document and eccentric prose-poetry bastardization of conventional literary forms often runs afoul in the extremity of his refusals and the noise of his angers. We can take rebellious literature for what it peculiarly is, aware of its limitations and oddities, without denying the literary rebel's distinctive values of provoking and extending awareness. Even if one can't live with it alone.

But that may be put too mildly. Literary rebels carry out some special functions we should be aware, and perhaps wary, of in their writing. Currently, especially in America, many of those identified as literary rebels use literature for personal therapy, in rather direct and unartistic ways. However curative this may be for the author in his "unblocking" and release and psychodrama of violations, the conveyable medical utility seems doubtful. Many readers, not diagnostically interested in literary symptomology, can only acquire from the rebellious literary ragings an easy—probably too easy—pattern for therapeutic imitation. (The best therapies are more likely arduously created, and often unique, than aesthetically copied.) But this also points to a larger function of the literary rebel. Much of his writing has always been for a distinctive audience—other rebels and would-be rebels. Rebellious literature often serves programmatic functions, creating therapies, jargons, rituals and styles of sensibility for groups of the socially and culturally marginal. Uncertain and endemic discontents receive morals and manners from the works of literary rebels. These I may not have discussed, here, in adequate detail since the focus has been on more broadly public points than marginal in-group mores and rebel mutual aid methodologies. (My academic concern with intentionally practicing varied "critical methodologies"—analytical, thematic, social and speculative—may also partly distort my choice and handling of literary material.) Once again we must note that the rebellious are distinctive types, groups, values and arts whose understanding requires appropriate perspectives which frequently turn out contrary to much of the popular and learned irrelevancy about literary rebels.

Perhaps my selection of rebels and their works appears arbitrary. *De gustibus.* The "field" is an open one, and my examples of literary rebels, chosen often for illustrative and dialectical purposes, makes no claim to completeness. (Also: in focusing on modern modes of the rebel, with special emphasis on those that seem particularly significant to the literature of this time and place, but in insisting on putting them in several traditional and historical contexts, I have refused any stock definable subject matter. My choice of refusing chauvinistic fashion, and not delimiting "our" rebels from several "foreign" contexts, also suggests endless heritages and linkages which undercut convenient formulations.) The missing rebels that bother me the most are the truly "missing ones." For rebellion not only takes special forms in art, it also takes forms quite outside art. Does our literature fairly represent the rebellious responses and possibilities? I doubt it. If, both historically and contemporaneously, we admit that literature is often a drastically partial and incomplete recording and reordering of social realities and psychic phenomena—and few seem to deny this—then the incompleteness of the record of rebel sensibility must be even more marked. The record-keepers of our society and culture are not primarily rebels, and certainly and necessarily not largely sympathetic to denials and defiances. Without joining a full-scale "conspiracy" view of the established—as do some rebels who exasperatedly over-rate the conscious repressiveness of the powers that be (and thus under-acknowledge the automatically shrewd self-protectiveness of power)—we can nevertheless grant that many rebellious things and beings must have been kept out, put down and twisted around until the actual nature of the rebel, and his literature, must be quite uncertain. Our knowledge, like the rebel himself, remains perplexed and limited.

Some significant rebellious literature—to take up an old argument—must literally be missing. Unsung Miltons, complacently said that shrewd self-publicist and earlier *avant-kitsch* writer Gertrude Stein, are never unsung for long. No doubt the Miltonic type avoids being muted. But what of the others? Unless your deity happens to be a first-rate literary critic (and the evidence given is usually against that, not least because most believers make Him a quite peculiar poet), part of our subject is in oblivion. *Belles lettres*, for example, must sometimes suffer at least as capricious and harsh fates as good communities and good men. The rebellious in spirit must also often be the victims of the very institutions of literature, which are part of the rigidities that are. Not just censorship (which, in America, has markedly lessened precisely when other forces—mass media, technological neutralization of values, etc.—may lessen the effectiveness of the dissident word) but the organizations that promote and reproduce art, the culti-vated groups that call for and consume edification, and the authorities and sycophants that comment upon and evaluate culture—certainly these are no better (and they may, as so many rebels insist, be much worse) than the other fixities of society. In sum, there must be literary rebels who never get seen, and others who rise belatedly, if at all, to the surface of general literate consciousness. Therefore, any selection of past rebels must remain inherently fortuitous, any discussion of contemporary rebels more than personally arbitrary. My purpose here is more than a humbling of the commentator on rebels, and not just a tear for anyone's sad fate: the exasperating insistence and irritable flamboyance of rebellious art comes from a practical as well as basic sense that the rebel cannot hold other men's faiths in the justice of past, present and future.

The repeated denouncements of false literature by so many rebels, and their efforts at anti-literature, confirm a more general rebel hostility to literature and its institu-tions. If one wishes to deny things as they are, and defy the powers that be, why be literary at all about it? Most rebels, after all, insist on the directest possible confrontations of life, the intensification of individual and immediate values, and resistance to established institutions and accepted responses. No need to be a primitive mystic or a Reformation Puritan or a later Leo Tolstoy to suspect almost any dominant literature of being essentially trivial, conformist and existentially dishonest, and to hold that the "literary life" is both corrupt and a waste of greater powers and urgencies. Despite the romanticisms which have led some rebels to exalt art as the process itself of defiance—not merely compensatory for their frustration of more direct and communal rebellions, for by art they often meant something so exceptional as not to be contained in the actual literature—the rebel often finds his literary efforts at odds with the imperative sense to live the personal reality. The rebel demands something more than reading, not least of himself. He desperately wants to engage actuality, confront it, change it.

Only by perverse twisting, then, is literature the true and appropriate end for the rebel. Rebellious literature is often drastically limited in that the rebel, more than most men, must suffer the anguish of the discrepancies between his avowals and his living, since anger over such falsities provides his identity. To be truistic, we can say that the quite particular limits of the rebel are both his virtues and his vices. To be polemical, we can say that the literature of the rebel must be comprehended in essentially rebellious ways, which is often not done. Much literature is not extreme, nihilistic, defiant, exacerbated, but the literature, traditions and purposes of the rebel are, and we falsify more than the rebellious if we try to read them as moderate, "aesthetic," and pious of the things that disgustingly are. Rebellion, a fundamental response and authenticity, should not be confused with revolution, reform, religion, art, though these may, at times, assume rebellious shapes. If, for example, God is a worthy notion, so is the completing pursuit of the demonic; if social criticism is a valid activity, so is its fullest form, social defiance; if the perfection of art is a desirable way of consciousness, so is "anti-literature" which opens and perplexes its possibilities. If existence is worth affirming, then rebellion against the perpetually arbitrary limits imposed on life, and against the false loyalties so many pretend to live by, is proper for brave men. (Perhaps a crux of rebelliousness in our world is not to confuse significant identity with institutional identification—including the "institutions" of literature—and to pledge nonallegiance.) So let us conclude this limited apologia for the literary rebel with appropriate anger. One may not be able to live just within the rebel's limits—though there also seems to be a unique serenity sometimes achieved by rebels—but those unrebellious and anti-rebellious people who refuse the deep imperatives in all of us to revolt, and the courage and value of the rebels who do, deserve our contempt. May the rebels continue to deny their world and defy their ways.

1 — The Diogenes Style

1. My most immediate source for the passage is Dostoevsky; it was a favorite of his (it appears twice in *The Possessed*).

2. For example, see the traditional stridencies of Allen Ginsberg (*Howl* and *Kaddish*). While I am indebted to some of the literature on the Old Testament prophets, the summary, and probably impertinent, nature of my comments suggests not citing any scholar.

3. After previously writing a lengthy discussion of the Beats as analogous to the Cynics — "The Literary Rebel," *Centennial Rev.*, VI (Spring, 1962) — I searched through many books and articles for what then seemed the obvious comparison. The only one I found was by Lewis S. Feur, "Youth in the '60's," *New Leader*, XLIV (March 6, 1961), 18–22. While he notes the basic similarity, he also follows the stock contempt of the liberal ideologue and the usual charges of lack of productivity, political program, normal ambitions, etc.—points I try to answer below.

4. The general characteristics of the Beat style seem to be public information. For examples, bibliographies and selected commentaries see the various anthologies: *The Beat Generation and the Angry Young Men*, ed. G. Feldman and M. Gartenberg (New York, 1959); *The Beats*, ed. Seymour Krim (New York, 1960); *A Casebook on the Beat*, ed. Thomas Parkinson (New York, 1961); *Marginal Manners*, ed. F. J. Hoffman (Evanston, 1962). In later sections, but not here, I discuss several writers labeled Beat. For the material on Diogenes and the Cynics I have drawn on the standard sources in translation: *Diogenes Laertius*, trans. R. D. Hicks (2 vols.; London, 1925); *Dio Chrysostom*, trans. J. W. Cahoon (5 vols.; London, 1932); *The Works of the Emperor Julian*, Vol. II, trans. W. C. Wright; *Epictetus*, trans. W. A. Oldfather (2 vols.; London, 1932). See also Farrand Sayre, *The Greek Cynics* (Baltimore, 1948—a considerable improvement over

the earlier edition). The half-dozen histories of philosophy that I have consulted have not been very helpful on the aspects of Cynicism that concern us here. See, for example, W. Windelband, *A History of Philosophy*, Vol. I (New York, 1958), 86 ff. Neither are the standard reference works helpful; see, for example, Robert Eisler, "Cynics," in the *Encyclopedia of the Social Sciences* who provides a quasi-Marxist polemic. By far the most useful scholarly study for our purposes is Donald R. Dudley, *A History of Cynicism* (London, 1937) who astutely gives much of the essential information. My interpretations, of course, go beyond his suggestions.

5. See A. O. Lovejoy and George Boas, *Primitivism and Related Ideas in Antiquity* (Baltimore, 1935). My comments throughout intentionally de-emphasize historical sources and significances of the literary rebels, which is not to deny them but to focus on the permanent qualities of rebellion.

6. The main source here is Dudley, *op. cit.* Prof. Marvin Singleton brought to my attention the importance of Crates' wife and daughter.

7. For a pleasant but rather too fervently rational-ascetic moralist view, see Gilbert Murray, *Five Stages of Greek Religion* (New York, 1951), pp. 86–91. The educational role of the Cynics is generally and falsely ignored; none of them, for example, are discussed in H. I. Marrou, *A History of Education in Antiquity* (New York, 1957).

8. Henry De Montherlant, "The Death of Peregrinos," *Selected Essays*, trans. J. Weightman (London, 1960), pp. 39–54. Montherlant, of course, expounds a view paralleled in many of his fictional figures, such as Costals.

9. Franz Kafka, "Diogenes," *Parables and Paradoxes* (New York, 1961), p. 95. While the crucialness of this parable could only be demonstrated by a broad discussion of Kafka's work, its *un*ironic seriousness is certainly confirmed by the adjoining parables, "Alexander the Great" and "The New Attorney," which treat willful power as positive.

2—Variations of Defiance

1. Some of my examples here are drawn from Walter Nigg, *The Heretics*, trans. R. and C. Winston (New York, 1962)—informal studies from a sympathetic Protestant view of representative heretics. Franck is quoted by Nigg, p. 339. On the Brethern, see also Wilhelm Fränger, *The Millennium of Hieronymous Bosch* (Chicago, 1951). For a criticism of Fränger see Enrico Castelli, *Le Démonique* (Paris, 1959), pp. 65–66 and 71.

2. *Commentary*, XXXV (April, 1963), 336.

3. See Nicolas Berdyaev, *Slavery and Freedom* (New York, 1944).

4. Gertrude Huehns, *Antinomianism in English History* (London, 1951), p. 172. See also the discussion of the antinomian traditions in A. L. Morton's book on William Blake and his sources, *The Everlasting Gospel* (London, 1958).

5. These points never seem to be noted by such expositors of Zen as Alan Watts, Suzuki, etc.

6. Holmes Welch, *The Parting of the Way: Lao Tzu and the Taoist Move* (Boston, 1957), p. 165.

7. Quoted in Arthur Waley, *Three Ways of Thought in Ancient China* (New York, 1956), p. 28.

8. Herbert Read, *The Politics of the Unpolitical* (London, 1943) —itself, a not very adequate statement of the position of the political values of the artist-saint-nonconformist. The rebel, of course, should not be confined to art and religion, nor to Read's religion of art. Modern anarchism, in considerable part, took a similar role under the guise of politics. As George Woodcock points out, anarchism "was really a movement of rebellion rather than a movement of revolution." *Anarchism* (New York, 1962), p. 469. For the point below on manners, perhaps the most authoritive insight was that of a six-year-old who explained to me, "You gotta be polite because that's the best way to be mean."

9. The opening sentence of "Walking," *The Portable Thoreau*, ed. Carl Bode (New York, 1947), p. 592.

10. "Life Without Principle," *Ibid.*, p. 653. Curiously, even the sometimes smug radical cliques who draw a "nonviolent" politics of protest from Thoreau badly distort him here (for a recent example see *Liberation* magazine, Feb. and April, 1963).

11. *Books in My Life* (New York, 1952), p. 95. For some further parallels see my *Henry Miller* (New York, 1963).

12. For a list of examples, and sources, see my "Our Demonic Heritage: D. H. Lawrence," *A D. H. Lawrence Miscellany*, ed. Harry T. Moore (Carbondale, Ill., 1959).

13. For sometimes suggestive, if ponderous, comments on Genet's endless revolt towards authenticity, see Benjamin Nelson, "*The Balcony* and Parisian Existentialism," *Tulane Drama Review*, VII (Spring, 1963), 60–79.

14. *We* in *An Anthology of Russian Literature in the Soviet Period*, ed. and trans. B. B. Guerney (New York, 1960), p. 298.

15. While this emphasis is rarely made, even Enid Welsford's *The Fool* (London, 1935) provides, in such material as the linkage of the buffoon and the philosopher, possible evidence for the argument.

16. The view of Prince Hal as a purely mythic hero type and of Falstaff as holy man and prophet is suggested by Lord Raglan, *The Hero* (London, 1949), chap. xix. The nihilistic emphasis in Shakespeare is usually gotten around, except by innocent students, though Wyndham Lewis did, in his own peculiar way, argue the point in *The Lion and the Fox* (New York, 1927).

17. Rochester deserves further discussion as a rebel type. The point has at least been touched on by the unspeculative Vivian De Sola Pinto, who connects Rochester with Blake and Lawrence, "Introduction," *Poems of John Wilmot, Earl of Rochester* (Cambridge, Mass., 1953), p. xxxix.

18. Found in most of the standard studies of seventeenth- and eighteenth-century English comedy and satire, the more general theory has also been grossly over-stated in such different anti-rebellious views of comedy as Albert Cook, *The Dark Voyage and the Golden Mean* (Cambridge, Mass., 1949) and Northrup Frye, *Anatomy of Criticism* (Princeton, 1957).

19. Wylie Sypher, "The Meanings of Comedy," *Comedy*, ed. Sypher (New York, 1956), p. 195. He suggests some rather rebellious meanings of the comic, including some for Falstaff, though his attempt to get too much under his shifting rubrics makes them pretty fluttery.

20. See the discussion, throughout, of Martin Esslin, *The Theatre of the Absurd* (New York, 1961) and the *Anthologie de L'Humour Noir*, ed. André Breton (Paris, 1950).

21. One of the more charming arguments sympathetic to occultism essentially grants the disparity between literary rebels and their occult interests: John Senior, *The Way Down and Out: The Occult in Symbolist Literature* (Ithaca, N. Y., 1959). A crucial point—the linkage of gnosticism and nihilism—is suggested in Hans Jonas, *The Gnostic Religion*, rev. ed. (Boston, 1963).

22. See Paracelsus, *Selected Writings*, ed. Jolandi Jacobi (New York, 1951) and *Four Treatises* (Baltimore, 1946). One of the more judicious accounts in English, with emphasis on his philosophical medicine, is Walter Pagel, *Paracelsus* (Basel, 1958). See Wilhelm Reich, *Selected Writings* (New York, 1961), which includes a bibliography. Writers discussed below, who have been strongly influenced by Reich include Bellow, Mailer, Goodman, O'Connor, and some of the Beats. See also, such "left wing" Freudians as Norman O. Brown, *Life Against Death* (Middleton, Conn., 1959) and Herbert Marcuse, *Eros and Civilization* (Boston, 1956). There are also a number of less learned prophets of the orgasm.

23. Even a Christian-moralist polemic against extreme modern rebellion grants that it is quite different from hopelessness and is marked by a "will to truth." Helmut Thielicke, *Nihilism,* trans. J. W. Doberstein (New York, 1961), p. 28.

3—The Marriage of Heaven and Hell

1. All quotations are from *The Complete Writings of William Blake,* ed. Geoffrey Keynes (New York, 1957), pp. 148–60. While I am indebted, often in disagreement, to a large number of the studies of Blake, only a few examples are cited below.

2. For example, the uninsightful study of Robert F. Gleckner, *The Piper and the Bard, A Study of William Blake* (Detroit, 1959), pp. 185 ff. Since the *Marriage* is not usual poetry, and rather extreme, he finds it poor art, though he does not seem very clear on what it is about.

3. This is true of Northrup Frye, *Fearful Symmetry, A Study of William Blake* (Princeton, 1947), who doesn't say much about it because he is so busy with Blake's "system."

4. Several of the points below—the shape of the work, the meaning of proverb No. 70, Blake's demonic emphasis, etc.— contrast with the most detailed critical study, Martin K. Nurmi, *Blake's Marriage of Heaven and Hell, Kent State University Bulletin,* Research Series III, Vol. LXV (1957) which is an informed and pleasant monograph over-qualifying Blake's extremity.

5. Recent tiresome examples of this sort of approach are Peter F. Fisher, *The Valley of Vision* (Toronto, 1961) and George Mills Harper, *Neoplatonism of William Blake* (Durham, N. C., 1961).

6. "Jerusalem," pl. 11, Keynes, *op. cit.,* p. 630.

7. For the covert political significance, see David V. Erdman, *Blake: Prophet Against Empire* (Princeton, 1954), pp. 160 ff. I am pleasantly indebted to Mr. Erdman for earlier criticisms of my interpretation of Blake.

8. "Jerusalem," pl. 54, Keynes, *op. cit.,* p. 687.

9. An obvious substantiation is in Blake's use of the same line in "America," Keynes, *op. cit.,* p. 199: "For everything that lives is holy, life delights in life;/ Because the soul of sweet delight can never be defiled." When, two lines later, Blake speaks of "lustful fires" which perfect the prophetic man, the metaphor has some literal significance—and morality and piety only a negative one.

10. In the probably earlier prophetic narrative "Tiriel," Blake used a variant of the same statement: "Why is one law

given to the lion and the patient Ox?" Keynes, *op. cit.*, p. 109. The following deleted lines contrast the deceitful and the wrathful, which do not quite fit the comparison but do suggest part of what Blake had in mind.

11. Harold Bloom has rightly noted that Blake "does not build truth by dialectic." "Dialectic in *The Marriage of Heaven and Hell*," *PMLA*, LXXIII (Dec., 1958), 502. Contrast Nurmi, *op. cit.*, and others. Bloom also notes, within a quite obscure commentary, Blake's emphasis on "enmity" and "antinomianism."

12. See Blake's marginalia to Swedenborg, Keynes, *op. cit.*, pp. 89 ff. and 131 ff.

13. See my "Milton's Iconography of Renunciation," *E L H*, XXV (Dec., 1958).

14. This is not to deny the doctrine of "correspondences" which Blake apparently took from Swedenborg and Böhme—and perhaps from Paracelsus who gave it a more libertarian cast—but since Blake defies Swedenborg and the others here, the correspondences take a minor role.

15. "Jerusalem," pl. 69, Keynes, *op. cit.*, p. 708. For a neat proverbial argument on the basic oppositional nature of proverbs—and literature—see Karl Shapiro, *The Bourgeois Poet* (New York, 1964), p. 20.

16. And apparently a fairly aggressive masculinity: "Let man wear the fell of the lion, woman the fleece of the sheep" (No. 30). As Harold Bloom comments, Blake has "a diabolical formula: sexual excess leads to antinomian perception." *The Visionary Company* (New York, 1961), p. 65.

17. A few other commentators on Blake have partly put emphasis on his gnomic utterances rather than his obsessional mythological machinery: see Bernard Blackstone, *English Blake* (Cambridge, 1949), p. 102.

18. Some of the imagery may be antinomian in origin; in any case, the antinomian tradition is probably the most crucial, and underemphasized, background for Blake. See note 13, above.

19. The point is not sufficiently noted; Erdman, *Blake*, p. 163, is one of the few to comment on the irony of the title.

4—Bartleby

1. All citations to the novella are from *The Complete Stories of Herman Melville*, ed. Jay Leyda (New York, 1948), pp. 2–47.

2. See Newton Arvin, *Herman Melville* (New York, 1950), p. 242; see also, Charles G. Hoffmann, "The Shorter Fictions

of Herman Melville," *South Atlantic Quarterly,* LII, No. 3 (July, 1953), 420.

3. Arvin mentioned the writer allegory. Richard Chase was more emphatic: "on the internal evidence . . . Melville was consciously writing a parable of the artist." *Herman Melville* (New York, 1949), p. 146. The internal evidence is not provided. Leyda notes possible biographical sources, p. 455. But the most forced biographical allegorizing is Leo Marx, "Melville's Parable of the Walls," *The Sewanee Review,* LXI (Autumn, 1953). Besides the points discussed below, he makes his reading depend on elaborate symbolic interpretations of details, such as incidental colors, and on bits from letters and novels of other periods. Then he finds that the story must fail, for it is "a grave defect of the parable that we must go back" to these earlier works to understand this story.

4. Marx, *op. cit.,* pp. 622, 627.

5. Richard Harter Fogle, *Melville's Shorter Tales* (Norman, Okla., 1960), p. 23. He rightly sees Bartleby as an "absolutist," but, too aware of the dominant interpretations, inconsistently makes Bartleby a vague "victim of his environment." A mechanical view of the story's development and a listing of some other interpretations may also be found in Marvin Felheim, "Meaning and Structure in 'Bartleby,' " *College English,* XXIII (February, 1962), 365–68.

6. Leyda, *op. cit.,* "Introduction," p. xxiv.

7. Fogle, *op. cit.,* p. 26. Melville's characteristic mockeries of Protestant Christianity, as on pp. 25 and 34 of the story, also further the case against rather than for predestination. While critics like Laurence Thompson (*Melville's Quarrel With God*) have obviously over-elaborated the case, there is little justification for denying "father-killing" Melville's persistent mockeries of Christian determinism. This is, just as in Blake's attack on Swedenborg, one of the favorite subjects of literary rebels.

8. Arvin, *op. cit.,* p. 244; Chase (who gets everything in), *op. cit.,* p. 143.

9. Melville, of course, shows similarities here with Dostoevsky and Conrad, and the literary perspective, rather than the social-biographical, is most informative. For some different detailing on this subject, see Mordecau Marcus, "Melville's Bartlby as a Psychological Double," *College English,* XXIII (February, 1962), 365–68, though he, too, sometimes falls into the dubious socio-economic interpretation of Melville's metaphysical "Wall Street." For a discussion of the "double" as an ironist's technique for playing the

demonic against common morality, see my "Conrad's Pyrrhic Victory," *Twentieth Century Literature*, 5 (October, 1959).

10. And so will at least three of the commentators, who start discussing Melville's eyesight, thus again confusing a possible source of a motif with its meaning.

11. Hoffmann, *op. cit.*, p. 420. He says the end violates the theme of "the element of mystery in the world, against which all reason is helpless."

12. Lyda, *op. cit.*, "The Encantadas" (Sketch 8), p. 94.

13. Burning the dead letters can also be made into biographical allegory. Alfred Kazin dogmatically stated in a public lecture a few years ago (I have not been able to find a printed version) that the story was about two things: Melville's horror of Wall Street economics and his horror at the destruction of some manuscripts in a fire at Harper's. But neither does a "philosophical" emphasis always help; for a fatuous and poor summary of *Bartleby* that intends to pass as existentialist see Maurice Friedman's unproblematic and unrebellious *Problematic Rebel* (New York, 1963), pp. 93 ff.

5—Les Amours Jaunes

1. All citations to the poems of Corbière are to the most complete edition of *Les Amours Jaunes*, ed. Yves-Gérard Le Dantec (Paris, 1953)—hereafter *LAJ*. There has been some critical divergence on just why the "yellow loves" of the general title (and the section title of the love poems). Albert Sonnenfeld, for example, emphasizes yellow as the symbolical color of Judas, and therefore Corbière's love as a betrayal. *L'Oeuvre Poétique de Tristan Corbière* (Paris, 1960), pp. 48 ff. That seems forced. If we take the use of yellow in the poems, we find the yellow beak of the legendary self-lacerating pelican in the seventh of the Paris sonnets (*LAJ*, p. 30), which seems appropriate. In "A L'Etna" the volcanic mountain is identified with the poet and treated as a diseased lover with a "ris jaune" (p. 111). In "Bohême de Chic" the mocked (and self-mocked) bohemian poet has a humor of "sauce jaune / De chic et de mépris" (p. 38). Other uses of yellow are less significant, such as the yellow flower of "Duel aux Camélias" (p. 60) and the yellow star of "Bonsoir" (p. 63), but not inconsistent with an emphasis on a self-lacerating humor, a jaundiced love and laughter which may also be a literal description of the sick Corbière's complexion. For another version of the modern relevance of Cobière's style of revolt, see Jean Rousselot, *Tristan Corbière* (Paris, 1951).

2. "A Mon Chien Pope," *LAJ*, p. 90. For the balancing

reversal into the doggy role with women, see "Sonnet a Sir Bob." Corbière also named one of his dogs after himself.

3. *LAJ*, pp. 204–5.

4. A number of French critics have over-emphasized the positive Breton side of Corbière: Jean Trignon, *Tristan Corbière* (Paris, 1950); Alexander Arnoux, *Tristan Corbière* (Paris, 1929); Le Dantec, *op. cit.*; and others. Sonnenfeld's useful book attempts to partly qualify this parochialism by giving, in current fashion, the book a symbolic-moralistic structure of Brittany vs. Paris. But this is just more of the same since he makes the outcast state and perversity qualities of Paris. Sonnenfeld, *op. cit.*, pp. 70 and 120. If we see Corbière as essentially a rebel, then the Breton and Paris poems provide different and complementry aspects of his essential role.

5. *LAJ*, p. 205.

6. *LAJ*, p. 169.

7. *LAJ*, p. 165.

8. *LAJ*, pp. 147–55. There is a discussion of this poem in the suggestive essay of G. M. Turnell, "Introduction to the Study of Tristan Corbière," *Criterion*, XV (April, 1936), pp. 404 ff.

9. *LAJ*, pp. 138–40. This, Corbière's only poem directly concerned with social-political events, is a harsh attack on a stupid Breton military adventure. Given from a conscript's point of view, it has the anti-patriotism we expect from a real rebel.

10. *LAJ*, pp. 138–40. This poem, as often noted, also has minor (and by now clichéd) forms of literary rebellion—the parodistic mixture of popular song and Latin prayer, and a complete absence of punctuation.

11. *LAJ*, pp. 128–35. Contrary to many weirdly pious comments on "Le Pardon," C. F. MacIntyre rightly speaks of it as an "indictment against God." See the note to his English translation in *Selections from Les Amours Jaunes* (Berkeley, 1954), p. 222. The surreal images of heightened crippling, disease and misery (without benign balance), the constant ironic praise of divine kindness in creating and continuing them, and the parodistic figure of the "saintly" "rapsode foraine" (*Misère*)—it is she who is the controlling figure, the poet's surrogate, and the one who mockingly gives the "vrai signe de croix"—establish a repeated undercutting of the pious materials. This is also supported by Corbière's recurrent use of religious materials for bizarre incongruity and outright blasphemy.

12. *LAJ*, pp. 124–25.

13. *LAJ*, pp. 155–56. The renegade-pariah-burlesque

troubadour type appears in various sections of the book, casting further doubt on moralistic divisions of the work into Breton vs. Paris, earnestness vs. mockery, etc.

14. *LAJ*, pp. 118–19. For one to exist "par hazard"—gratuitously in Corbière's emphasis—is a favorite characterization also applied to his book ("Ça?"), figures of misery ("Le Pardon"), and himself ("Epitaphe").

15. Corbière's contumacious trademark, as it were, is the semiprivate joke (sometimes obscure) given in a parodistic title, incongruous epigraph, fantastic place or date of composition, burlesque literary borrowing, etc.

16. "Toit," *LAJ*, p. 73. Adaptions often catch the quality of a poem better than translations. Here is a version of "Toit," "Drumming Above," kindly provided by Stewart Millpond:

> Hear it? Like thunder, or the big drum.
> I know, in my attic, what's above:
> the tattoo of clams dropped by the gulls.
> Message? There's ripe meat in those shells.
>
> But I fast, on the bread and the wine . . .
> till the belly and the arteries harden,
> turning the hope and the desire to stone.
> Death? Just the breaking of shells.
>
> Calcified, then smashed on the roof,
> my head will go like a shell on the tile,
> sharp rim-shot, full slam of the bass,
> bursting the ear, and the skin of the drum.
>
> My window is a box of tranquil sky,
> a translucent blued skin—monkey hide?—
> covering the hardest damn drum—
> the ear of a deaf old man. Te Deum.

17. *LAJ*, pp. 56–57. Other poems, such as "Heures" and "Le Poète Contumace," also use invocations to insomniac anguish.

18. *LAJ*, pp. 97–101—one of his untranslatable, and hardly paraphrasable, pieces.

19. See André Breton, *Anthologie de L'Humour Noir* (Paris, 1950), pp. 163–64. The point has been elaborated by most of the writers on Corbière since Breton's comment.

20. *LAJ*, pp. 200–203. My first example here is obviously loaded since Corbière seems to have himself rejected the poem for inclusion in his one book. Ida Levi persuasively suggests, contrary to some hopeful critics, that anything not

published in *LAJ* was not intended for another volume. "New Light on Tristan Corbière," *French Studies*, V (July, 1951), 243.

21. *LAJ*, pp. 53–56.

22. The rather brittle stock bohemian materials—the drinking artist, the theater, venereal disease, the abused poet, the prostitutes, urban despair—as in the eight sonnets entitled "Paris," are not Corbière at his best. That part of Corbière which most belongs to his time, such as the café and theater décor, the espagnolism and melodramatic mannerisms of his contemporary poets, has the least permanent value, as is usual with historical materials.

23. *LAJ*, pp. 76 and 89. "Le Phare" in the sea poems also seems to be a phallic double-play. In almost all of Corbière, the shrewdly aware sense of sex and death breaks through in affirmation of the instinctual order of life.

24. *LAJ*, pp. 108 ff.

25. *LAJ*, pp. 94–95.

26. *LAJ*, pp. 181–84. These slight poems belong in Blake's Beulah land. Only with such pieces is there much relevance in the bracketing of Corbière with Laforgue. See, for example, the generally fatuous discussion of Peter Quennell, who finds a "timorous fragility . . . the chief characteristic of many of Laforgue's and Corbière's poems." *Baudelaire and the Symbolists* (rev. ed.; London, 1954), p. 123. J. G. Legge is equally irrelevant in finding most of Corbière "coarse." *Chanticleer, A Study of the French Muse* (New York, 1935), pp. 247–51.

27. *LAJ*, pp. 25–26. It must be granted here, as in the other prefatory poems, the Paris sonnets and the rondels, that Corbière falls into some rather literary archness—probably the result of his preparing his until then poems-for-himself for publication. Nothing does more damage to the rebel tone than the shoddy self-important awareness of publication —but that may be even more generally true in the past century. For an often suggestive technical discussion of other aspects of Corbière's poetics, see Christian Angelet, *La Poétique de Tristan Corbière* (Brussels, 1961).

28. Randall Jarrell, for a representative example, finds these poems "antagonistic, obstinate, and monotonous wit." *Poetry and the Age* (New York, 1953), p. 146. This is not just antagonism to Corbière, whom he admires on his sentimental side, because Jarrell's condemnation sweeps the whole type, including Raleigh's fine poem, "The Lie." Turnell finds excessive such "perpetual use of antithesis" which he blames on the desire to express the irrational. *Op. cit.*, p. 411. Sonnenfeld also finds these poems unpleasant and denies

that there is any meaning to hold the antitheses together. *Op. cit.*, p. 174. It is just this eláborate irony which has been Corbière's main, and persistent, influence on modern poetry. See C. M. Shanahan, "Irony in Laforgue, Corbière, Eliot." *Modern Philology* (Nov., 1955), pp. 117–28. Or, better, Sonnenfeld.

29. *LAJ*, pp. 31–33. There is also a shorter, and somewhat different, version, pp. 240–41. There is another, and weaker, epitaphe, entitled "Sous un Portrait de Corbiere," pp. 205–6.

30. *LAJ*, pp. 92–93. The remarks of bright contemporary adolescents sometimes catch similar qualities, such as the one of a youngster devastatingly catching me in a mistake who then hung his head and said, "Gee, I guess I'm just a dumb nihilist."

31. *LAJ*, pp. 87–89.

32. See the practical jokes and quips reported by René Martineau, *Tristan Corbière* (Paris, 1925).

6 – The Art of Wandering

1. The point is made, and over made, by most of the sociological writers on the subject. See, for example, Alexandre Vexliard, *Introduction a la sociologie du vagabondage* (Paris, 1956), who systematically reduces wandering to the wickedness of capitalism but makes some suggestive points along the way.

2. Besides Vexliard, see (for diverse representative examples) A. Marie and R. Meunier, *Les Vagabonds* (Paris, 1908); Helen Waddell, *The Wandering Scholars* (New York, 1961); and William O. Douglas, *Vagrancy and Arrest on Suspicion* (Albuquerque, New Mexico, 1960). The usual emphasis traces vicious treatment of wanderers to the late Medieval period, which has some appropriateness, but Greek and Roman comments on the horrors of exile and the facts of slavery do not justify interpretations based mainly on the history of law and social welfare.

3. For a recent description of the passive negator, see Elmer Bendiner, *The Bowery Man* (New York, 1961), especially his "totally adjusted" and tranquilized failure in chapters ix–xii. Many accounts rightly qualify this by insisting on the arduousness of marginal living, its widespread diversity, and the rebellious fascination with outcast ways by many more settled citizens. A popular example would be the slight and sentimental sketches of "twilight people" in New York by Edmund G. Love, *Subways Are For Sleeping* (New York, 1958).

4. See Philip O'Connor, *Britain in the Sixties: Vagrancy* (London, 1963), pp. 86 ff. and 130 ff. See also O'Connor's personal account of tramping, *The Lower View* (London, 1960), pp. 57 ff. Though heavily burdened with didactic abstraction and obsessive socialist arguments against "competitive individualism," he has several suggestive points which will be drawn on below. The best, though slick, accounts of the contemporary professional tramp—a rather different type than our main subject here—that I know are those of Jim Phelan, such as *Tramping the Toby* (London, 1953), and *We Follow the Roads* (London, 1949). A poignant novel on the subject, ending on defeated rebellion, is that of the Swedish writer, Harry Martinson, *The Road*, trans. M. A. Michael (London, 1955). Other examples will be discussed later, though I have not attempted any fully systematic or complete account of this literature.

5. Sebastian de Grazia, *Of Time, Work and Leisure* (New York, 1962), pp. 144–45. This suggestive study of the crucialness of leisure—the author somewhat old-fashionedly divides the world into the "majority" and the leisure minorities—is often marred by the association of leisure with aristocratic social and political power, though he properly grants at one point that they are antithetical (p. 431). Politics can lead to far more obtuse treatments of the meaning of work and even to a complete ignoring of uncivic leisure. See, for example, the highly arbitrary discussion of Hannah Arendt, *The Human Condition* (New York, 1959), who does not even recognize vagabondage as existing prior to modern times (p. 358) because of a quasi-Marxism in which alienation from work derives from certain political-economic forms instead of from much more basic discontents. Her pleasure-pain analysis also misses the crucial roles of freedom and authority in other than hedonistic senses in the meanings of work and labor.

6. For an abridged version of my comments on the novels dealing with this subject, see "The Academic Comedy," *Partisan Review*, XXV (Summer, 1960).

7. See, besides the works previously cited, some of the usual historical studies: C. J. Ribton Turner, *A History of Vagrants and Vagrancy and Beggars and Begging* (London, 1887), and the large literature on Renaissance vagabondage, such as the pedantic summary of Frank Aydelotte, *Elizabethan Rogues and Vagabonds* (Oxford, 1913). There is also much material which expresses the genteel fascination with crime, partly connected with the road, such as Ronald Fuller, *The Beggar's Brotherhood* (London, 1936). The largest part of writings on people of the road, from Martin Luther's vicious *Liber Vagatorum* (1528) on, are hostile. I believe this

goes beyond the Protestant glorification of work to the fear of the mixture of cynicism and messianic longings which give a special tone to the wanderers in all periods. There have, of course, been times when the "class of wayfarers" may have contributed significantly to intellectual community and consequent revolution. For their possible influence on the Peasant's Revolt of 1381, see J. J. Jusserand, *English Wayfaring Life in the Middle Ages* (London, 1889, 1950), p. 153. A later example would be the Wobbly doctrines carried by many American hobos, discussed briefly below.

8. See, in contrast, most of the studies previously cited. Harlan W. Gilmore, *The Beggar* (Chapel Hill, N. C., 1940), chaps. i and iv, more reasonably gives some recognition to adventure and discontent, and allows some motivation to leisure, sport and philosophy, as part of taking to the road. We must grant, of course, that literary discussions usually ignore the economic and psychological forces in the literature of the road, as in the decorous appreciations of Arthur Rickett, *The Vagabond in Literature* (London, 1906). Such polite views of the road find an appropriate wandering hero in Robert Louis Stevenson.

9. *The Goliard Poets*, trans. and ed. George F. Whicher (Cambridge, Mass., 1949), p. 4. The poems mentioned above are also given there in what may be the best translations. For a less rebellious emphasis, see Waddell, *op. cit.*

10. "Je suis Francoys, dont il me poise, / Ne de Paris emprès Pontoise, / Et de la corde d'une toise, / Scaura mon col que mon cul poise."

11. The standard indiscriminate summary is F. W. Chandler, *The Literature of Roguery* (2 vols.; Boston, 1907).

12. *The Life of Lazarillo de Tormes*, trans. Harriet de Onis (Great Neck, N. Y., 1959), p. 74.

13. Vexliard, *op. cit.*, p. 173.

14. For apt comment on why Baroja preferred to write of vagabonds, see Anthony Kerrigan's Foreward to Baroja's *The Restlessness of Shanti Andia* (New York, 1962), pp. xi and xx.

15. H. J. C. Grimmelshausen, *The Adventurous Simplicissimus*, trans. A. T. S. Goodrich (Lincoln, Nebraska, 1962), p. 104.

16. *Ibid.*, p. 97.

17. Günter Grass, *The Tin Drum* (New York, 1962), p. 328.

18. *Ibid.*, p. 342.

19. For a quite different interpretation of the relevance of the picaresque to modern fiction, see R. W. B. Lewis, *The Picaresque Saint* (Philadelphia, 1959). His best discus-

sion is of Silone. In later chapters I comment on some examples of American picaresque.

20. Though not in the unprobing summary of Joseph Gaer, *The Legend of the Wandering Jew* (New York, 1961).

21. See my *Henry Miller* (New York, 1963), chap. iii, III, "The Imaginary Jew," and "The Imaginary Jew," *International H. Miller News Letter* (Netherlands, April, 1964).

22. Alex Comfort, *On This Side Nothing* (New York, 1949), p. 43.

23. Leslie A. Fiedler, *The Second Stone* (New York, 1963), p. 252. Probably nothing more need be said about this novel (or about the similar stories in *Pull Down Vanity*) with its archly murky fable about the crotch-culture of an intellectual coterie.

24. See the poem by Bob Kaufman quoted in "Introduction," *Marginal Manners*, ed. F. J. Hoffman (New York, 1962). The editor raises several suggestive points about the outsider's identification with an unpious Christ, pp. 4–5 and 10–11. A shrewdly done Beat-jargon poem on Christ is Lawrence Ferlingetti's "#5," *A Coney Island of the Mind* (New York, 1959).

25. Nikos Kazantzakis, *The Saviors of God: Spiritual Exercises*, trans. Kimon Friar (New York, 1960), p. 113. Finally, of course, God "DOES NOT EXIST" (p. 131) because if he did that would destroy the deepest antinomian freedom of the rebel on the road. Kazantzakis often seems (in translation, anyway) a not very satisfactory writer—perhaps at his best in less ambitious works such as *Zorba the Greek*. Like so many literary rebels, he has difficulty in finding a form and a style for his ecstatic nihilism and stoic vitalism.

26. It should also be granted that much of the war novel genre is repetitious and noisy on the subject. On re-reading Barbusse, Dos Passos, Remarque, Mailer, Burns, Lowry, etc., only a few works seem to effectively make their point about authority—the brilliant tactic (but tediously developed) of Jaroslav Hasek's *The Good Soldier: Schweik*, the cool "separate peace" of *Farewell to Arms*. A quiet reportorial account such as Lester Atwell's *Private* (New York, 1958) seems more often to catch honestly the qualities of arbitrary authority than many of the more ambitious fictions.

27. See, for examples, many of the prison accounts of "Conscientious Objectors" in the U. S.: *Prison Etiquette*, ed. H. Cantine and D. Ranier (New York, [n. d.]); Lowell Naeve and David Wieck *A Field of Broken Stones* (Denver, 1960); Jim Peck, *We Who Would Not Kill* (New York, 1958); etc. Even when the writing is mediocre and the in-

sights minor, the details often reveal a special awareness. Also to the point here would be the concentration camp literature of Rousset, Nansen, Cohen, etc.

28. For example, see the raggedly fervent report of John Howard Griffin, *Black Like Me* (New York, 1962), pp. 85 ff. He clearly saw, in his hitchhiking through the South disguised as a Negro, what some have great difficulty in recognizing, such as the insistently sexual basis of the "white's" mistreatment of the Negro.

29. See the anonymous *Streetwalker* (New York, 1961) who notes her sympathy for "the individualists, the wanderers, the eccentrics" because they developed their own codes and styles of life in thoughtful, if self-centered, ways (pp. 82–83). She also insightfully notes the special limits of the rebel: "I had thought to find complete personal freedom in that ultimate flouting of convention, yet I became hag-ridden by hate, guilt, fear, despair, disgust." For "independence is invalid without the power to appreciate it" (p. 222). One only truly rebels to the degree that he responds beyond compulsions, and thus outside guilt and self-destruction. To be a rebel is also a discipline.

30. "Le Voyage": "Mais les vrais voyageurs sont ceux-là seux qui partent. / Pour partir. . . ." Despite the Gothic exoticism and Baudelaire's inability to really rebel (as J.-P. Sarte argues in his *Baudelaire*), this is surely one of the profound paradigms of the wandering psyche. Dostoevsky presented a similar insight when Stepan, one of his wise fools, takes to the road which ends with his death: "The road [he thinks to himself] is very, very long, and has no end to it; it is like a man's life, like a man's dream. There is a grand idea in the open road." *The Possessed*, trans. A. R. MacAndrew (New York, 1962), p. 649. But for Dostoevsky, the road is too painful, absurd, fatal, and so he ends it in the pathetic comedy of salvation. There are many more examples; patently, my introduction is inadequate since I ignored Jason and the Prodigal Son, the Franciscans and the seventeenth-century French vagabond poets, Bruno, Goldsmith, Rousseau, Rimbaud, Synge, etc.—a rich tradition!

7—The Hobo Style

1. For an insufficiently analytic but useful compendium of the images, see George N. Fenin and William K. Everson, *The Western* (New York, 1962).

2. The point on atheism is implicitly suggested by Philip Asthon Rollins, *The Cowboy* (rev. ed.; New York, 1936), pp. 83–84. In demythologizing the type, Rollins may reduce the cowboy too much to economics and "code"—he says little

about the extreme alienation and psychological weirdness—but I follow his evidence in seeing the cowboy too bound by his trade to represent significant freedom.

3. Apparently the last of the Anglo-Saxon whalers, a few years ago, still had some of the Melville qualities: highly competent and rebellious misfits—"healthy psychopaths"—driven by "some deep, unexpressed, and inexpressible religious urge." R. B. Robertson, *Of Whales and Men* (New York, 1954), p. 172.

4. In his essay on Whitman in *Studies in Classic American Literature*.

5. *Sister of the Road, The Autobiography of Box-Car Bertha*, as told to Dr. Ben L. Reitman" (New York, 1937), p. 228.

6. Vachel Lindsay, *A Handy Guide for Beggars* (New York, 1916), p. 204.

7. See Eleanor Ruggles, *The West-Going Heart, A Life of Vachel Lindsay* (New York, 1959).

8. While obviously indebted to Nels Anderson, *The Hobo* (Chicago, 1923) in the following summary discussion, I have gone through most of his published sources, and drawn on some ex-hobos, to come out with a rather different emphasis. In Anderson's later comments (Preface to the 1961 edition) he insists even more on the purely economic ("industrial frontier") role and motives, contrary to most of the memoirs and individual sources. His later anti-lore addition to hobo lore, *The Milk and Honey Route* (New York, 1930), a burlesque of hobo literature which turns into tedious documentary, reasonably aims to deny both leftist and romantic myths but ends in its own puritanic economic myth.

9. Quoted in Anderson, *The Hobo*, p. 87.

10. Mr. Justice Douglas, *op. cit.*, p. 7, cites government reports indicating half a million hobos in America in the early 1950's, but obviously much contemporary wandering takes more varied and less countable forms. Douglas, incidentally, warmly cites his own early experiences riding the rods and tramping, and perhaps therefore recognizes wandering as partly a desire for independence and rebellion.

11. Hobo songs are briefly commented on in the next chapter.

12. Jack London, *The Road* (New York, 1907), p. 53. London's hobo experiences were primarily in the early 'nineties. His use of tramp materials in his fictions, as in the mawkish story "The Princess," is inferior to his journalistic accounts. A recent academic literary discussion of some of this material is John D. Seelye, "The American Tramp: A Version of the Picaresque," *American Quarterly*, XV (Winter, 1963), 535–53. He childishly assumes that tramps were

mostly "filthy, bestial," fearsome and predatory, and debili-
tatingly idle, which is nonsense, though he recognizes the
special mocker role of the hobo-image (but not of the actual
hobo).

13. London, *The Road*, p. 197.

14. Harry Kemp, *Tramping On Life* (New York, 1922),
p. 339. He was one of the hobo intellectuals who ended as a
fixture in bohemia—there is an historically long and important connection between the road and bohemianism.

15. Josiah Flynt, *My Life* (New York, 1908). Flynt's
hoboing and tramping goes back to the 1880's; he has a
number of earlier writings on the subject which may have
had considerable influence on later writers.

16. W. H. Davies, *Autobiography of a Super-Tramp* (New
York, 1917). His minor but sometimes effective poetry rarely
concerns his years as an American tramp.

17. For this cosmic fantasy, see Jim Tully, *Beggars of Life*
(New York, 1924), pp. 289 ff. His summary of what the
road meant is on p. 327. Tully became a professional writer
on vagabondage and has many books about it.

18. The "radicalism" is discussed in the next chapter.
Most of them knew nothing of the more profound literary
wanderers, such as Rimbaud, nor of the more specialized
ones, such as Gipsy fellow-traveler George Burrows.

19. William Edge, *The Main Stem* (New York, 1927),
pp. 40 and 198. My examples are intended to be representative rather than complete, and those of the 1930s are left
aside for later discussion.

20. Gilmore, *The Beggar*, p. 77.

21. Clancy Sigal, *Going Away*, "A Report, A Memoir"
(Boston, 1962), p. 52.

22. *Ibid.*, p. 188. He also has other claims on the experience of the road, ranging from cheap therapy (p. 191) to his
ostensible report on the 1956 politics of America. The road
as, now, an exploitable sub-genre which identifies a rebel,
should not be ignored.

23. *Ibid.*, pp. 370, 396 and 139.

24. *Ibid.*, p. 482.

25. *Ibid.*, p. 512. Sigal's more focused and intense documentary, *Weekend in Dinlock* (New York, 1961), achieves
more, perhaps because it is less self-justifying. Sigal's worker
and artist ideologies find dramatic issue in the English coal
miner who struggles between alienated worldly artist and
coal miner in a limited but meaningful communion with the
mines, his mates and a whole organic way of life.

26. Jack Kerouac, *The Lonesome Traveler* (New York,
1960), p. 64.

27. *Ibid.*, p. 107.

28. Jack Kerouac, *The Dharma Bums* (New York, 1959), p. 189.

29. For a defense of Kerouac's style, see Warren Tallman, "Kerouac's Sound," *Evergreen Review*, IV (Jan.-Feb., 1960), 153–69. In debating the issue, Professor Tallman granted me my points but insisted that detached and mocking criticism undercut the responsiveness that was required. The trouble is that such rebels don't stick to their own responsiveness but get pretentious. For Kerouac's restatement of the Whitman-Miller aesthetic, with a flavoring of surrealist dogma, see "Essentials of Spontaneous Prose," *Evergreen Review*, II (Summer, 1958) and "Belief Technique for Modern Prose," *Evergreen Review*, II (Spring, 1959).

Another example: Alexander Trocchi, one of the addict-cult writers associated with the Beat, demonstrated a narrow but lucid talent for harsh melodrama in his novella "Young Adam," *The Outsiders* (New York, 1961). Yet when he wrote a long confessional work, *Cain's Book* (New York, 1959), he violated his one small talent by on principle insisting that he would not falsify his experience by knowledge-able organization. Which was the more sincere and responsive work?

American literary rebels of late seem to suffer from the usual ambitions which they should be scorning. They insist that they are poets, artists, aestheticians, tragic philosophers; we know from their work at its best that they are primarily rebels. It had been better if they had played it straight.

30. Jack Kerouac, *On the Road* (New York, 1958), p. 11.

31. *Ibid.*, p. 49.

32. *Ibid.*, p. 89. Sigal, *Going Away*, p. 60, makes a similar point: "Negroes have a *dense* life." Part of the issue here is the intensity of outcast sensibility, which has a broad recurrence not specifically Negro (despite James Baldwin, *The Fire Next Time*).

33. Jack Kerouac (New York, 1962). Some of what is said about Kerouac could also apply to others, such as Thomas Wolfe.

34. *Lonesome Traveler*, p. 176.

35. John Rechy, *City of Night* (New York, 1964), p. 357.

8—Naturalism and the American Joe

1. As Vladimir notes, *Waiting for Godot* (New York, 1954), p. 76. This may also be an ironic identification with the "aesthetes."

2. For the circularity, see Fredrick J. Hoffman, *Samuel Beckett* (Carbondale, Ill., 1962), p. 139. The repeated inversion of clichés is also circular: the cliché becomes a joke which reaffirms the cliché—the last reach of romantic double irony. So does the constant double-play of the actors aware that they are characters who are actors.

3. See Martin Esslin, *The Theatre of the Absurd* (New York, 1961), p. 37, who says a favorite Beckett quote was Democritus, "Nothing is more real than nothing."

4. Frederick R. Karl, *The Contemporary English Novel* (New York, 1962), p. 9, argues that Beckett is the "real rebel" (in contrast to merely "angry" writers) who protests "against the entire order of the universe." But there is something essentially undefiant—no opposition—about Beckett's tone, and the other works rarely have any rebellious quality, especially the novels.

5. These, and others, can be found in *The Hobo's Hornbook*, "A Repertory for a Gutter Jongleur," collected and annotated by George Milburn (New York, 1930). Over all, a not very impressive collection. Some of the more famous examples cited below can be found in standard folk song collections: *A Treasury of American Folklore*, ed. B. A. Botkin (New York, 1944), pp. 882 ff.; *The Folk Songs of North America*, ed. Alan Lomax (New York, 1960), pp. 435 ff. Some of the fine obscene songs are hard to come by.

6. See *IWW Songs, To Fan the Flames of Discontent* (30th ed. Chicago, 1962)—the famous "Little Red Song Book." Most are bombastically bad and make a Marxist misuse of the hobo material. Most of Joe Hill's have been overrated because of the sentimental legends created about him.

7. John Greenway, *American Folksongs of Protest* (Philadelphia, 1953), p. 203. The very words, of course, suggest a political-actionist bias. While Greenway provides good summaries of Joe Hill and some of the other figures, we must ignore the folklorists' tiresome pedantry of non-qualitative definitions about the folkish. When it is found out that a self-conscious intelligence has improved a slopped-up popular version of a piece probably done by an exceptional individual in the first place, they reject the piece—an anti-intellectual and anti-individualist bias which pervades such discussions.

8. Examples of the more primitive blues about traveling are given by Paul Oliver, *The Meaning of the Blues* (New York, 1963), chap. ii. See the well-known distinction, "When a woman gets the blues she hangs her head and cries. When a man gets the blues, he flags a freight train and rides."

9. For authorship and comment, see Greenway, *op. cit.*, p. 175.

10. Professor Leonard Frye kindly brought this poem to my attention.

11. Hart Crane, *Collected Poems*, ed. Waldo Frank (New York, 1933), pp. 13–18. The following comments are not intended as a complete explication of this section.

12. *Ibid.*, pp. 32 and 34.

13. *Ibid.*, p. 53.

14. *Ibid.*, p. 113. The only detailed explication I can find of this poem is my own: "Crane's 'Key West,'" *The Explicator*, XVIII, No. 17 (December, 1959). Crane indicated its capstone relation by making it the first and title piece of his final volume.

15. I have come across very little other American poetry of the road deserving comment. In dozens of Beat volumes of verse there is hardly anything about the road, though there are some indications that it is an underlying experience. Perhaps the best one is William Margolis, "The Hegira-Cycle" in F. J. Rigney and L. D. Smith, *The Real Bohemia* (New York, 1961), pp. 177 ff.

16. Edward Dahlberg, *Bottom Dogs* (New York, 1930). There is a new Preface to the later edition (San Francisco, 1961) in which Dahlberg expresses drastic dissatisfaction with his naturalistic style, but his later fervent poetic-moralist ornateness is a doubtful improvement. See my review-article on Dahlberg's autobiography, *Because I Was Flesh*, *Shenandoah* (Fall, 1964).

17. Jack Conroy, *The Disinherited* (London, 1934), pp. 180 ff. and 240 ff. Since "proletarian novels" are simply an inverted extension of Victorian fiction, one might ignore the final moralizings.

18. Nelson Algren, *Somebody in Boots* (New York, 1935). See, also, comments on Algren below.

19. George Orwell, *Down and Out in Paris and London* (New York, 1933, 1959), p. 150. It is part of Orwell's usual limitation that he missed much of the real tramping side—see Phelan's works cited above and Philip O'Connor's *Vagrancy*. But implicitly, Orwell experienced what many make much of and what O'Connor insists upon: "Once one has at all seen outside normal society, one cannot forget . . . the complete enclosure of the respectable against the rest." *The Lower View*, p. 67.

20. The standard history of the Wobblies is Paul F. Brissenden, *The I. W. W.: A Study of American Syndicalism* (New York, 1919, 1957) which, whatever its factual merits, quite lacks necessary interpretation. The sentimental attachment to the Wobbly as image of the rebel is amazing; rebels taking a spokesman posture, such as Kenneth Rexroth and

Jack Kerouac, identify themselves with the Wobbly tradition.

21. John Dos Passos, "Vag," *The Big Money* (New York, 1937), pp. 559–61.

22. Some of the popular attitudes to the "Cult of the Good Joe" are discussed by Orin E. Klapp, *Heroes, Villains and Fools* (New York, 1962), pp. 108 ff.

23. William Faulkner, *Light in August* (New York, 1950), p. 197.

24. *Ibid.*, p. 296.

25. *Ibid.*, p. 407.

26. *Ibid.*, p. 322. For a discussion of the major theme, see William Van O'Connor, *The Tangled Fire of William Faulkner* (Minneapolis, 1953), chap. vi, to which I contributed numerous points. However, I see no evidence for O'Connor's curious statement that some of the characters move "inside the religion" since Hightower renounces his, Lena never has any, and Byron—in taking to the road after Lena—effectively becomes the ex-Everyman of Christian duty. O'Connor also seems to miss that Faulkner's sexual scenes are usually his worst writing.

27. See Leslie A. Fiedler, "Dead-End Werther: the Bum as American Culture Hero," *An End to Innocence* (Boston, 1948), pp. 183–90, who seems right about Jones but misses the other qualities in the bum as American hero.

28. I am summarizing an unpublished study of *Night Rider, At Heaven's Gate, All the King's Men, World Enough and Time,* and *The Cave.* The later, incidentally, reverses the father-killing pattern and expiation into a son-killing pattern, which gets attempted justification.

29. The imagery of the road is both a stock part of our experience and of our literature. For example, when a minor poet, with some skill at the small turn-of-wit piece, gets unduly ambitious he turns to the subject. See Louis Simpson, *At the End of the Open Road* (Middletown, Conn., 1963). The main poems are exercises in a mild mood of cultivated disillusionment, and mediocre comments on the Whitmanian images rather than on any experiences. The images and the morals are the obvious ones: "The Open Road goes to the used-car lot." "At the end of the open road we come to ourselves." And so forth.

9—Contemporary American Outcasts

1. I must confess to having made a partly antithetical argument in "Poetic Naturalism in the Contemporary Novel," *Partisan Review* (Summer, 1959).

2. *The Assistant* (New York, 1958), p. 99. Most of the discussions of Malamud fail to note his moralistic naïveté and heaviness. In Malamud's first novel, *The Natural*, the author even more elaborately poeticized his naturalistic American Joe in allegorizing a baseball story into a grail quest for corruptive American success. His later heroes, such as Levin in the academic-picaresque *A New Life* (a mild satire on the usual second-rate American college) and in many of his stories, are essentially Wandering Jews.

3. *Ibid.*, p. 100.

4. *The Man Who Was Not With It* [republished as *The Wild Life*] (New York, 1957), p. 218. Gold's two flat earlier novels, and his ambitious and sententious later fictions, do not merit comment. Counterfeit rebelliousness can take some peculiar involutions; see, for example, Jack Ludwig, *Confusions* (New York, 1963). Outside of some amusing bohemian reportage ("Thoreau in California"), fearfully undercut, the author does awkward convolutions around why an ambitious academic Harvard-type nice-guy-snob can't be a rebel, wants to be a rebel, and hopes he is/isn't a rebel.

5. Defensively, I note that my commentary on Salinger was written more than half a dozen years ago, before some of the long, pretentious and self-indulgent Glass family stories brought out properly unfavorable criticism of Salinger.

6. *The Adventures of Augie March* (New York, 1953), p. 117. Bellow does well with some of his women characters, but that is not my subject here. His best single work, as is usually pointed out, is the novella *Seize the Day* with its devastating presentation of the corruption of a weak innocent who yearns for success, led on by a con-man sage. (Bellow's popular reputation—not altogether his fault—has also mislead some readers into finding an ameliorative solace in its self-pitying and death-longing final scene.)

7. *A Walk on the Wild Side* (New York, 1957), pp. 249–50.

8. *Ibid.*, p. 261. Probably Algren is more successful in the limited ambitions of the sketches in *Never Come Morning* (New York, 1942) where he more directly carries out the Whitmanian injunction to "belong to those convicts and prostitutes myself." But, as his later writings (including the coyly antique "Preface" to the 1962 edition) indicate, that takes some forcing. In his most recent pastiche, *Who Lost An American?* (New York, 1963), his mixture of travel sketches, weak verses, burlesques of other rebels (such as Mailer), and punchy ruminations too often mix merely personal whimsey and ponderous off-key proclamations "The artist's usefulness has always been to stand in an ironic affiliation to his society"

(p. 257), he writes—and practices by hitting marshmallows with sledgehammers, and vice-versa.

9. *One Flew Over the Cuckoo's Nest* (New York, 1963), p. 255.

10. *Ibid.*, p. 30.

11. *Ibid.*, p. 57.

12. *Ibid.*, p. 46.

13. *Ibid.*, p. 104. The Combine's conforming apparatus may derive from the fantasy anti-utopian mechanisms in William Burroughs' *Naked Lunch*, discussed below.

14. *Ibid.*, p. 134.

15. See, for example, the discussion by Ihab Hassan, *Radical Innocence: Studies in the Contemporary American Novel* (Princeton, 1961), pp. 194–200, who seems to quite miss this main point. He concludes his sometimes stimulating discussion viewing the book as "a mad, nugatory snarl," which doesn't fit at all. Uplift must be the besetting sin of literary criticism.

16. *The Ginger Man* (New York, 1958), p. 231. This is the expurgated edition. The earlier unexpurgated edition has been republished (London, 1963), but, with the exception of a few nice details about oral intercourse and some homosexual advice to his miserable mirror-image (and some tiresome over-detailing of an exhibitionist scene), the abridged edition is as good, and even, because of the tightening in expurgation, better than the unexpurgated. Part of the novel has also been directly transmitted into a play of the same title (London, 1960) with a dryly amusing preface. The author's other play, *Fairy Tales of New York* (New York, 1961) is dull and flat fantasy. His later novel, *A Singular Man* (New York, 1963) has a few nicely perverse comic bits but the verve mostly disappears in pathetic and paranoid whimsey about a vaguely rich eccentric in New York. The mannered concerns (such as with a mausoleum), the shoddy plot devices (such as the auto accident death of the heroine), etc., badly deflate the self-indulgent burlesque and the occasional concern with commitment in a madly lonely society. Most significant rebel works, it is certainly fair to say, are single shots.

17. *Ibid.*, p. 318.

18. *Ibid.*, p. 256.

19. *Ibid.*, p. 236.

20. *Ibid.*, pp. 244 and 256.

21. *Ibid.*, p. 168. The ditties are in an oral tradition, and must be read appropriately to get the relevant effect (this one, perhaps, read gaily for the first three lines, hard and dropping on the last line).

22. *Ibid.*, p. 327. There are, of course, other contemporary novels that could be discussed here, such as John Barth, *The Sot-Weed Factor* (New York, 1960). But that would be a most peculiar example since Barth seems to be an abstruse diabolist counterfeiting as an allegorical moralist (and not just in an inhumanly forced parable such as *End of the Road*). My crime, says the hero of the mock-seventeenth-century picaresque *Sot-Weed*, is "the crime of innocence. . . . There's the true Original Sin . . . (p. 788). But all the "proof" for this carefully built up moral is hilariously fantastic. The reality of this cleverly manipulated work is all demonic, the moral gloss all pyrrhic.

Other works of this period, such as Ralph Ellison's *Invisible Man* and Joseph Heller's *Catch-22*, obviously partly fit into my suggested pattern (and also suffer from ambiguous over-poeticization and archness).

10—Rebellion Against Rebellion?

1. For an example of the skittish point on rebel fashionableness, see Leslie Fiedler, "Foreward" to J. Hasek, *The Good Soldier: Schweik* (New York, 1963); see also *No! in Thunder* (discussed below). The point is also a commonplace with book reviewers.

2. I am, of course, thinking of the gross categories of C. P. Snow, *The Two Cultures* (Cambridge, 1959).

3. Paul Goodman develops the point in *Growing Up Absurd* (New York, 1960), chap. viii, "An Apparently Closed Room." His label is given in *Making Do* (New York, 1963), p. 142, where he also identifies *Evergreen Review, Esquire*, etc., as places of such psuedo-rebellion. See, for a related example, *Writers in Revolt*, ed. Richard Seaver, Terry Southern and Alexander Trocchi (New York, 1963).

4. In shaping several of these points, I am indebted to discussions with Elbridge Rand.

5. For an academic example, see the discussions in *The American Style*, ed. E. Morrison (New York, 1959).

6. See the discussions of Mailer, Fiedler, Wilson and Camus, below. Sir Herbert Read, in his many discussions of poetry and art, provides an even more obvious example. The artist-as-rebel is a bohemian commonplace. Typically, Maxwell Bodenheim wrote, "The artist's role is to disturb." *My Life and Loves* (New York, 1961), p. 56.

7. Geraldine Pelles summarizes, somewhat loosely, some of the aesthetic background of this "fetishism" of the artist as a "model of deviance and creativity." "The Image of the

Artist," *Journal of Aesthetics and Art Criticism*, XXI (Winter, 1962), 119–38. My emphasis is broader.

8. See Albert Parry, *Garrets and Pretenders* "A History of Bohemianism in America," (rev. ed.; Gloucester, Mass., 1960), and "Enter Beatniks" by Harry T. Moore. Parry constantly refers to "jollity" in his compendium of bohemian detail—something no more recent writer would certainly do, as Moore makes clear. While Parry has a few suggestive points, including the "declassed" role of the bohemians (p. xxxi), the revolt against work (p. 163), etc., he quite misses the connections with utopianism and other forms of marginal living. Philip O'Connor aptly notes the major point: "the essence of Bohemianism is an ideal life (or the attempt at it) according to some dim vision of communality." *Vagrancy* (London, 1963), p. 39. An ex-bohemian, O'Connor elsewhere awkwardly argues for a natural exile from conventional life rather than a forced rebellion against it. *Living in Croesor* (London, 1962), p. 106. Actually, in this badly written book, he is just holding forth for another form of genuine bohemianism, equally based on the crucial principle of the rebel: "Failure is nearly divine," p. 104.

9. See, for example, Seymour Krim, *Views of a Nearsighted Cannoneer* (New York, 1961). The novels mentioned below provide the evidence.

10. For bibliography, see *Garrets and Pretenders*. See, also, the rather slick retelling of Allen Churchill, *The Improper Bohemians* (New York, 1959), p. 28.

11. See London, Whitman, Kerouac, Sigal, etc. O'Connor and "Box Car Bertha" detail the fusion of utopian, bohemian and hobo elements. Michael Harrington comments on the purposive rebellion into poverty as quite different from forced poverty. *The Other America* (London, 1963), pp. 87–89.

12. Weirdly enough—and with amazing sociological naivete—the point is usually made in indignation in the studies of bohemias.

13. My point here is not the usual one in either praise or blame of Beat poetry. If one takes as representative (though it is not very good) *The New American Poetry*, ed. Donald Allen (New York, 1960), the general level is low. There are a few interesting bits by Ginsberg, Blackburn, Welch and Leroi Jones, but reading their collections does not much raise the estimate since the re-Victorian bubbling about love and beauty, the too easy rages, and the imitation of each other do not achieve much. Undoubtedly, future discussions of rebellious poetry in this period will not include many

poets in this anthology, nor hardly anyone directly connected with these movements. Contrast a more genuine, though uncertain and excessively literary, rebellious poet: Karl Shapiro, *The Bourgeois Poet* (New York, 1964). His suggestive directions could bear further discussion in this context, despite his refusal to follow out his rebellion.

14. Lawrence Lipton, *The Holy Barbarians* (New York, 1959, 1962), p. 308.

15. See Francis J. Rigney and L. Douglas Smith, *The Real Bohemia* (New York, 1961). They put undue emphasis on "creativity" in their summary, pp. 177 ff.—against their own evidence.

16. Ned Polsky, "The Village Beat Scene: Summer 1960," *Dissent*, VIII (Summer, 1961), pp. 339–59. An apt study, though drugs and Gregory Corso get more than their due. Allen Ginsberg's "America" and Bob Kaufmann's *Abominist Manifesto* provide good examples of Beat wisecracks as literature (see the anthologies given in Note 4, chap. 1).

17. See the essays in the anthologies mentioned above. For some representative muddy and shallow Beat pronouncements on revolt, see Michael McClure *et al.*, *Journal for the Protection of All Beings,* I (San Francisco, 1961).

18. Churchill, *op. cit.*, p. 329.

19. Mill is appropriately quoted in many of the studies of American eccentricity. See the start of Gerald W. Johnson, *The Lunatic Fringe* (New York, 1957)—a newspaper level account of some slightly more daring than usual American political figures. See also Irving Wallace, *The Square Pegs* (New York, 1957), p. 24—a picturesque account of oddities (mostly minor belle-lettrists)—who also notes the relative lack of eccentricity in America. To go a separate way in America obviously requires more self-conscious and willed rebellion. Contemporary American fiction also has far less eccentrics—almost the main stock of such witty British writers as Iris Murdoch. This may be what the literary officializers, such as Lionel Trilling, should be talking about when they discuss the lack of "social texture" in American literature. But, as the above works on American eccentrics indicate (including their authors) much of the eccentricity here is so minor as not to deserve detailed consideration.

20. The several intellectual "best-sellers" each year are usually bohemian reportage—most often "upper-bohemian" and anti-rebellious.

21. The phrase is Wolfe's in *The Magic of Their Singing* New York, 1961). This over-written didactic attack on hipsterism by an intelligent writer takes "left-wing New York" radical values (discussed in Mailer and Goodman,

below) as a happy ending: orgiastic potency, meaningful work, Zionism, and adds being well-dressed. William Gaddis, *The Recognitions* (New York, 1955), is a thousand ornate pages of obsessive religious pedantry, macabre effects and satire on more old-fashioned New York and international bohemianism. Pynchon's *V.* (New York, 1964) is mostly an exotic-bizarre symbolist dallying with bohemians ("The Sick Crew") in an elaborate and arbitrary quest for the usual rebel illumination—"a dream of annihilation" (p. 190), the ultimate nothing on which one could found a true awareness of existence. Lawrence Durrell is the British counterpart of these writers, though he has a somewhat more antique romantic cultism of the artist which he ornately imposes on a naturalistic and commonplace moral view of reality.

22. The works mentioned, and similar ones, could provide the subject for another book on literary rebels since such prose-poetry accounts may provide a penultimate rebel literary form. Also practiced by lesser writers, such as the mawkish Kenneth Patchen in *The Journal of Albion Moonlight* (New York, 1961), contrast a more learned and less rebellious but equally tedious British counterpart such as David Jones, *In Parenthesis* (New York, 1962); it provides one of our major literary traditions, rarely examined as such, as I pointed out in some inadequate remarks on the subject in "Timeless Prose [E. E. Cummings]," *Twentieth Century Lit.* (Summer, 1958). But the tradition of rebelliously independent poetic sensibility has become much obscured, not only by *avant-kitsch* and the archly psuedo-rebellious novels published every year (apparently the "serious" taste of commercial editors) but by the loss of communal and formal values which provide the necessary footing for the rebel's individual defiances and literary violations.

23. Citations are to the first edition (Paris, 1959). There has been an American edition since this was written. The continuations, *The Soft Machine* and *Novia Express*, do not add anything. For a restrained discussion of all three, see Ihab Hassan, "The Subtracting Machine: the Work of William Burroughs," *Critique*, VI (Spring, 1963), 4–23.

24. See the author's quite defensive remarks in the "Atropied Preface" at the end of *Naked Lunch*, p. 212.

25. See "Introduction . . . ," *Evergreen Review*, VI (Jan.–Feb., 1962), 99–109. (This issue also contains a blurb disguised as a critical discussion which presents *Naked Lunch* as a "novel of revolt": E. S. Selden, "the Cannibal Feast.") See, also, Burroughs, "Deposition: Testimony Concerning a Sickness," *Evergreen Rev.*, IV (Jan.–Feb., 1960).

26. Mary McCarthy, "Déjeuner sur l'Herbe," *The New York Review of Books* (Special Issue, n. d.), pp. 4–5—one of the better reviews.

27. *Naked Lunch*, p. 69.

28. *Ibid.*, p. 18.

29. *Ibid.*, p. 157. But the theme receives very little narrative or intellectual development.

30. *Ibid.*, p. 114.

31. *Ibid.*, p. 220. I have not discussed literary "experimentalism" as such because much of it is not significantly rebellious. While, from the Dadaists to the Situationists, avant-garde techniques appear to be iconoclastic, they are more often merely pedantic, despite their use by a few incisive literary rebels. The exaggerated technocracy of artistry not only violates the most essential rebel commitments but also often serves as a substitute for, and escape from, meaningful revolt. Burrough's "cut-up" method is generally a narcissistic surrogate which neutralizes his content (as well as anyone else's). The most rebellious styles these days may be "semi-conventional" in appearance, controlled reversals of accepted modes. It is not accidental that "avant-kitsch" is often practiced by and for the unrebellious.

11—Ambiguous Rebels in Literature

1. Of course the more insulting remarks here apply to the author of this book.

2. My citations are to a revised and shortened version of "The Middle Against Both Ends," *Literary Censorship*, ed. E. and K. Widmer (San Francisco, 1961), pp. 84–91. An earlier version appeared in *Encounter*, V (February, 1955), 16–23. Similar essays of Fiedler's are collected in *An End to Innocence* (New York, 1948).

3. *Literary Censorship*, p. 91.

4. Fiedler (New York, 1959).

5. Fiedler (Boston, 1960), p. 5.

6. *Ibid.*, p. 4.—Fiedler's italics. The preceding quotes, pp. 10 and 7. Various other essays in the volume exemplify the points made below. In a later literary polemic, *Waiting for the End* (New York, 1964) Fiedler again maps out the contemporary cultural scene and supposed decadence and deploys idiosyncratic-chic platoons in a burlesque of official-style literary surveys. While his individual discussions are exceptionally thin and arbitrary (compare him on Henry Miller with the critics discussed in my *Henry Miller*) there are some poignant eccentricities on literary sex, literary Jewishness, inverted literary hero worship, etc., which could

provide an interesting case history of the purely literary rebel.

7. There are a number of other examples. A variation is provided by Kenneth Rexroth, ex-proletarian poet with some skill as a translator-adaptor who writes amusingly cranky and egomaniacal literary ruminations. Actually a learned but un-housed pedant with idiosyncratic manners and an I-was-there rebel posturing, he writes most often on esoterica. His sensible rages on racial injustice and fraudulent political and social claims—all part of our overwhelming "Social Lie"—support a longing for "an elite in permanent revolt and alienation." *Assays* (New York, 1961), p. 101. Unfortunately, he attributes this rebellion to student movements or various writers who will not carry the burden. The wisely declassed nostalgia for the heroic rebellion of times past seems badly vitiated by radical uncertainty about any possible rebellious role. See also his essays in *Bird in the Bush* (New York, 1959).

8. Colin Wilson (Boston, 1961). There is some arch satire on bohemians and a portrayal of a modern follower of Crates the Cynic (pp. 182 ff.), handled with his usual chatty and flat didacticism. Another novel, *Ritual in the Dark* (New York, 1961) is a fanciful but poorly written Jack-the-Ripper tale—Wilson's defiance so often turning out to be an obsessive but pedantic interest in sexual-sadist violations.

9. *The Outsider* (Boston, 1956), p. 160.

10. *Ibid.*, pp. 67 and 118.

11. *Ibid.*, p. 197.

12. *Religion and the Rebel* (Boston, 1957), p. 20.

13. *Ibid.*, p. 25.

14. *Ibid.*, pp. 1 and 40.

15. *Ibid.*, p. 148; see, also, pp. 132 and 289. Every third assertion, so to say, seems patently false, such as that all great men are puritans, that there are no middle-aged rebels, etc.

16. *Ibid.*, p. 144. The new discovery of Lawrence (probably Wilson's first reading of a significant portion of the works), however, only shows the usual shallowness when we see it in more detail. See the superficial analysis of Lawrence's fictions in *The Strength to Dream* (Boston, 1962), pp. 182 ff. This book, incidentally, is another moralizing literary excursion with short simple-minded summaries and paraphrases of dozens of additional modern writers. He is perhaps at his best in the common-sense rejection of passive nihilism, "The Implications of Total Pessimism." The by-the-way remarks are as bad as ever, such as that leisure results in neurosis and crime (p. 96). His over-all point, again, is the hortatory affirmation of moral values as necessary to

literature. If he ever wrote better, one would suspect him of "writing down" in such books.

17. *The Stature of Man* (Boston, 1959), p. 75.

18. *The Sex Diary of Gerard Sormes* (New York, 1964), pp. 15 and 17. The rather naive call for super-orgasm is summarized on p. 196. For essays on superman consciousness, see pp. 63 and 130. This is perhaps Wilson's best book, for its unintentional typology of a bland autodidactic (which is one dead-end of the rebel tradition); its pedestrian sexual descriptions (Wilson has gotten over part of his earlier puritanism), and sceptical but fascinated dalliance with magic are its weakest parts.

19. *The Rebel* (New York, 1956), p. 252.

20. *Ibid.*, p. 271.

21. See several of the essays in *Camus*, ed. Germaine Breé (New York, 1962). Philip Thody notes the rhetorical pompousness of much of the latter part and gives a liberal-moralist criticism of Camus' negativism. *Camus* (London, 1961), pp. 138 ff.

22. Albert Camus, *The Rebel* (New York, 1954), p. 21.

23. *Ibid.*, p. 100.

24. *Ibid.*, p. 25.

25. *Ibid.*, p. 288.

26. *Ibid.*, p. 100.

27. *Ibid.*, p. 101.

28. *Ibid.*, p. 303. There are, of course, other suggestive points in Camus' discussion because of this intermittent sympathy with rebellion as an ultimate value.

29. *Resistance, Rebellion and Death* (New York, 1961), p. 256.

30. *The Myth of Sisyphus* (New York, 1955), p. 40.

31. *Ibid.*, p. 90. His morally (but not intellectually or stylistically) admirable essay against capital punishment (like his earlier one against war, "Neither Victims nor Executioners") is essentially vague and hortatory.

32. Several of my points are indebted to discussions with Professor James R. Baker. Much of my commentary shows obvious impatience with many of the discussions of the novella which earnestly aim to find more "positive" values, in a liberal-humanist sense, than it contains. See, for example, Germaine Breé, *Camus* (New Brunswick, N. J., 1961), pp. 141 ff.

33. *The Stranger*, pp. 25, 41, 23 and 52.

34. *Ibid.*, p. 80.

35. *Ibid.*, p. 81.

36. *Ibid.*, p. 124.

37. *Ibid.*, p. 132.

38. *Ibid.*, p. 138. I am ignoring many of Camus' other works, such as *The Plague*. That "novel is paralyzed by its own form," rightly notes Gaëton Picon, "Notes on *The Plague*," *Camus*, ed. Breé, p. 147. The ambiguousness of the plague and the sententious moralisms of "health" and "hard work" also do not allow much rebellious awareness, despite a few curious motifs such as Tarrou wanting to be "a saint without God."

12—Several American Perplexes

1. My comments are based on the two miscellanies, which will be discussed below, some periodical pieces, and his collection of verse, *Death for the Ladies and Other Disasters* (New York, 1962). His doggerel has some aptness when mocking the demi-monde, but more often he is rather spluttering and coy on cancer, the disinherited, phonies, and his own bored search for extremities.

2. *Advertisements for Myself* (New York, 1960), pp. 205 ff.

3. *Ibid.*, p. 20.

4. *Ibid.*, p. 246. Mailer's real terror of failure, of insignificance, militates against his rebellion. See, for example, *Presidential Papers* (New York, 1964), p. 174.

5. *Advertisements*, p. 15.

6. *Ibid.*, pp. 142 ff.

7. *Ibid.*, p. 97.

8. *Ibid.*, pp. 299 ff. Actually, this one was rather less self-flattering and trivial than many of his other ostensibly defiant gestures on the mass media.

9. *Ibid.*, pp. 272, 171 and 463.

10. *Ibid.*, pp. 353 ff.

11. *Ibid.*, p. 200. For an example of his obsession with being "used up" in sex and in writing, etc., see *Presidential Papers*, p. 144. As with so many of Mailer's "far out" gestures, such as his Manicheism, this turns out to be ancient mythology: the sexual "dying" of seventeenth-century poetry (but the translation into artistic gonads is slightly more modern in temper).

12. *Advertisements*, p. 308. I am applying to Mailer his own arguments for the Hipster.

13. *Ibid.*, p. 294.

14. *Ibid.*, p. 348. The other quotes are from "The White Negro."

15. The cancer magic (sometimes similar to Reich's *The Cancer Biopathy*) appears obsessively, even in verses in *Death*

for the Ladies. In *An American Dream* "cancer is the child of madness denied" and comes close to being used to characterize any "bad guy" as well as castrating female. At its best, Mailer's magic is more "white" than this, expressing qualities of spirit, will, conviction and faith, as in his psychological-religious interpretations of Buber's interpretations of Hassidic tales.

16. See *Papers*, p. 88. Mailer's only good descriptive writing in the volume, unfortunately, comes in parts of the scene setting for Kennedy and for the Liston-Patterson fight. Mailer also gets grossly sentimental about a somewhat faded hero of his, Castro, pp. 67 ff. Only Mailer's envious adulation of power could explain why he looks for existential heroism in the ordinary political realms.

17. *Ibid.*, p. 256.

18. My argument that Mailer is an incomplete rebel might be contrasted with an opposite interpretation. See George Alfred Schrader, "Norman Mailer and the Despair of Defiance," *Yale Review*, LI (Winter, 1962), 267–80. He sees Mailer, in Kierkegaardian terms, as attempting to annihilate existence in a futile, sickly romantic (aesthetic) stage. While he makes several suggestive points, such as that Hipsterism combines nihilism and pagan faith in instinctual power, he arrives at the usual and disappointing Kierkegaardian answer, but that ethico-religious stage never shows much relevance to the original problem. (And while one is drawing existential analogies, Mailer's occasional desperate pieties towards figures of power characterize that tradition: Kierkegaard's final submergence in an authoritarian deity, Nietzsche's dubious statements on the "Will to Power," Unamuno's and Heidegger's curious relation to dictators, Buber's partial support of chauvinistic Zionism, Sartre's dalliance with the French Communists, etc. While existentialism can be seen as a philosophy of revolt, it cuts several ways.)

19. *Advertisements*, p. 458.

20. *Ibid.*, pp. 427 ff.

21. My references to *An American Dream* are to the serialized version. This quote is taken from the final installment in *Esquire* (August, 1964), p. 103. The arbitrary and sensational playing with synthetic inner and outer decor loses most of its possible effects by going off in trivial directions, not least at the end. The use of hatred, violence, nausea, etc., to heighten existence is similar to one of the few other self-consciously existential American novels, Richard Wright's *The Outsider.* Wright and Mailer use extreme melodrama as naturally appropriate to the existential search centering in dread, destructively free actions and the ambi-

guity of meaning in a nihilistic universe. In both, however, the violence also points back to social and psychic compulsions—and to the literary form of the sex-murder thriller. There is more rigor to Wright's more bitter—and rhetorical—version of violently guilty knowledge, but neither are satisfactory novels. See my discussion of Wright and existentialism, *Wisc. Studies in Contemp. Lit.*, I (Fall, 1960), 13–21.

22. *Papers*, p. 134 and "Norman Mailer, An Interview," *Paris Review*, VIII (Winter–Spring, 1964), 58.

23. *Papers*, p. 198. As with most writers identifying themselves as existentialists, there is also a strong antipathy to scientism (p. 197).

24. *Ibid.*, pp. 291 ff. I suggest that the over-writing indicates that Mailer himself is uncertain as to just how much in earnest he is about this animism.

25. *Ibid.*, p. 136.

26. *Ibid.*, p. 11. Camus' "Reflections on the Guillotine" appear in *Resistance, Rebellion and Death*, pp. 171 ff. Neither follow out the perplexities of the issue, including the problem of "killing" a large part of a man's life by prolonged imprisonment.

27. Among others, *Papers*, p. 142.

28. *Papers*, p. 170. He is, of course, right—though very awkwardly so—about American political "conservatism" but probably irrelevant from a rebellious point of view in falling into the stock and often meaningless liberal-conservative arguments in his desire to find a visible public role. Rebel politics lie in quite different directions (as in Paul Goodman's "Strike Against Voting").

29. *Papers*, p. 213.

30. *Ibid.*, pp. 128, 139 and 134.

31. *Ibid.*, p. 290.

32. Paul Goodman (New York, 1945). Occasional curious notions never find adequate language or form, even in the title story (the best).

33. Paul Goodman (New York, 1960). Some detailed comments on the stylistic and human inadequacies of Goodman's writing, though marred by a lack of sympathy with and clarity about his ideas, appear in a long review-article of several of Goodman's books by John J. Enck, *Wisconsin Studies in Contemp. Lit.* I (Fall, 1960), 89–103.

34. Paul Goodman (New York, 1959). Outside of a few wisecracks (Joy Scouts for Boy Scouts) and here and there suggestive ruminations on pedagogy and on Schweikish resistance to authority, not much is readable. The fourth volume, *The Holy Terror*, is probably the best. It consists of

abstract reflections on things like "speed," parodies of the *Herald Tribune*'s support of Eisenhower, a surprisingly well-written attack on Parent-Teacher's Association activity (pp. 530 ff.), some Taoist bits, and even—at last—a little concrete description of the city the series is supposedly placed in.

35. Paul Goodman, *Making Do* (New York, 1963), p. 197.

36. *Ibid.*, p. 102. American society, he emphasizes, specializes in making it difficult even to retain one's own sensibility.

37. *Ibid.*, p. 230.

38. *Ibid.*, p. 237.

39. Paul Goodman, *The Lordly Hudson* (New York, 1962), p. 132; Parts 46 and 51 of "Mathew Ready"; and p. 158.

40. *Ibid.*, p. 223; see, also, pp. 30, 43, 45, 56, 57, 77, 91, 157, 163, etc.

41. Paul Goodman, *Drawing the Line* (New York, 1962), p. 87. The best essay in this collection is the critique of liberal professors and similar people failing to act, "The Ineffectuality of Some Intelligent People," pp. 97 ff.

42. Paul Goodman (New York, 1946). The social essays are reprinted in *Drawing the Line*.

43. Paul Goodman (New York, 1963).

44. Paul Goodman, "The Freedom to Be Academic," *Growing Up Absurd* (New York, 1962), pp. 256 ff.

45. Paul Goodman, *The Community of Scholars* (New York, 1962), p. 74.

46. But Goodman is sometimes more earnest than serious, and does not probe the issues. He fails to note, for a representative example, that grading systems partly impersonalize—and free the intransigent from—the vicious "laying on of hands" traditions of academic recommendations and sycophancy. Similarly, much of the "value" of administrative neutralization of values is in allowing contradictory values, and people, to exist, which would not happen (especially to the best and rebellious) if a likely pedagogical ideology were in control. The freest places are rarely the small and committed institutions—and this probably applies broad scale through out social organizations.

47. *Drawing the Line*, p. 41—one of his hedges on drawing the line.

48. *The Community of Scholars*, p. 139. I discuss Goodman's academic piece at such length less from personal bias than because it expresses some of the basic concern of the rebellious intellectual with his own place in society, and has some paradigmatic value for all social organizations. I am

not denying his basic point that much of our educational system and style is an outrageously hypocritical fraud carrying us toward "1984."

49. *Ibid.*, p. 162.

50. *Drawing the Line*, p. 11 — in rejecting "utopian."

51. Paul Goodman, *Utopian Essays and Practical Proposals* (New York, 1962), p. 9.

52. *Ibid.*, p. 34.

53. *Growing Up Absurd*, p. 104.

54. *Utopian Essays*, p. 63.

55. For just one example: he assumes that no jurists have defended the right of literature to arouse sexual feelings. Yet that point has repeatedly been made in books as well as in decisions by Justice William O. Douglas, among others.

56. *Utopian Essays*, p. 78.

57. *Drawing the Line*, p. 84.

58. (New York, 1960 — this is a revised edition).

59. *Utopian Essays*, p. 208.

60. The other citations, such as Kant and Mallarme — or his inordinate admiration for such homosexual fantasists as Cocteau and Genet — obviously lack tangible relevance to American writing, his subject.

61. *Utopian Essays*, p. 227.

62. *Growing Up Absurd*, pp. 177–78. As so often with such writers, who feel unappreciated, personal relationships with related souls override judgment.

63. *Ibid.*, pp. 170 ff.

64. *Utopian Essays*, pp. 249 ff. His one concrete reading — Job — is dully conventional, and misses any emotional crux in the work.

65. *Growing Up Absurd*, p. 96. One of his repeated demands has been for more direct and genuine sexuality for adolescents. It seems to be a good test issue, not only in terms of moral conflict but because it expresses the affirmative belief in human instinctual life and freedom, is basic to any educational philosophy (Toynbee, for instance, argues that early sex and intellectual development are antithetical; rebels almost invariably hold the opposite view), and because it raises some real psychological, social and practical perplexities.

66. *Ibid.*, pp. 102 and 123.

67. *Ibid.*, p. 160. Part of Goodman's trouble is much hasty and sloppy writing; this often seems indigenous to rebels, who frequently have a faith in spontaneity, an impatience to get out their "content," a dubious aesthetic rationalization in terms of "free-flow," and a despairing sense that they will not be heard or understood anyway.

68. Reading the descriptions of puritanic labor in American literature—as with Sherwood Anderson's Jesse Bentley and William Faulkner's McEachern—sharply poses the problems Goodman ignores.

69. *Growing Up Absurd,* pp. 16, 69, 130 and 233. After all, independent life-style is *the* main subject of literary rebels.

Agee, James (poetic-natural-ist), 155

Alexander (King of Kings): counterpart to Diogenes, 8, 15, 16

Algren, Nelson: heroic bum, 103; *Somebody in Boots*, 114, 130; *A Walk on the Wild Side*, 130–31; *Never Come Morning*, 233; *Who Lost an American?* 233–34

American culture: pathology of, *passim*

Anarchism: of Cynics, 6; of Blake, 38, 43–44; of wanderers, 78–84; of hobos, 97, 116; in general, 178, 213

Anderson, Nels: *The Hobo*, 227

Anderson, Sherwood (incho-ate rebel), 104, 122, 247

Angelet, Christian: on Cor-bière, 221

Arendt, Hannah: as political falsification of wandering, 223

Aristotle (Aristotelianism), 9, 40, 46, 136, 161, 196

Art: antithetical to rebels, 13–14; drastic limits of, 48, 205–9; substitute for rebellion, 143–58; as op-position, *passim*; confused with rebellion. *See* Read, Fiedler, Mailer, Camus, Wilson, Goodman, *et al.*

Atwell, Lester (and war lit-erature), 225

Avant-kitsch (chi-chi rebels):

other contemporary exam-ples, 139, 143–58, 237–38; as defined, partly by Good-man, 144, 195, 235; as partly practiced by Good-man, 187–98, 235; earlier form, 208

Baldwin, James: bohemian pseudo-novel, 124, 154; outcast misconceived, 229

Baroja, Pio: picaresque im-petus, 86, 87

Barth, John: moral diabolism of *The Sot-Weed Factor*, 235

Baudelaire, Charles: paro-died by Corbière, 61, 71; nihilistic dream voyage, 90, 226

Beats (American Beat Gen-eration): as latter day Cynics, 4–14, 211; as pseudo-Orientalists, 19–20; confused with politics, 22, 23; "kicks," 31; as masqueraders, 81; as child-cult, 101–6, 123; as vic-tims of Age of Counterfeit, 143–53; attached by Mailer, 182; defended by Goodman, 195; failure in art, 211, 235–37

Beckett, Samuel: tragic-bur-lesque, 29; dumb-show, 48; *Waiting for Godot*, 108–9; as arcane anti-rebel, 155, 229, 230

Bellow, Saul: search for hero (and *Henderson*), 103,

130; *Adventures of Augie March*, 129–30; *Seize the Day*, 233

Bendiner, Elmer: on bums, 222

Berdyaev, Nicolas: anarchist theology, 18

Bion: *also* Menippus, Dio Chrysostom, Oenomaus as literary Cynics, 9

Blackstone, Bernard: on Blake, 216

Blake, William: as antinomian, 18–19, 35, 213, *passim*; mythologizing lonely confusions, 31–32; *Marriage of Heaven and Hell* as epistemology and ontology of rebellion, 35–47; as optimist, 48; as overabstract, 60; as wisely foolish, 69; as cynosure, 167; miscriticized, 215–16

Blechman, Bert (hysterical art-rebel), 139

Bloom, Harold: on Blake, 216

Bodenheim, Maxwell: bohemian pathos, 235

Bohemianism: role of, 10–12; contemporary failure of, 148–54; some literature of, 154–55, 235–38; rebel as spokesman for, 206–7. *See* Beats; Cynics; Goliards; Goodman; Hobos; Mailer

Böhme, Jacob (antinomian mythographer), 18, 38, 46

Bosch, Hieronymous (Brethren of Free Spirit), 17, 212

Bourgeois, épater le (traditional rebel manners), 5–6 *passim*

Box-Car Bertha (as told by Ben Reitman), 92–93, 236

Breé, Germaine: liberal apologetics for Camus, 241

Breton, André, 220. *See also* Surrealism

Brissenden, Paul F.: archivist view of I. W. W., 231

Brossard, Chandler: neonaturalism, 114

Buber, Martin, 243

Burroughs, William: *Naked Lunch*, 155–58; influence on Kesey, 234; critics missing his anti-rebellion, 238–39

Camus, Albert: *The Rebel*, 167–70; *Resistance, Rebellion and Death*, 170; *Myth of Sisyphus*, 170–71; *The Stranger*, 171–73; humanist quasi-rebel, 173–74; critics on, 241–42

Castro, Fidel: masked as rebel, 22; sentimentalized by Mailer, 243

Céline, Louis-Ferdinand: major influence on poetry of disgust, 156

Cervantes, Miguel, 77, 81, 98

Chaplin, Charlie: tramp imagery, 108

Chaucer, Geoffrey: sly minor reporter, 81

Christ, Jesus: Middle Eastern vagrant, 17, 106; as rebel, 18; as Lawrencean lover, 26, 88; as Blakean demon, 39, 40, 41; as sacrificial nihilist, 57; as hobo, 77, 106; as Wandering Jew, 88–89; as Beckett bum, 109; as "American Joe," 118–20; in Kesey's insane asylum, 135

Christianity: prophecy, 4;

similarity to Cynicism but bureaucratized, 10, 17, *passim;* antinomian heretics, 17–19, 31; Blake's rebellion against, 35, 36, 37, 40–42, 44, 46, 47; as disguise of rebellion, 81; mocked by Kazantzakis and Lawrence, 88; mocked by hobos, 110; similar to Marxism, 114; mocked by Melville, 217; loss of elan, *passim*

Chuang-Tzĕ (Taoist): rebellious morality of desire, 19–20

Churchill, Allen: urbane bohemian nostalgia, 152, 236

Clare, John: poetic individualism, 167

Comfort, Alex: *On This Side Nothing,* 87

Conrad, Joseph: as Faustian moralist, 133, 218

Conroy, Jack: proletarian novel, *The Disinherited,* 114

Conservativism: defensiveness of, 22; pervasiveness of, 152, 201; irrelevance of, 203; disguised as rebellion, *see* Fiedler and Wilson; Mailer on, 244

Cook, Albert: pseudo-Aristotelian theory of comedy, 214

Corbière, Tristan: Cynic style, 8, 61; significance of, 33–34, 72–73; young rebel archetype, 60, 72–73; *Les Amours Jaunes,* 60–73; critics on, 217–22; symbolism of, 218

Corso, Gregory (Beat unpoet), 236, 237

Crane, Hart: sense of American road, 78; contradiction in *The Bridge,* 111–13; "Key West," 112, 231

Cranks (rebel eccentricity): 19, 31, 45, *passim*

Crates: Cynic saint, 9, 13; Colin Wilson using, 240

Cummings, E. E., 155

Cynics: basic style of revolt, 4–17, 18, 19, 20, 21, 23, 25, 27, 35, 71, 84. *See* Diogenes

Dahlberg, Edward: *Bottom Dogs,* 114; poetic-naturalist, 231

Davies, W. H.: as American tramp, 98, 228

De Grazia, Sebastian: aristocratic theory of work and leisure, 223

De Sade, Marquise: power as pain, 26; limits of demonic, 26, 171

Devil (demonic): as heroic exploration, 25–27; as wit, 29; as Blake's muse, 37–47; as Melville's method, 53, 59; as Corbière's awareness, 67, 72; Fiedler's exploitation of, 163; Mailer looking for, 183–85; justified, 209

Dio Chrysostom (Cynic), 9

Diogenes of Sinope (the Cynic): as wise man, 4–18; as wit, 4–18, 27; feared by Kafka, 16; as creator of traditionalism, 21, 25; as Falstaff, 28; as joyous, 31; as profound, 33; as Blake's prophet, 35–37; as Corbière's hero, 61, 63, 67; as recurrent rebel type, *passim*

Donleavy, J. P.: search for American hero, 103; *The Ginger Man,* 136–39; *A*

Singular Man and other works, 234–35

Dos Passos, John: "Wobbly" and "Vag" in *U. S. A.*, 116–17; tired naturalist moralist, 128

Dostoevsky, Feodor: spider self-consciousness, 46; mockery of morality of self-interest, 54; part of rebel education, 98; ethic of suffering, 125, 126; Ivan and paradoxes of rebellion, 199–201, 205, 211; explanation for Melville, 217; his flight from freedom, 226

Douglas, William O.: on vagrancy, 222, 227; on censorship, 246

Dudley, Donald R.: main commentator on Cynicism, 212

Durrell, Lawrence: as ersatz-rebel, 238

Edge, William (representative earlier student hobo), 98–99

Education: Cynics as teachers, 7, 12–14, 212, *passim*; academic principle of excluding the best teachers, 82; hoboism as, 96–97; as polite fraud, 128; as auto-didacticism, *see* especially Colin Wilson and Philip O'Connor; Goodman's attacks on universities, 189–92, 245–46; education of rebels, *passim*

Ellison, Ralph (mildly rebellious poetic-naturalist), 235

Enck, John J.: academic criticism of Goodman, 244

Epictetus, 14

Erdman, David V.: on Blake, 215, 216

Esslin, Martin: on Beckett, 29, 230

Excremental vision (rebel mysticism), 138, 157, 185

Existentialism: Cynic similarities, 5; Melville as, 59, 122, 218; Wilson's discovery of, 166; Camus' relation to, 170, 172; Mailer's Americanization of, 181–86, 243–44; Wright's, 243–44; general, 243, *passim*

Failure, positive philosophy of: Cynics and Beats, 5–9; as point of American satire, 130–31; as principle of rebel, 199–210, 236. *See also* Beats, Bohemians, Cynics; Hobos

Faulkner, William: American Joe in *Light in August*, 118–20; style of, 119, 123; Protestant ethos, 119, 247; transvaluing of rebel, 120, 126; W. O'Connor on, 247

Ferlingetti, Lawrence: on Christ, 225

Feur, Lewis S.: unlibertarian liberalism, 211

Fideism (temporary rebellion to re-enforce conformity). *See Avant-kitsch*; Fiedler; Gold; Hipsterism; Salinger; Warren

Fiedler, Leslie A.: on the Imaginary Jew, 87; cultural politician's polemics, 160–64; sneering energy of, 166; as typical case, 173–74; as fiction writer, 225; on bums, 232; usual skittishness, 235; *Waiting for the End,* 239–40

Flynt, Josiah (tramp writer), 97–98, 228

Fogle, Richard: on Melville, 217

Folk literature: "Western," 91–92; of road, 94–96, 108, 110–11, 230; Fiedler on comicbooks, 161–62; anti-rebellious, 201. *See* Hobo

Fourier, François: utopian imagination, 194

Frank, Sebastian (heretic), 17

Friedman, Maurice: academicized existentialism, 218

Frye, Northrup: poeticized pedantry of humor, 214; solipsistic theologizing of Blake, 215

Gaddis, William (gothic *advance-kitsch*), 155, 238

Gellert, Lawrence (folk songs), 110

Genet, Jean: homosexual fantasist, 26, 246; dubious rebel, 171; Nelson's ruminations on, 213

Ghandi, Mahatma: ambiguous ideology of, 185

Gilmore, Harlan: on beggars, 224

Ginsburg, Allen: Old Testament manners, 211; role as Beat poet, 236, 237

Gleckner, Robert F.: pedantic view of Blake, 215

God: non-existence of and how to recreate, 65, 73, 199, 209, *passim*

Gold, Herbert: *The Man Who Was Not With It,* 126–27, anti-rebellious

views of bohemianism, 154, 233

Goliards: as Medieval literary rebels, 77, 78, 84–85, 87

Goodman, Paul: on *avant-kitsch,* 144, 188, 195–96, 235; New York parochialism of, 175, 176, 198; literary works criticized, 186–89; millenarian ideas discussed, 189–98, 244–47; criticism rejected, 195–96

Gorki, Nikolai (socialist influence on hobos), 98

Grass, Günter: *The Tin Drum,* 86–87

Greenway, John: progressivist view of hobo songs, 230

Griffin, John H.: perception from the road, 226

Grimmelshausen, J. J. von, *Simplicissimus,* 86, 87

Guthrie, Woody (folk songs), 110

Harrington, Michael: on rebellious poverty, 236

Hasek, Jaroslav: *The Good Soldier Schweik,* 27, 225; "Schweikism," *passim*

Hassan, Ihab: fashionable criticism of rebels, 234, 238

Hawkes, John: gothic experimentalism, 164

Heller, Joseph (popular rebel writer), 103, 235

Hemingway, Ernest: not source of "hardboiled" style, 110; adolescent manly poses, 123; exploited by Fiedler, 163; copied by Camus, 172; pose used by Mailer, 181; not understood by Goodman, 195; early war writing praised, 225

Heretics: tradition of, 17–19; examples of, *passim*

Herlihy, James Leo (minor "sensitivity" novelist), 128

Hipsterism: as demonic revival, 26; as *avant-kitsch*, 144; Mailer's power obeisance to, 181–82

Hobos: broad significance of, 77; psychology of, 80–81, 93–97; as social and moral rebels, 82–84, *passim*; American style, 91, 92, 93–97; literary hobos, 97–99; Beat and related figures re-doing hobo, 99–105; end and effect of, 106–7; in naturalistic literature, 108–18; in post-naturalism, 118–21, *passim*; commentaries on, 222–24, 227, 230, 231

Hoffman, Fredrick J.: on Beckett, 225; on Christ metaphors, 230

Hoffmann, Charles G.: on Melville, 216

Holmes, John Clellon: on Beats, 105

Homer, 77, 81

Huehns, Gertrude: on political antinomianism, 18

Humor (special rebel qualities): Cynic wit, 8–14; the rebellious black mock, 27–29; Blakean mockery, 45, 46, 47; linked to suffering, 48; in Melville, 54–56; twisted and hysterical in Corbière, 61, 63, 65, 67, 69, 70, 71, 72; in Villon, 85; in picaresque, 85–86; hobo's parodistic, 110–11; of mock rebel, 130; satiric in Kesey, 133–34; dark

farce in Donleavy, 136–38; sick in Burroughs, 157–58; buffoonish in Mailer, 178, 185; earnest-unintentional in Goodman, 187–88, 189, 196; sardonic and grotesque, *passim*

Ibsen, Henrik, 27

Ionesco, Eugene, 29, 48

Ivan (Karamazov). *See* Dostoevsky

James, Henry (polished renunciation), 136

James, William: insight on war, 193

Jarrell, Randall: prefers sentimentality over perversity, 221

Jeremiah: prophet, 3; anti-Zionist, 87

Jewish rebel in literature. *See* Wandering Jew

Joachim of Flora, 18

Job: Melville on, 46; Blake on, 57; Goodman on, 246

Johnson, Gerald W.: rebelliousness as liberal tolerance, 237

Jonah, 3

Jonas, Hans: gnosticism as nihilism, 214

Jones, David: example of poeticized incomprehension, 238

Jones, James: rebellion as masochism, 120; he-man pose, 181

Jones, Leroi (slight Beat poet), 236

Julian (misnamed "the apostate"): "purifying" Cynicism, 14

Jusserand, J. J.: on wanderers, 224

Justice (rebel demand for). *See* Freedom; Love; Passion

Kafka, Franz: fear of rebellion, 16; "Bartleby" similar to, 49; Goodman's Freudian interpretation of, 196; basic worship of power, 212
Karl, Frederick: over-statement of Beckett, 230
Kaufman, Bob: Beat poem on Christ, 225; wisecrack role, 237
Kazantzakis, Nikos: on vagrant and rebel Christ, 88; on fervent nonexistence of God, 225
Kazin, Alfred: example of imposed liberal morality, 218
Kemp, Harry (tramp poet turned bohemian), 97, 111, 228
Kennedy, John F.: power called nice, 15; as "golden goy," 181; Mailer on, 183, 184
Kerouac, Jack: intensification of experience, 31; holy delinquency, 78; *Dharma Bums, On the Road, Lonesome Traveller, Big Sur,* 101–6; beyond doctrine, 113; supposed aesthetic of, 229
Kerrigan, Anthony: on Baroja's rebellious taste, 224
Kesey, Ken: seeking vital hero, 103; *One Flew Over the Cuckoo's Nest,* 133–36
Kierkegaard, Soren: authoritarian streak in, 243
Klapp, Orin E.: on American Joe, 232

Krim, Seymour: on bohemian mores, 236

Laforgue, Jules: contrasted with Corbière, 68, 221
Lautrémont: contrasted with Corbière, 60
Lawrence, D. H.: Black Mass of, 26–27; responsiveness of, 31, 32; double-ethic like Blake's, 39; wanderer, 78, 88; on Whitman, 92; rejection of WASPs, 104; on Dahlberg and American failure, 114; influence on Bellow, 129; about American literature, 132; falsified by Wilson, 165, 240; recognized as existentialist, 166; thoughtfully studied, 213
Lazarillo de Tormes: example of picaresque attitude and form, 85–86, 87
Levi, Ida: on Corbière, 220
Lewis, R. W. B.: for moralizing of picaresque, 224
Lewis, Wyndham: nihilist criticism, 214
Liberalism: irrelevance to understanding rebels, *passim*; rebels provide test of genuineness, 22; failure of, 50—and *see* Melville; lack of range, 153; attacked by Fiedler, 163–64; of Camus, 168–71; disguised, 180; attacked by Mailer, 181; basically antipathetic to rebels, 203; for further examples, *see* various academic critics cited (Feur, Trilling, etc.)
Liberation (quasi-rebel political coeterie), 213
Lindsay, Vachel: on road, 93, 111

Lipton, Lawrence: Beat pathology, 150

London, Jack: on road, 78; *On Road*, 97; influence on hobo writers, 98; more than naturalist, 113; mawkishness, 227

Love. *See* Freedom; Justice; Passion

Love, Edmund G.: sentimentalizing of marginals, 222

Lucian: attack on Cynics, 15

Ludwig, Jack: example of Ivy-bohemian literature, 233

McClure, Michael (Beat diatribe), 237

MacIntyre, C. F.: on Corbière, 219

Mailer, Norman: as antinomian, 18; his "White Negro," 104, 180–82; similarity to Goodman, 175–78, 198; rebel writings and confusions discussed, 175–86; attacked by Goodman, 188, 195; other criticisms of, 242–44

Malamud, Bernard: *The Assistant* as transvaluation of American Joe, 124–26; other novels, 233

Marcus, Mordecai: on Melville, 217

Margolis, William: road poem, 231

Martineau, René: on Corbière, 222

Martinson, Harry: on road, 223

Marx, Leo: quasi-Marxist view of Melville, 50–52, 217

Marxism: rebels confused with, 21–22; application to Melville illustrates falsity of, 50–52; mythology used by hobos, 81, 98; Sigal's dependence on, 99, 100; naturalist's imposition of, 113, 115; disguised by Fiedler, 162; attacked by Camus, 168, 169; mars Mailer's style, 181, 182; deleterious influence on sociology of work and wandering, 222, 223

Melville, Herman: with rebels, 33; "Bartleby" analyzed as existential rebellion, 48–59, 109; relative ambiguity, 60; as tramp, 92; as generally metaphysical rebel, 122; used by Fiedler, 163; criticism of, 216–18

Millburn, George: hobo poetry, 230

Mill, John Stuart, 153

Miller, Henry: as modern Thoreau, 24–25; as crank-buffoon, 32; as rogue, 103; in mainstream of American style, 123; as influence on Donleavy, 136; influence on Burroughs, 156; as criticized, 239

Milton, John: Satanist source, 25, 41; as authoritarian, 216

Millpond, Stewart (eccentric poet), 220

Montherlant, Henry de: aristocratic-rebel defense of Peregrinos, 15–16, 212

Moore, Harry T.: on bohemianism, 236

Morton, A. L.: on antinomianism, 18

Murdoch, Iris (novelist of eccentricity), 237

Murray, Gilbert: on Diogenes, 212

Mysticism: *see* excremental vision

Nabokov, Vladimir: *Lolita*, 121

Naeve, Lowell, 225

Naturalism (literary): as in conflict with Crane's mythic purpose, 112–13; using American road as subject with revulsive morality, 113–18; given mythic form of American Joe, 118–19; adapted by Faulkner, 118–20; poeticized in amorphous culture, 122–24; meaning of poetic-naturalism, 123, 129, 132; stylized in Malamud, 124–26, 233; fideistic ornateness in post-World War II fiction, 126–31; cerebralized by Bellow, sentimentally burlesqued by Algren, 129–31, 233–34; schizophrenic extreme in work of Burroughs, 155–58; neo-naturalism, *passim*

Negro: rebel identification with defeated, dark and demonic, 104, 181–82, 229; Wright, 243–44

Nelson, Benjamin N.: a metapsychology for Genet, 213

Nietzsche, Frederich: aristocratic rebel, 28; imagery similar to Blake, 39; inverted by Camus, 170; his rebel hyperbole followed by Mailer, 178; authoritarian strain, 243

Nigg, Walter: on heretics, 212

Nihilism: of power and technological-bureaucratic society, 8, 11, 16, 20–23, 133–35, 143, 192, *passim*; counter-nihilism (will to truth) of rebels, 199–210 *passim*; as basic characteristic of life, *passim*

Nurmi, Martin K.: on Blake, 215

Obscenity: justified as style for linking disparities, 5–6. *See also* individual writers (Burroughs, *et al.*)

O'Connor, Philip: on psychology of vagrancy, 80–81, 96; as writer, 223, 231; on bohemianism, 236

O'Connor, William Van: on Faulkner, 232

Organized System. *See* American culture; Paul Goodman; Nihilism

Ortega y Gasset, Jose, 144

Orwell, George: *Down and Out in Paris and London*, 114–15, 231

Paracelsus, Theophrastus: rebel philosopher, 32; influence, 38, 45, 214, 216

Parodistic form (and mockery, burlesque, buffoonery, artistic inversion, poetic pot-pourri, etc.): as basic rebel literary mode, 9, 10, 11–14, 19, 23–25, 26, 27–28, 31, 32, 33, 35–47, 48, 53, 56, 59, 67–73, 84–85, 86, 87, 88, 110, 130, 133, 136, 155, 156, 175–86, 209–10

Parry, Albert: on nice American bohemians, 236

Patchen, Kenneth: example

of self-indulgent rebel rhetoric, 195, 238

Peck, Jim, 225

Pelles, Geraldine: loose discussion of bohemian aesthetology, 235

Peregrinos (Cynic), 15, 178

Phelan, Jim (tramp writer), 223

Picaresque literature: general tradition, 77–78, 81, 83; in European writings, 85–87, 88, 115, 223–25, 227; in American autobiography, 87, 91, 92, 98–106, 114, 227–29; in contemporary poetic-naturalism, 122–39, 231, 232–35

Plato: dislike of Diogenes, 6, 9

Politics (as institutional power claiming moral good): only negative relevance to rebel, 8–10; rebel as antithesis of revolutionary, 18–19, 20–22; some rebels confused by revolutionary sentiments, 21, 98–100, 114, 115; rebel tests quality of politics, 22; political ideals as greatest form of destruction, 25; Blake's politics, 38; outsider protests, 94, 97, 209, 244; politics usually against genuine outcasts, 107, 115–16; Camus' concern with, 168, 241, and confusion about, 169; Mailer's confusion about, 178–80, 181–84, 186; Goodman's anti-politics as major rebel tradition, 189, 191, 193–97. See also Conservativism; Liberalism; Marxism; Wobbly

Polsky, Ned: on Beats, 237

Protestantism: contained rebellion, 3; antinomianism, 18–19; destructive pattern to be rebelled against, 119–20; rebellion against puritanism, passim; necessary rebellion against work ethos, 196–97, 247. See Beats; Hobos

Psychology: of anti-rebels, 10–12, 78–79, 88, 94–95, 200–210, passim; of rebels, passim; of sexual orgasm, 32, 42, 181–82, 193–94, 242, 246; of wandering, 77–86, 89–92, 94–107

Purdy, James: example of "child-cult" writer, 128

Pynchon, Thomas: example of ornate bohemian literature, 155, 238

Quennell, Peter: on Corbière, 221

Raglan, Lord: on Falstaff, 214

Raleigh, Walter: as rebel poet, 221

Read, Herbert: confusion of art and rebellion, 21, 213, 235

Rechy, John: City of Night, 106

Reich, Wilhelm: metapsychology of sexual rebellion and pervasive influence, 32, 183, 184, 214, 242

Revelation, Book of: quoted, 3

Revolution (as antithetical to rebel). See Politics

Rexroth, Kenneth: "Crow-Jimism," 104; as professional rebel, 231, 240

Rigney, F. J. (and L. D. Smith): on Beats, 237

Rimbaud, Arthur: demonic, 27, 31; contrasted with Corbière, 60; mentioned, 228

Robertson, R. B.: on rebellious whalers, 227

Rochester, John Wilmot, Earl of: as rebel poet, 28, 214

Rollins, Philip A.: on cowboy, 226

Rosenfeld, Isaac: on bohemia, 152

Roth, Henry (minor ghetto fiction), 164

Rousseau, J, -J., 184, 193

Salinger, J. D., *Catcher in the Rye*, 127–28, 233

Sartre, J. -P.: on Baudelaire, 226; anti-rebellious politics, 243

Seelye, John D.: recent genteel criticism of hobo, 227

Senior, John: on limitation of occultism in modern literature, 214

Sexual orgasm: favorite rebel metaphor—often taken literally—for intensity of response and passionate freedom, 32, 42, 181–82, 193–94, 242, 246

Shakespeare, William: Falstaff as rebel, 27–28, 214

Shapiro, Karl: convert to literary rebellion, 216, 236

Shrader, Alfred: existential moralizing of Mailer, 243

Sigal, Clancy: *Going Away* as post-hobo rebel account of the road, 99–101, 102, 228; *Weekend in Dinlock* as best work, 229

Simpson, Louis: decorous slight verse on road tradition, 232

Snow, C. P.: view of cultural bureaucrat, 144

Socrates: as moderate Diogenes, 6, 7, 21

Sonnenfeld, Albert: on Corbière, 218, 219, 221

Southern, Terry (shrewd *avant-kitsch*), 139, 235

Stein, Gertrude, 208

Steinbeck, John: example of sentimental rebelliousness, 114, 129

Stendahl (Henri Beyle): Julien Sorel as rebel type, 172, 173

Streetwalker: prostitute as rebel and her perception, 226

Styron, William: high serious mode of bohemian reportage, 124, 154

Swedenborg, Emmanuel: Blake's use of, 38, 40, 41, 46, 216

Surrealism: as modern demonic, 26; humor of, 29; questionable application to Corbière, 66, 67; Camus on bad politics of, 168

Tallman, Warren: defense of Kerouac, 229

Taoism (oriental Cynicism), 19–20, 195, 245

Thielicke, Helmut: Christian view of nihilistic rebel, 215

Thody, Philip: on Camus, 241

Thompson, Laurence: on Melville, 217

Thoreau, Henry David: as related to Diogenes, 7; as antinomian mocker with rebel aesthetic and related to Diogenes and Miller, 23–25; positive nihilism, 31; as philosophical tramp, 92; paradoxically, part of American cult of experience, 122; Kesey marching to Thoreau's tune, 136; comparison to Goodman, 194; distortion of, 213

Tolstoy, Leo: as antinomian rebel, 17, 18, 209

Toynbee, Arnold: view of sexual reactionary, 246

Trilling, Lionel (as New York literary coeterie spokesman), 237

Trocchi, Alexander: example of Beat aesthetic contradiction, 229, 235

Tully, Jim: on hobos, 98

Turnell, G. M.: on Corbière, 219

Twain, Mark: as Western writer, 91; Huck Finn vs. Holden Caulfied, 123; simplicity pose, 128; Fiedler on, 162

Utopianism (often synonym for rebellious, millenarian, apocalyptic, radical, *outré*, unselfish, etc.): Cynics, 7, 19; rebel anti-utopianism, 27; bohemian, 148–49; Beat, 151; Goodman, 189–94, 197. *See also* Bohemianism; Hobo; Politics of rebel

Vagrancy (and vagabondage). *See* Hobo; Picaresque

Vexliard, Alexandre: on vagabondage, 222

Villon, François: like Cynic,

8; influenced Corbière, 71; essential rebellious manner and tone, 85, 87, 224

Wandering Jew: Old Testament prophets, 3–4; defined and as used by Comfort and Fiedler, 87; as Christ and used by Beats, Lawrence and Kazantsakis, 88; outsider experience, 90; related to Malamud, 125, 133; implicit in Bellow, 129–30; part of secularized Jewish heritage of rebelliousness, 176

Warren, Robert Penn: anti-rebel novelist, 120, 164, 232

Washington, George, 196

Watts, Alan: ellipsis on Zen, 213

Welch, Holmes: on Taoism, 213

Welsford, Enid, 213

West, Nathanael: on art as trick, 146; scorned unjustly by Goodman, 195

Whitman, Walt: contradiction in poetry of road, 78, 92–93; major influence on hobo writers, 98; influence on Beat writers, 103, 106; influence on American style and egotism, 122, 129, 178, 233

Widmer, Eleanor, 239, *passim*

Widmer, Matthew, 213

Wilson, Colin: *The Outsider, Religion and the Rebel,* and other works discussed as unrebellious and drastically inadequate rebel commentaries, 164–67, 173–74, 240–41

Wobbly (I. W. W.): songs

discussed, 110; basic character of movement and use by Dos Passos, 116–17, 230

Wolfe, Bernard: parochial New York school rebellious fiction, 155, 237–38

Wolfe, Thomas: similar to Beat writers, 122, 229

Woodcock, George: on anarchism, 213

Work: reasons for rebelling against usual forms of, 9, 10–11, 21, 23, 78–80, 223; wanderers and hobos view of work, 81–84, 94–95; sense of purpose against, 100; increasing technological-bureaucratic corruption of, 146–47, 153, 194, 197; rightness of refusing or sabotaging many jobs, roles and values, *passim*

Wright, Richard: as existential melodramatist, 243–44

Zamiatin, Eugene: rebel anti-utopianism, 27

Zen (Buddhism): contemporary rebel use of, 19, 31, 103, 105, 213